WITHDRAWN

D1712945

THE READING OF SILENCE

The
Reading of Silence

VIRGINIA WOOLF IN THE
ENGLISH TRADITION

Patricia Ondek Laurence

STAFFORD LIBRARY
COLUMBIA COLLEGE
1001 ROGERS STREET
COLUMBIA, MO 65216

STANFORD UNIVERSITY PRESS
STANFORD, CALIFORNIA

823.912
W8835L

Stanford University Press
Stanford, California
© 1991 by the Board of Trustees of the
Leland Stanford Junior University

Original printing 1991
Last figure below indicates year of this printing:
02 01 00 99 98 97 96 95 94 93

CIP data appear at the end of the book

For Stuart

Acknowledgments

ALTHOUGH THIS BOOK is about silence, it was always a delight to talk during its early stages with Mary Ann Caws, whose encouragement and criticism—then and now—I greatly value. Jane Marcus's comments on my work were invaluable, and her professional and scholarly energy remain an inspiration. I also benefited from conversation with Vincent Crapanzano, Gerhard Joseph, Marvin Magalaner, and Jane Tompkins, who are now or once were associated with the Graduate Center of the City University of New York.

Helen Tartar of Stanford University Press offered gracious and timely support. And my editor, Julia Johnson Zafferano, has been an especially attentive auditor of the whole manuscript, and I thank her for her continuing good will and patience. Dean Paul Sherwin of the City College of New York also deserves special thanks for his support of this project in its final stages.

And to my husband, Stuart, always a wry counselor, and to my children, Ilana and Jonathan—all of whom love to talk—I am grateful for the spaces of silence that enabled me to write this book.

P.O.L.

Contents

Illustrations

THE READING OF SILENCE

Introduction

S T. AUGUSTINE SAID that his master Ambrose was the first man of An-
tiquity to practice silent reading. It may also be said that Virginia
Woolf is the first woman novelist in Modernity to practice silence rather
than speech. Terence Hewet, an aspiring writer in Woolf's first novel,
The Voyage Out, announces her lifelong preoccupation with silence and
the barrier between the sayable and the unsayable: "I want to write a
novel about Silence, he said; the things people don't say. But the difficulty
is immense" (p. 216). Seeking to "devise a method for conveying not only
what people say but what they leave unsaid, not only what they are but
what life is" (*Common Reader,* p. 14), Woolf confronts the narrativity
of silence and the cultural constraints of her time. Distinctions are made
in her novels between what is left "unsaid," something one might have
felt but does not say; the "unspoken," something not yet formulated or
expressed in voiced words; and the "unsayable," something not sayable
based on the social taboos of Victorian propriety or something about
life that is ineffable. What Woolf does, as a novelist of subjectivity, is to
confront and narrate these silences between islands of speech, inviting
us, as readers, to enter into the obscurity and to consult our own minds.

To the Lighthouse provides examples of these three types of silence:
Woolf's subjective modes of being rather than doing. When Mr. Ramsay
dampens everyone's hopes of going to the lighthouse, Mrs. Ramsay despairs of her ability to say anything to him at such times: "There was
nothing to be said." Later the narrator comments, "That was typical of
their relationship. Many things were left unsaid" (*To the Lighthouse,*

p. 263). Lily Briscoe, the artist, ruminating about expression, illustrates the second kind of silence, the things not yet spoken: "For how could one express in words the emotions of the body? express that emptiness there? (She was looking at the drawing-room steps; they looked extraordinarily empty.) It was one's body feeling, not one's mind" (p. 265). Third, there are things that are unsayable. Mrs. Ramsay's daughters, Prue, Nancy, and Rose, observe her orchestrating dinner and the conversation:

She was now formidable to behold, and it was only in silence, looking up from their plates, after she had spoken so severely about Charles Tansley, that her daughters, Prue, Nancy, Rose—could sport with infidel ideas which they had brewed for themselves of a life different from hers; in Paris, perhaps; a wilder life; not always taking care of some man or other; for there was in all their minds a mute questioning of deference and chivalry, of the Bank of England and the Indian Empire, of ringed fingers and lace. (p. 14)

The daughters mutely question the mother's role, which, the narrator implies, serves patriarchy, the Empire, and colonialism: a web of relations that Woolf will develop more fully in *Three Guineas* in 1938, eleven years later. In her diary, Woolf also writes of "a fin passing far out. What image can I reach to convey what I mean? Really there is none" (3, p. 113). This is another aspect of the "unsayable," the ineffable.

The narration of such distinct silences is difficult because, like Terence Hewet, Woolf wishes to write a novel "about" or embodying silence and not a novel that refuses expression. Rejecting the "realist" demands of fictional discourse advocated by the Edwardians—Arnold Bennett, John Galsworthy, and H. G. Wells—Woolf uses experimental techniques to suggest what is unsaid, unspoken, and unsayable by giving sensation, mind, feeling, and "life" a narrative and thematic place in the novel. Suspicious of talk and of those who try to record it, she states: "It turns hither and thither, seldom sticks to the point, abounds in exaggeration and inaccuracy, and has frequent stretches of extreme dullness" (*Second Common Reader*, p. 233). She turns to techniques of silence, organizing her narration in such a way that what is unsayable— the cultural silences or repressions of her time—is revealed in her novels.

Going beyond received taxonomies of fiction, Woolf, through the formal uses of silence, interrogates the nature of the novel and the "literary." She creates new representations of mind and self amid changing notions of the relationship between word and world in the twentieth century. Although, as George Steiner claims, fundamental breaks in the history of human perception are rare, in the twentieth century "there are fault lines . . . that break open the preceding constructs of identification.

. . . It is the break of covenant between word and world which constitutes one of the very few genuine revolutions of spirit in Western history
and which defines modernity itself" (*Real Presences*, pp. 87, 93). The
loss of trust in words, the covenant between word and world, can best
be expressed, according to Steiner,

by saying that our inward history, that the codes of perception and self-perception
through which we situate our relations of intelligibility to others and to "the
world," have entered upon a second major phase. In shorthand: the first which
extended from the beginnings of recorded history to the later nineteenth century
is that of the Logos, of the saying of being. The second phase . . . must now be
understood as coming "after the Word." (Ibid., p. 93)

It is this phase, after the Word—with its focus on the unsaid, the unspoken, and the unsayable—with which this book is concerned. It is a
phase when certain aspects of being, as represented in Woolf's novels,
can only be revealed through various configurations of silence: a lexicon,
punctuation, metaphor, space, or rhythm of silence.

To understand the riddle of silence in Woolf's novels is to enhance
one's interpretation of other layers of fictional and historical silence. This
book is about a theory of reading silence in narration not for the sake
of theory but as a means of engaging the multiple levels and the meaning of silence that one experiences in a Woolf novel and, potentially, in
other writers. As Woolf varies her experimental intention in each of her
novels, the meanings of silence shift, as do the methods used to represent
it. In "Modern Fiction" she states that "nothing—no method, no experiment, even of the wildest—is forbidden, but only falsity and pretence
. . . . Any method is right, every method is right, that expresses what
we wish to express, if we are writers" (*Common Reader*, pp. 158, 156).
But what methods express "silence" in a text? How do we locate it in
narration? Is it a sign or a "floating signifier" or a word? Is it simply a
concern? A theme? Is it a figure or a symbol? A discourse or a rhetoric?
Is it a strategy? Is it a presence or an absence? Is it a physical space in
the text or an implicit structure? A psychological space for the reader or
the writer? Is silence a rhythm or a feeling patterned with sound? How
do we empirically grasp it? How does a writer mark silence with words?
Where is silence—in the writer's or the reader's experience? How does
a writer "write" it? How does a critic "sound" it, making it into expressive discourse for the reader? Finally, how does a reader "read" silence?
"How," as Shoshana Felman asks in *Writing and Madness*, "can we read
the unreadable?" (p. 187). Only, she suggests, through a modification of
the meaning of reading itself: "To read on the basis of the unreadable

would be, here again, not what does the unreadable mean, but how does the unreadable mean. Not what is the meaning of the letters, but in what way do the letters escape meaning?" (ibid.). Such questions may seem to subvert their own terms, but they underlie the explorations of this book. We, as readers, must discover in Woolf's many kinds of silence not, as Søren Kierkegaard urges, "an alphabet that has just as many letters as the ordinary one" (*Repetition*, p. 145), but, in keeping with the spirit of this book, a "new rhetoric" of silence, a new form of writing that escapes the alphabet—perhaps expressed metaphorically by Woolf's "wedge-shaped core[s] of darkness"—a cuneiform that is not encoded like an ordinary alphabet.

Woolf both uses and escapes the alphabet in creating these narrative silences capturing the "rushing stream of broken dreams, nursery rhymes, street cries, half-finished sentences and sights—elm trees, willow trees, gardeners sweeping, women writing" (*The Waves*, p. 255): the polyphony of self, language, and culture in the twentieth century.

This subject of silence has particular appeal in the word-clogged reality of the twentieth century, a time when we are bombarded with words from the public spaces of advertising, public relations, and journalism. It is a time when, as Gérard Genette reports, one must pay for a period of silence on a jukebox, a blank record, equal in its playing time to that of a tune, illustrating that "in a civilization of noise silence must also be a product, that it is the fruit of a technology and a commercial object" (*Figures of Literary Discourse*, p. 43). It is a time when we distinguish acts of silence in the face of the unimaginable inhumanity of the Holocaust; it is a time when we note that post-structuralist novelists like Joan Didion write of death and political inhumanity in Central America as if people no longer exist—"the corpse nourishes the symbolic," she writes in *Salvador*—except as an opportunity for the self-reflection of writers. This too is a kind of silence.

Silence is usually the ground against which talk or sound is perceived, but silence "figures" itself in the writing of Woolf. Although there are many types of literary interest that generate meaning in her novels, particularly the recent focus on her "realism" and the problem of the "subject," the focus of this book is on Woolf's configurations of silence—the lexical, syntactical, metaphorical, thematic, and structural embodiments—a critically uncharted field. However, in order to read and discuss it, we must establish a new rhetoric, as Genette suggests, which will include the semiotics of all discourses—literary, visual, musical, sociological, anthropological, psychological, philosophical, bodily.

And in this discourse of silence we must, as Foucault urges, "try to determine the different ways of not saying . . . things . . . . There is not one
but many silences, and they are an integral part of the strategies that
underlie and permeate discourses" (*Foucault Reader*, p. 931). This effort
may be as futile as Virginia Woolf's pursuit of the elusive "it" of life, but
this is, nevertheless, an attempt to give the moment and my reading of
Woolf "whole."

As I will make clear, a philological and an epistemological concern
is present throughout this study. In probing silence, I was soon treading
ground not mapped by literary criticism, and I needed to approach some
of the aforementioned questions in other discourses of knowledge. My
own post-structuralist view of Woolf emerges from structuralism, associated with the disciplines of linguistics and anthropology; deconstruction, springing from a philosophical perspective; feminism, connecting
with a historical sense of women; and psychoanalysis, revealing aspects
of the mind hitherto ignored: all leading sources of energy and innovation in twentieth-century literary theory. Although these discourses will
be used here to provide an articulation and interpretation of silence, it
need hardly be said that Woolf was a writer, not a philosopher or feminist or linguist; nevertheless, she expresses the concerns of her time. She
anticipates certain philosophical themes to be found in modern thought,
and the critical theories emerging from various disciplines, unlike earlier
critical perspectives, provide a stance and vocabulary for approaching
her evanescent concept of silence.

My post-structuralist position springs from reading Woolf's silence
as one of the "signs by which literature draws attention to itself and
points out its mask" (Genette, p. 22). Woolf's narrative silence is found
not only in "marked" contexts but also in the "unmarked" ideography
of the novels—as if silence were of the same order as the readable, the
same order as words on the page. She seeks, through her adventurous
and ever-changing narrative methods, to express silence, its nature, its
meanings, and its uses. Structural and deconstructive analysis reveals
that Woolf's flowing style, like Lily Briscoe's painting, is poised upon a
weight: "Beautiful and bright it should be on the surface, feathery and
evanescent, one colour melting into another like the colours on a butterfly's wing; but beneath the fabric must be clamped together with bolts of
iron" (*To the Lighthouse*, p. 255). This study of Woolf's uses of silence
reveals the textual weight and gravity that support the lightness of style
and being in her novels.

Using narrative techniques to capture "being" and point out the mask of language, silence becomes in her novels the equivalent of "interior distance" as described by George Poulet: "How can one find in language something equivalent to this multiple, interior 'whirling about' which is the lived moment, and to this vertiginous gliding which is lived time" (p. 28). This interior "whirling about"—the lived moment, lived time—which includes silence as well as sound, is what Woolf attempts to spatialize and temporalize in her novels. For example, in the "Time Passes" section of *To the Lighthouse*, she attempts to embody the emptiness of a house when no one lives in it, but time passes and takes its toll. Orlando muses and expresses Woolf's problematic: "Life? Literature? One to be made into the other? But how monstrously difficult" (p. 257). Woolf, trying to capture the expressiveness of the living, lived moment, must develop narrative methods that rely on the nonverbal as well as on the verbal. She, like Rousseau in his account of the origins of language, realizes that "Writing, which would seem to crystallize language, is precisely what alters it. It changes not the words but the spirit, substituting exactitude for expressiveness" (p. 21). Or as Derrida expresses it, "What writing itself, in its nonphonetic moment, betrays is life" (*Of Grammatology*, p. 25). From Cubism and Stravinsky onward, much of modern art relies on motion, and though she has her own stasis in "moments of being," Woolf is more sensitive to conveying motions of mind and time and language than other modern writers. This sense is what gives her style its immediacy and flow and what gives the reader the sense of participating in, indeed living, the sensation, the thought, the feeling—the sounds and the silences—while reading.

Woolf's narrative use of silence is related to the modern preoccupation with "inwardness" and the use of techniques of indirection in twentieth-century literature. For example, Henry James is obsessed with "not telling" in *The Golden Bowl*; Samuel Beckett refuses expression in *Malone Dies*; Gustave Flaubert is absorbed with the incidental leading him to "say nothing" in *Madame Bovary*; James Joyce invents an artist who vows "silence, exile and cunning" in *Portrait of the Artist as a Young Man*; Harold Pinter dramatizes a complex of conversational silences in *The Homecoming*; and Gertrude Stein exclaims that "silence is so windowful" in *What Happened*. Ezra Pound, T. S. Eliot, and Wallace Stevens also employ indirection and silence, using minimal poetic forms to dramatize the limitations of language and withdrawal from a fragmented culture into an interior world. Woolf prefigures some of the modern notions of silence in Beckett and Jean-Paul Sartre, though not their interest in the silences of the absurd; in Julia Kristeva and her discussions of the expressiveness of the body in space; and in Maurice Blanchot's presentations of the ineffability of life. Contemporary literary and critical ideas can also be glimpsed in Woolf's narrative experiments: her interest in subjectivity perhaps now carried to its extreme in the novels of Nathalie Sarraute and Alain Robbe-Grillet; her emphasis on kinetic rather than static processes now revealed in performance art; her interest in the participation of the reader and audience in contemporary novels, literary theory, and theater; her concern with ineffability and the limitations of language and interpretation in contemporary philosophy and literary theory; her interest in multiplicity of selves, dream, and the expression of the unconscious developing in tandem with Freud and now part of contemporary psychological theory; and, finally, her interest in the music, art, and "architecting" of words reflecting a now-fashionable interdisciplinary and structural approach to writing and art.

The motif of the inadequacy of language is an ancient one. From Woolf's perspective, words are false to the experience of "Reality dwelling in what one saw and felt, but did not talk about" (*The Voyage Out*, p. 37). The people she admires most keep silent in the important moments of life. She writes in a letter to Ethel Smyth: "For months on knowing you, I said to myself here's one of those talkers. They don't know what feeling is, happily for them. Because everyone I most honour is silent—Nessa, Lytton, Leonard, Maynard: all silent; and so I have trained myself to silence; induced to it also by the terror I have of my own unlimited capacity for feeling" (*Letters* 4, p. 422). Silence here is a space for feeling that she respects and creates a narrative place for in her novels. By using a metalanguage in her narration—as expressed through a lexicon and rhetoric of silence (punctuation, metaphor, rhythm, shapes, space, and structure) to delineate thought, feeling, and character in her novels, she develops a novelistic technique for representing this silence and securing ideological closure on what cannot be expressed through the ordinary alphabet. Writing with the realization that "language bears within itself the necessity of its own critique" (Derrida, *Of Grammatology*, p. 254), Woolf incorporates silence into her narration as a critique of words, of "talkers" and "phrase-makers," of the "speaking subject," and of Western notions of knowing and being. She both uses and questions language in creating a narrative space for silence.

It is also useful to recognize the connection of Woolf's interest in silence with the traditions of English fiction as well as contemporary literary theory. Though my discussion in this book follows typological lines representing the various kinds and strata of silence to be found in a

Woolf novel, I do not disregard the literary or philosophical tradition of defining "reality" and what is "outside" and "inside," or the historical dimension of the inner life that presents new problems to each generation of writers. In Chapter 1, I begin with a brief survey of the history of interiority in English literature. This leads to a discussion of Woolf's deepening sense of tradition and of the kinds of silence to be found in her novels. Her treatment of silence relates to the "unsaid" in eighteenth- and nineteenth-century novels and to writers like Wordsworth and Rousseau who sometimes idealize people who cannot speak, connecting perhaps with the pastoral tradition that invests gesture and song with an eloquence lacking in speech. I proceed in Chapter 2 to examine a separate female tradition, as Woolf suggests in *A Room of One's Own*, revealing silence as a ritual of truth for women in selected novels of Jane Austen, Charlotte Brontë, and Virginia Woolf. Woolf extends the tradition of Austen and Brontë in "figuring" the developing inwardness of women. In contrast, this configuration is rendered as "absence" by a sample of male novelists—Samuel Richardson, Charles Dickens, George Meredith, and Thomas Hardy, also discussed in Chapter 2. They view women from the "outside," like the legendary Mrs. Brown rendering women's silences as a ritual of oppression. It is in this tradition, in these authors, and in this fabric of language that the interest of Woolf's modern novel develops with a nod and yawn toward the Edwardians and "this appalling narrative business of the realist: 'getting on from lunch to dinner'" (*Diary* 3, p. 209). Woolf's valuing of the silence of women undermines not only patriarchal but also Western notions of talk and silence.

After this historical sweep, I focus on methods for narrating silence. In Chapter 3, the philosophies of Rousseau, Derrida, Poulet, and Blanchot further illuminate our understanding of silence. Woolf's notions of the reader and the writer are presented from the critical perspective of Deconstruction, which is acknowledged as conferring "a new kind of readability" (Johnson, *Rigorous Unreliability*, p. 279) and complexity on the element of silence in Woolf's novels. In allowing more silence into the text than other modern authors, Woolf creates a space for the subjectivity of the reader. A discussion follows that provides a methodology for the linguistic identification of Woolf's "scenes of silence" through the formal construction of a lexicon of silence and that examines the expression of silence through punctuation of suspension and metaphors of silence. Scenes of silence are selected from Woolf's novels—*The Voyage Out, Mrs. Dalloway, To the Lighthouse, The Waves,* and *Between the Acts*—each being chosen as the best text to illustrate a particular kind of silence, though it may occur in diluted or involuted forms in other places. Chapter 4 demonstrates a way of reading the spatial dimension of silence in Woolf's novels by reinterpreting the bodily expression of hysteria and delusion in women as another form of "silence." Using the methodology of intertextuality, the mind-body-feeling states of Rachel in *The Voyage Out* and Rhoda in *The Waves* are compared to Freud and Breuer's descriptions of hysteria in their case studies of Dora and Anna O., and to male and female surrealist painters' representations of women. The last chapter presents alternating rhythm in thematic, temporal, and spatial patterns as a fact of Virginia Woolf's style. That rhythm is her notion of "form": "Form in fiction is emotion put into the right relations" (*Letters* 3, p. 133). This chapter juxtaposes the harmonic and sweeping rhythms of *The Waves* to the modern counterpoint of *Between the Acts*, and it describes the different patterning and lexicon of silence in each work. Taken together the chapters indicate the layers of silence in Woolf's novels. Although, for purposes of discussion, silence is categorized and stratified and analyzed in these chapters, it is important to keep in mind that silence in Woolf's novels is a vast nest of Chinese boxes.

For at least a century, the literary avant-garde—from Mallarmé to Joyce and Artaud—has presented the multiplicity in language and self through such silences: ruptures, holes, and spaces in the text. Mallarmé calls this "the music in letters." It is important to note that the concern is not new, for even St. Augustine acknowledges the "spaces" in writing and recommends listening for silence between syllables in his *De Musica* (Mazzeo, p. 189). What is new is the self-consciousness, frequency of appearance, and labeling of narrative spaces and blanks, reflecting a change in consciousness. It is what Elaine Showalter and *l'écriture feminine* school label "the holes in discourse, the blanks and gaps and silences . . . the blinds of a 'prison-house' language" (*New Feminist Criticism*, p. 255), and it is what this book, encouraging a new reading, labels a discourse of silence. From this perspective, "blanks" are not blinders but are infused with the psychic life and historical sense of a woman. As Kristeva notes, "All these modifications in the linguistic fabric are the sign of a force that has not been grasped by the linguistic or ideological system" (*Desire in Language*, p. 165). One of the forces that has not been grasped is women.

Woolf's turning of the theme of silence to effect in her novels is determined not only by modernism but also by the strategies of a woman in modern culture. Though other writers also challenge the narrative function and turn consciousness inside out on the page, Woolf maps gender metaphors onto literary processes, challenging "the literary," by more frequently marking women's minds on the space of her page through a lexicon of silence, a punctuation of suspension, an undertext of rhythm, and metaphors of silence.

In this book some of the critical assumptions of Woolf scholars—from J. Hillis Miller and Geoffrey Hartman to more recent critics such as Elizabeth Abel, Elaine Showalter, and Julia Kristeva—are revised. Acknowledging that there have been a series of useful "centers" that have structured Woolf criticism over the past five decades, I now suggest that we question our "centers," our assumptions, and examine how they have functioned in this criticism and in ourselves as critics. These centers of Woolf criticism receive different forms and names, but they each refer to a foundation for her writing, the deciphering of a central "truth," or the designation or loss of an influence. In reviewing Woolf criticism, one cannot help but observe that the Virginia Woolf of Alex Zwerdling, Woolf as a novelist in the real world, is not the Woolf of James Naremore, a poetic novelist in a world without a self; E. M. Forster's "Invalid Lady of Bloomsbury" is not the same as Jane Marcus's "guerilla fighter in a Victorian skirt"; F. R. Leavis's morally censured Bloomsbury does not have the same exemplary appeal of Nigel Nicholson's and Mary Ann Caws's portraits; Geoffrey Hartman's vision of Woolf's romantic unity is shattered in Lucio Ruotolo's presentation of Woolf's aesthetic anarchy and "interrupted moment"; Hugh Kenner's dismissal of Woolf as a lesser modernist than Joyce, Eliot, and Pound is rebuked by Jane Marcus and Makiko Minow-Pinkney; Harvena Richter's subjective metaphors shift to exterior London in Susan Squier's Woolf, who stalks London storing up images; William Empson's totalizing tendency is resisted by Minow-Pinkney, Ruotolo, and Perry Meisel; and Quentin Bell's Aunt Virginia is not Louise deSalvo's abused child.

This book, admitting silence and language and deconstruction as part of the Woolf problematic, presents a new stance toward Woolf criticism. It views one critic as de-centering the structure proposed by the critic before—not necessarily replacing what is said, but multiplying the forces at work in the field of interpretation. It views Woolf and the criticism surrounding her with an oscillating vision, acknowledging the poetic, "real," philosophical, psychological, cultural, and multiple selves of Woolf. This is a critical stance that rejects the totalizing tendencies of New Criticism, which seeks a "well-wrought" literary interpretation of

Woolf. It is a stance that acknowledges the inaccessibility and inconsistencies of language, literature, and indeed Virginia Woolf's life. Previous criticisms then flicker with various significance, differences, and oppositions, creating the dancing rhythm that is so much a part of reading as well as interpreting Woolf. The opposing senses of self, reality, presence, being, and language that underlie the critical discourses cited above attest to the loss of a "center" in Woolf criticism and affirm Derrida's sense of "différance": "a structure which encompasses the freeplay of differences in a network of meaning." And though there's a trace in the word "freeplay" that suggests easy pleasure, this book attests to the critical knowledge needed to enter into the free but rigorous play of differences in the critical domain. Woolf critics, now peering with the "fifty pairs of eyes" she longed to see with, should acknowledge their joyous multiplicity and, as Derrida suggests, "This affirmation then determines the non-center otherwise than as a loss of the center" ("Structure," p. 264).

The exploration of the theme and narration of silence in Virginia Woolf's novels in this book brings under scrutiny nothing less than her perceptions of the nature of gender, being, mind, feelings, knowledge, and language. In defining silence, particularly women's silence, as an enlightened "presence" and not just an absence in the conventional sense of "lack" or "emptiness" in life and narration, Woolf displaces the "speaking subject" and speech or dialogue in the novel. This book, then, breaks new ground both in its theoretical treatment of silence and in the explications of silence in Virginia Woolf's novels. Like Derrida and Rousseau, she "is suspicious . . . of the illusion of full and present speech [and] . . . it is toward the praise of silence that the myth of a full presence wrenched from différance and from the violence of the word is then deviated" (*Of Grammatology*, p. 140). Woolf's "writing" of silence, or perhaps "archewriting"—"to think the unique within the system" (ibid., p. 112)—creates a "presence" that we are now learning to read or decipher. She, searching for a language of mind in the midst of concepts of mind in the twentieth century, creates a lexicon of silence, a punctuation of suspension, and metaphors of silence that signal mind and feeling, particularly the unconscious, in fiction.

This marking of the presence of mind and feeling in narration is not just a formalist preoccupation of Woolf's, however; it is intertwined with her perceptions of the social roles of men and women and with her worldview. Talk, which is often associated with men in Woolf's novels, has traditionally been valued as "presence mastered" (Derrida, *Of Grammatology*, p. 159); women's silence, on the other hand, is marked as "absence." Woolf, however, infuses this narrative space with a new psychic life, a rhetoric of silence, and the women in her novels are often present in this narrative space we are learning to read, refining our notion of Woolf's characteristic lexicon of silence of gaps, gulfs, pauses, fissures, cracks, and interludes. For example, in the character Rhoda in *The Waves* (incipient in Rachel in *The Voyage Out*), Woolf creates a new metaphor of the disembodied self, the dreaming mind, through the visualization of the body in space. Woolf's association of space with silence suggests that she approached the subject of form in the way that painters, composers, and architects do, using "negative" or "blank" spaces in a positive way, making them part of a style of alternating rhythm that is thematic and visual as well as musical, deconstructing the oppositional elements of time and space. Woolf's novels contain more "silence" than those of other modern authors, suggesting a different relation to language and writing than, for example, Joyce, who was much more preoccupied with the play and dissection of words. Finally, this book foregrounds rhythm as a structure and expression of sound and silence.

Woolf uses silence to mark her uncertainty about "what life is" and about "the reality of any feeling." Silence in her novels reveals the obscurities of self and human relationships and the difficulty of knowing anyone. Some silences express Woolf's preoccupation with and exploration of interiority and her desire to capture two strata of experience at once: the life of the mind, particularly on the unconscious level, and the surface world of facts. In addition, silence points out language's mask: the uncertainties and limitations of interpretation in literature and life. In narrating silence, Woolf implicates the readers of her novels in new ways by creating a space for them to interpret. Since silence has no one single meaning, the ambiguities of language and life are revealed.

The Narration of Interiority
in the English Novel

TERENCE HEWET'S PROJECT—to write a novel about Silence—reflects Woolf's preoccupation with rendering the mind itself, both conscious and unconscious, on the page. In her diary, she often writes of the capricious nature of the mind, its fluctuating, flitting, fluttering rhythms, and of the difficulty in arresting its movement with static language. While writing *To the Lighthouse*, she reflects in her diary, "I get it all too quick, too thin, too surface bright . . . how am I to get the depth without becoming static?" (4, pp. 149, 152). For Woolf it is "the old problem: how to keep the flight of the mind, yet be exact" (ibid., p. 298). It is only through writing that Woolf arrests the movement of mind and time, for as Lily observes in *To the Lighthouse*: "nothing stays, all changes; but not words, not paint."

Like Joyce, who in his defense of *Finnegans Wake* said that "One great part of every human existence is passed in a state which cannot be rendered sensible by the use of wideawake language, cutanddry grammar and goahead plot" (*Letters* 3, p. 146), Woolf is interested in finding a language and form for the novel that will enable her to narrate process and the living rhythms of life. She wants to capture both the movement of thought, feeling, and bodily sensations in the "depths" and the facts, events, and actions on the "surface" of life. In her essay "Modern Fiction," she writes: "Let us record the atoms as they fall upon the mind in the order in which they fall, let us trace the pattern, however disconnected and incoherent in appearance, which each sight or incident scores upon the consciousness. Let us not take it for granted that life exists more fully in what is commonly thought big than in what is commonly thought small" (*Common Reader*, p. 155). Woolf faithfully traces sensations of mind "however disconnected and incoherent in appearance." She states, "I see that there are 4? dimensions; all to be produced; in human life; and that leads to a far richer grouping and proportion: I mean: I: and the not I: and the outer and the inner" (*Diary* 4, p. 353). In describing the modern temper in her essay "The Narrow Bridge of Art," Woolf notes "the strange way in which things that have no apparent connection are associated. . . . Feelings which used to come single and separate do so no longer" (*Granite and Rainbow*, p. 16). Woolf is exploring, then, the mind and phenomenology of self: its borders in relation to the animate and inanimate, and inside and outside in relation to the body, mind, and definitions of "reality." Woolf (through her narrative explorations), like the field of psychology, which was then in its incipient stages, is demonstrating that the interior life is not beyond observation and expression.

This interior life or subjectivity is revealed in language as well as silence, which is the semiological system or the new rhetoric explored in this book. In studying silence, we study what is "literary" because, as Gérard Genette states, silence is one of "the signs by which literature draws attention to itself as literature, and points out its mask" (p. 29). At the same time that language is revealing something through words, it is concealing something else through silence. Since Woolf does not consider the essence and meaning of communication to be in language alone—in literature or life—she is content to have her writing throw new light on the need for a semiotics of sensation, feeling, and thought. Her interior reality has its exteriorization through the written word, which may represent a silent thought or feeling, a thought spoken aloud, a long passage of thinking aloud in a soliloquy, or the utterance of a word for the enjoyment of it or for the curiosity of its sound value.

Her expression of silence represents a passage from interiority to exteriority: it has a double existence. It functions in two ways in Woolf's novels, important as it is to respect her "adventuring, changing, opening [her] mind and [her] eyes, refusing to be stamped and stereotyped" (*Diary* 4, p. 187). First, silence is part of the rhythm of her narrative style as she moves "updown updown" from the surface events of life to the silent depths of the mind; second, there is a lexicon of silence and a punctuation of suspension that mark "scenes of silence." As she writes in a letter to Vita Sackville-West, "Style is a simple matter; it is all rhythm" (*Letters* 3, p. 247), and silence as well as words are a part of her rhythm for representing the conscious and unconscious movements of mind. The word "movement" is important to her style because she captures in the rhythm of her writing in time a "movement"—up, down / inner, outer—of the mind. Alternation is a fact of her writing, and the movement from surface, narrated events to the depths of character or life signaled by a certain lexicon, punctuation, and scenes of silence becomes an embodiment of the alternation. She juxtaposes what is present to what is seemingly absent, moving the reader from the known to the unknown, from the intelligible to the obscure. In 1928, after the publication of *Orlando*, she writes: "The idea has come to me that what I want now to do is to saturate every atom. I mean to eliminate all waste, deadness, superfluity; to give the moment whole; whatever it includes" (*Diary* 3, p. 309). Taking her stated intention not as a sole determinant but as a variable as important as any other in ascertaining the presence of silence in a text, we discover that silence, interlaced with words in rhythmic movement, is included in Woolf's "moment." The spaces and silences between words, chapters, and acts are as significant as the sounds.

In a scene in *Mrs. Dalloway*, everyone is looking up at skywriting, a metaphor perhaps for Woolf's sense of writing as it appears on the page (presence) and disappears (absence) into the mind of the reader: "As they looked the whole world became perfectly silent, and a flight of gulls crossed the sky, first one gull leading, then another, and in this extraordinary silence and peace, in this pallor in this purity, bells struck eleven times, the sound fading up there among the gulls" (p. 30). The skywriting that all strain to read is "sous-rature," under erasure, even as it is being read bringing us to the realization that "Through the word—already a presence made of absence—absence itself comes to giving itself a name" (Lacan, *The Language of the Self*, p. 39). This Derridean concept is realized beautifully in Woolf's "skywriting," because language, a "trace," is nothing but a moment of the discourse. The concept of experience is under erasure (*Of Grammatology*, p. 75) because it is represented by language that is not an entity. Sounds and sights (gulls, bells) as well as silences (silence, peace, pallor, purity, and repetitions that suggest trance or silence) are interlaced and momentary in this passage in the "zone of silence" that is art. Woolf first creates the zone, the suspended moment in time—"the whole world became perfectly silent"—and then crisscrosses and repeats patterns of flight and sound—the temporal and spatial movements of life—onto the aesthetic space of this rhythmic passage. In narrating the silences as well as the sounds, Woolf is multiplying the forces in the field of the novel and re-defining the "literary." As Lacan states: "It is still not enough to say that the concept is the thing itself, as any child can demonstrate against the scholar. It is the world of words which creates the world of things . . . by giving its concrete being to their essence" (*The Language of the Self*, p. 39). Woolf makes silence something that is almost palpable at times: she gives it a "being" through writing by marking its presence in the sky of the novel, knowing that it will disappear into the minds of her readers.

In addition to this rhythmic movement, there are a lexicon of silence and a punctuation of suspension that mark "scenes of silence" in Woolf's novels. These scenes are the contexts in which particular themes of silence emerge: linguistic, psychological, social, historical, and philo-sophical. Certain lexical configurations surround scenes of silence— "pauses, moments, gaps, suspensions, fixed moments, trances" and repe-titions like "Down, down"—as well as certain punctuation, dashes, and ellipses. The lexicon and punctuation of silence create points of sus-pension in the narrative, and they make "moments of being." Silence in Woolf's earlier novels does not necessarily "interrupt" a moment, as Lucio Ruotolo might say, and silence is not the "whole moment" but part of the "moment whole," an important distinction in perspective and emphasis in Woolf's writing until about 1937. For it is my thesis that, until then, silence was part of a Romantic harmony of vision, a "moment of being" in writing and life that was separate from the "cotton-wool" of ordinary experience, a moment when a character was in touch with some "whole" in nature, self, and "reality." After, perhaps, *The Years*, silence became a signal of a different organization of being, and we are now subject to a modern "music" of interruptions, abysses, and gaps. As George Poulet would say, "We are no longer in a universe where everything touches everything else, but in a world that remains eternally spacious and eternally populated by presences at a distance from each other" (p. 92).

The relational nature of silence to other elements in the text is im-portant. Barbara Johnson describes Mallarmé's style in a way that can be applied to Woolf: "Thus we can say that Mallarmé is to Chomsky as Copernicus is to Ptolemy as Freud is to Descartes, in that the former in each case works out a strategically rigorous decentering of the structure described by the latter, not by abandoning that structure but by multi-plying the forces at work in the field of which that structure is a part"

(*The Critical Difference*, p. 71). Woolf, in turn, decenters the structures of the Edwardian novelists Wells, Bennett, and Galsworthy, not by abandoning plot and character, as some critics claim, but by "multiplying the forces in the field" and attending to the inner life and silence. She writes, "When we speak of form, we mean that certain emotions have been placed in the right relations to each other; then that the novelist is able to dispose these emotions and make them tell by methods which he inherits, bends to his purpose, models anew or even invents for himself" (*Letters* 3, p. 133). Form embodies feeling.

Woolf's preoccupation with multiplying the forces in the field of the novel surfaces early in her essay on modern fiction, "Mr. Bennett and Mrs. Brown," written in 1910. Here she laments the inability of the Edwardian novelists to see the "reality," the inner life, of the legendary Mrs. Brown: "At this moment the form of fiction most in vogue more often misses than secures the thing we seek. Whether we call it life or spirit, truth or reality, this, the essential thing has moved off, or on and refuses to be contained any longer in such ill-fitting vestments" (*Common Reader*, p. 153). In lamenting the Edwardians' shortcomings, Woolf emphasizes that, as novelists, they "were interested in something outside" (*Collected Essays* 1, p. 327). She, however, overcomes Edwardian "realism," "the tiresome getting on from lunch to dinner," by tracing the patterns, as she says of Mrs. Dalloway, of an "ordinary mind on an ordinary day" (*Common Reader* 1, p. 154). She uses a technique commonly labeled "stream of consciousness," a term that, at times, belies the variety and complexity of methods for narrating "the unspoken."

Given that conventional dialogue is represented in only brief passages in a Woolf novel, and given her interest in capturing sensations, feelings, and states of mind in the novel and life, what formal methods can Woolf use to portray the inner life? And since life or mind in a novel can only be written on a page, how is the inner life of the character to be represented? "What is the formal structure," as George Steiner asks in his essay "The Distribution of Discourse," of "inward speech, of the language stream we direct towards ourselves?" (*Language and Silence*, pp. ix–x). These are difficult questions, but they are important to our understanding of Woolf, whose use of narrated monologue or "inward speech" relative to narrative "story" outweighs all modern novelists, with the exception of perhaps Marcel Proust and Nathalie Sarraute. What then is the structure of the inward speech of a fictional character in a Virginia Woolf novel?

Early explorers of "stream of consciousness" like Edouard Dujardin, who influenced James Joyce's development, have answered somewhat naively:

The essential innovation of the interior monologue consisted in its object, which was to evoke the uninterrupted flux of thoughts that traverse the mind of the character, at the moment they arise, without explanation of their logical link- age while giving the impression of haphazardness. . . . The difference is not that the traditional monologue expresses less intimate thoughts than the internal monologue, but that it coordinates them by showing their logical linkage. . . . Inmost thoughts (those lying nearest the unconscious) are portrayed without re- gard to logical organization—that is, in their original state—by means of direct sentences reduced to the syntactic minimum. (Cohn, p. 272)

Such a linguistically naive view that inner speech in its "original state" is syntactically minimal—almost a kind of baby talk generally lack- ing connecting words like conjunctions, prepositions, and articles—held sway in 1920. Dorothy Richardson, an early contributor to the stream- of-consciousness novel who influenced Virginia Woolf, conforms in her writing to Dujardin's thesis. Miriam ruminates:

Now in the boat, she wanted to be free for the strange grey river and the grey shores. But the home scenes recurred relentlessly. Again and again she went through the last moments . . . the good-byes, the unexpected convulsive force of her mother's arms, her own dreadful inability to give any answering embrace. She could not remember saying a single word. There had been a feeling that came like a tide, carrying her away. Eager and dumb and remorseful she had gone out of the house and into the cab with Sarah, and then had come the long sitting in the loopline train . . . "talk about something" . . . Sarah sitting opposite and her unchanged voice saying "What shall we talk about?" And then a long waiting. (*Pilgrimage*, p. 26)

New psychological and linguistic perspectives help us to approach the question of how the inner speech of characters is portrayed in fiction, and initially two kinds of thought or mental activity must be distin- guished: conscious thought, which is represented in fiction as conform- ing in structure and convention to outward speech and represented by coherent dialogue or reported speech; and unconscious thought, which is nonverbal "mind-stuff," represented in fiction through imagery, meta- phor, punctuation, and nonverbal signs. The latter category of thought, which includes the "silence" under discussion in this book, is what is generally labeled "stream of consciousness" by critics, and it appears more in modern novels than those of the eighteenth and nineteenth century. Even the first category, conscious thought and speech, admits the unconscious gaps into its linguistic fabric and appears in different form in modern novels, as J. F. Burrows notes: "The exclamations, repetitions, half-formed phrases and broken syntax of most 'utterance' are more directly registered in the dialogue of modern novels than in most novels of the eighteenth and early nineteenth centuries" (p. 215). If "consciousness," according to Derrida, is "a perception of self in presence," the "unconscious" differs in that it is characterized by "traces" and "delayed effects" (*Speech and Phenomena*, p. 152). However, using the thesis of Lacan, who expands Freud's notions of "language" in stating that the unconscious has the structure of a "form of writing" (*The Language of the Self*, p. 30), we can begin to decipher the unconscious and the silence of fictional texts in reading beyond language. Since the unconscious is structured like a form of writing, we must try to "read" the signs and silence that writers "write" in the strata that Virginia Woolf labels the "depths"—signs, symbols, ideography, metaphors, gaps, and dreams. The intricate interpretive strategies of deconstruction, poetics, psychology, and linguistics offer new insights, piercing the borders of self.

In exploring interiority, Woolf, as a novelist, is not interested in presenting clinical mental states but in finding narrative methods to represent thought and feeling, both conscious and unconscious. But the unconscious, by definition, is devoid of language: "The unconscious cannot be explored in its own unconscious form, since obviously this is unconscious. We can only infer it from symbols emerging in the conscious expression of the person" (Edel, p. 56). Ernest Jones, in *The Life and Work of Sigmund Freud*, further describes the disconnected characteristics of the unconscious:

(a) There is no sense of contradiction in the unconscious. Opposite or incompatible ideas exist happily side by side and exert no influence on each other; (b) Condensation of ideas and displacement of affect from one idea to another takes place freely without inhibition. These are features of what Freud had in *The Interpretation of Dreams* described as primary processes; (c) The unconscious has no conception of time. Ideas and impulses from different ages are telescoped together and only the present existed; (d) The unconscious has no relation to outer reality. (p. 324)

The language that produces the forms of literature has different conventions than the language of thought and consciousness in the context of everyday reality. Dorrit Cohn observes that "narrative fiction is the only literary genre, as well as the only kind of narration, in which the unspoken thoughts, feelings, perceptions of a person other than the speaker can be portrayed" (p. 7).

An examination of scenes of silence in Woolf's novels reveals that she indeed expands the possibilities of the genre of the novel as she extends her representation of the inner life and transforms the novel of fact to the novel of vision, moving from prose to poetry. Starting with *Jacob's Room*, Woolf's experimental method no longer allows for any absolute "outside," the world of facts or actuality, or any absolute "inside." Consequently, distinctions like speech and thought or narration and dialogue—which are incontestable in a novelist like Jane Austen—disappear in Virginia Woolf.

In Rousseau's essay *On the Origin of Language*, he states that "The art of writing does not at all depend upon that of speaking" (p. 19), challenging the Platonic view that speech is the origin of writing. Thought and speech, though clearly related, may at times be different orders of mind, and, therefore, physical "voice" need not be the metaphoric model for mind or "presence." In discussions of fictional techniques for narrating inner states, the nomenclature of speech is often applied to fictional thought, and terms that suggest speech as the origin of thought or writing emerge in the critical vocabulary: silent "discourse," internal "monologue," interior "discourse," inner "dialogue," inner "speech." Only the term "stream of consciousness," vague as it is, suggests the order of thought. M. M. Bakhtin, the Russian formalist critic of the novel, would approve of this dialogic terminology, believing that all thought is basically social (including dialogues within the self). However, such terms describe, in my view, the conventions of speech and not necessarily the dimensions of thought and writing. We are now in a phase, "after the Word," when as George Steiner says in his book *Real Presences*, we are exploring the arc of the "unspoken" or "unvoiced" and, therefore, need more refinement and distinction in our terms. We need a rhetoric of silence. Derrida writes that "the ethic of speech is the delusion of presence mastered" (*Of Grammatology*, p. 139), reminding us again of Western notions of presence as defined through speech. He broadens notions of "presence" by broadening notions of "writing," "inscribed ideology," to suggest the hidden aspects of language.

For example, three features that may distinguish the representation of thought and speech in fiction are coherency, audibility, and voicing, all of which relate to a speaker's and not necessarily to a writer's intention and sense of audience. Two of these features are confirmed by

Steiner: "The totality of human linguistic production, the sum of all significant lexical and syntactic units generated by human beings, can be divided into two portions: audible and inaudible, voiced and unvoiced. The unvoiced or internal components of speech span a wide arc" (*Language and Silence*, p. 91). Woolf's blurring of the normal distinction of thought as "silent" and speech as "sound" is revealed when the narrator narrating the inner life of Minnie Marsh comments, "Why look up? Was it a sound, a thought? Oh heavens! Back again to the thing you did" (*Complete Shorter Fiction*, p. 114).

Woolf as a novelist explores this wide arc of the unvoiced and the inaudible. The relationship between spoken, audible discourse, which includes but is not limited to "dialogue" in narration (i.e., soliloquies are "voiced"), and inaudible, silent thought, commonly termed free-indirect discourse or stream of consciousness, is problematic. It is not agreed even now among psychologists, let alone among literary critics and Virginia Woolf, whether thought (often referred to as "internal speech" or "unvoiced thought") is always expressed in words or sounded (Cohn, p. 260). We discern Woolf's early preoccupation with this issue as it affects fiction in her short stories. She blurs traditional distinctions between the "speech" of minds and actual dialogue by "sounding" internal speech or thought from the beginning—the genre of the novel lending itself to this kind of expression. In the short story, "An Unwritten Novel," written during the period 1917–21, the narrator observes about the character, Minnie:

But when the self speaks to the self, who is speaking?—the entombed soul, the spirit driven in, in, in to the central catacomb; the self that took the veil and left the world—a coward perhaps, yet somehow beautiful, as it flits with its lantern restlessly up and down the dark corridors. "I can bear it no longer," her spirit says. "That man at lunch—Hilda—the children." Oh heavens, her sob! (*Complete Shorter Fiction*, p. 114).

It is further developed as a pressing problem of narration in *The Waves*, where the physical voice of the characters (with the occasional exception of, perhaps, Bernard) is silent. Subjectivity speaks: " 'I see what is before me,' said Jinny. 'This scarf, these wine-coloured spots. This glass. This mustard pot. This flower. I like what one touches, what one tastes. I like rain when it has turned to snow and become palpable. And being rash, and much more than you are, I do not temper my beauty with meanness lest it should scorch me' " (p. 220). In her diary, Woolf notes that what is narrated can be thought or speech, yet she blurs the distinctions in her writing by using "said" and quotation marks, which conventionally indicate speech, and by using the present tense, which conventionally refers to thought. There is nothing colloquial in Jinny's voice above speaking to itself. "Speaks" and "thinks" are used interchangeably in this novel; indeed, she states in her planning of it: "It is to be a love story; she is finally to let the last great moth in. The contrasts might be something of this sort; she might talk, or think, about the age of the earth" (*Diary* 3, p. 139).

"Mind" in fiction is thus inevitably intertwined with language: indeed, mind is language and silence too. In observing "mind" or "thought" scattered on the page in a Woolf novel, what we are actually observing are forms of language and semiotics. What are her narrative preoccupations as a novelist? Who is speaking? Who is thinking? Do they speak aloud? Do they speak to themselves? And when the self speaks to the self, who is speaking? Is writing always silent? And if thought is sounded in life or on the page, is the presence of a listener or reader—audibility—necessary or peripheral? And if thought is audible or read, then how do we equate thought and silence? Locating the speaking subject in any of the various voices of a literary text proves to be difficult: what are the distinctions among the author, narrator, questioner, omniscient narrator, character? Woolf deconstructs the distinctions.

But if the distinctions are blurred, how is thought given audibility or visibility on the page? In *Between the Acts*, Woolf attempts the representation of "thoughts without words" when Bart muses, "Thoughts without words. . . . Can that be" (p. 68). In this novel, people "hear" when no words are spoken, challenging the criterion of audibility that we initially established to distinguish thought from speech (voicing, audibility, coherency). Silence then makes its "unmistakable contribution" to talk (p. 50) as Isa, Giles, and William say "without words" that they are unhappy (p. 205).

We note that Woolf pierces the membrane of inner/outer by transforming, among other things, traditional notions of punctuation, the use of quotation marks in narration. Sometimes Woolf's characters speak aloud when inwardly addressing themselves, and Woolf more often than other modern novelists couches unspoken thoughts in the form of direct speech through the use of quotation marks. This again begs the question as to who is "speaking." In *Night and Day*, Mary Datchet speaks both aloud and inwardly to herself of her disappointments in love with Ralph Denham:

She arranged the details of the new plan in her mind, not without a grim satis-
faction.

"Now," she said to herself, rising from her seat, "I'll think of Ralph."

Where was he to be placed in the new scale of life? Her exalted mood
seemed to make it safe to handle the question. But she was dismayed to find
how quickly her passions leapt forward the moment she sanctioned this line of
thought. Now she was identified with him and rethought his thoughts with complete self-surrender; now, with a sudden cleavage of spirit, she turned upon him
and denounced him for his cruelty.

"But I refuse—I refuse to hate any one," she said aloud; chose the moment to
cross the road with circumspection, and ten minutes later lunched in the Strand,
cutting her meat firmly into small pieces, but giving her fellow-diners no further
cause to judge her eccentric. (pp. 260–61)

Here Woolf encloses both a character's musings and her hasty outward
speech within quotation marks, exhibiting Woolf's collapse of the par-
titions of the mind, the outward and the inward, and, consequently,
notions of the objective and subjective. Conventionally, direct discourse
is signaled through the use of the word "said" and quotation marks,
but the form here is self-address, a self dramatically presented in inner
debate.

The importance of what is spoken and what is unspoken cannot be
underestimated, and we can observe the movement from the overt to the
covert in Woolf's narrative techniques from *The Voyage Out* to *Between
the Acts*. As Brenda Silver notes in her introduction to Woolf's *Reading
Notebooks*, her father would read aloud to her as a child, and "many
of the great English poems" seemed inseparable from his voice (p. 10).
Literature begins for Woolf as "spoken"—though by the end of her life,
when writing *Between the Acts* (1938–41), lines of poetry can only rum-
mage through Isa's mind and life internally, unvoiced. Nevertheless, they
are there as an unspoken but present poetic and historical commentary
on the times.

The movement from the overt to the covert is repeated in her comparison of the Elizabethan and the modern audience. The spectator of
Elizabethan drama transforms into a silent modern reader. In her "Notes
on an Elizabethan Play," Woolf observes the Elizabethan inattention to
the inner life, the focus on the public: "There is no little language, nothing brief, intimate, colloquial. . . . They could not enter into the private
world" (Silver, " 'Anon' and 'The Reader,' " p. 388). But in 1941, the
silent reader of the novel, attending to the private world of unspoken
thoughts, Woolf's psycho-narration, replaces the Elizabethan audience:

"The theater must be replaced by the theater of the brain. The playwright is replaced by the man who writes a book. The audience is replaced by the reader" (ibid., p. 398). In *Between the Acts*, literature becomes a pageant acted by the community even though the voiced words are blown away (Derrida's "sous-rature") in the atmosphere of the war, and literature is internalized in the lines of poetry that run through Isa's mind throughout the novel. The quality of attention to literature (Isa misremembers many lines) and to the inner life fails, and as the external drama of the war unfolds, the emergent popular art, the newspaper (for Isa's generation in *Between the Acts*) becomes "a book" (p. 19). Observing this, Woolf writes in despair of art and social and political institutions in 1941: "I cannot write any more. I have no audience."

In Woolf's view, then, the role of the narrator and the reader of the novel changes. The play that the Elizabethan spectator once watched becomes a book to be read. The book "gives a different pace to the mind":

It is here that we develop faculties that the play left dormant. Now the reader is completely in being. He can pause; he can ponder; he can compare, he can draw back from the page and see behind it a man sitting alone in a labyrinth of words in a college room thinking of success. He can read what is on the page, or drawing aside read what is not written. There is a long drawn continuity in the book that the play has not. It gives a different pace to the mind. We are in a world where nothing is concluded. (Silver, " 'Anon' and 'The Reader,' " p. 429)

This is different from the spectator of a play who must, more or less, externalize his attention and focus on the action of the play. In this essay, then, and in the development of her narrative techniques, Woolf transforms "theater" into a metaphor of the brain: what was once "outside" on the Elizabethan stage moves "inside"; what was once overt dramatization and realization of the self and character through dialogue with other characters now moves inward to a "self speaking to the self"; what was once voiced on the stage is now an unvoiced, silent dialogue between the writer and the reader. Woolf blurs the distinction between dramatist and audience, writer and reader in creating this "theater in the brain." In her first novel, *The Voyage Out*, we are placed inside the theater of the mind of one character, Rachel, by the narrator; in *The Waves* and *Between the Acts*, we are placed among the inner voices and minds of several characters, and there is a more complicated placement of the narrator and the reader.

In describing the relationship of narrator and character in "The Voice That Keeps Silence," Derrida asserts that "their intertwining is primordial" (p. 86). And so when the "self speaks to the self"—the self of the author to the self of the character or the self of the reader—"who" indeed is "speaking"? Who is "listening"? Such intertwining of the psychic processes of the character and narrator in narrated monologue is a favorite technique of Woolf's. Woolf articulates the narrative problems that cry out to be solved while writing *The Waves*: "Who thinks it? And am I outside the thinker? One wants some device which is not a trick" (*Diary* 3, p. 257). Woolf in this novel does not remain within the mind of one character as she does in her first novel, *The Voyage Out*: she enters and narrates multiple minds. Thus she questions herself as a narrator being "outside the thinker." Woolf's entry demonstrates Freud's notion of the "other" within the self, a narrating self who relates to the character's self, revealing, in this case, a double identity, at least. As narrator, is Woolf inside or outside of the character? Woolf, like Freud, re-defines self, but her diary entries concern a writing self, which can incorporate multiple perspectives and leave language open-ended so that the reader is invited into the novel in a way that differs from other modernists like Joyce and Faulkner. The most interesting question concerning modern literature, one that Woolf grappled with, is, then, "Who is speaking?"

Is this preoccupation with inwardness, silence, and indirection in Woolf's fiction "modern"? According to Dorrit Cohn, a theorist on novelists' techniques for capturing the inner life,

One could probably argue for a theory of cyclical (or spiral) return of the genre to its inward matrix whenever its characters get hyper-active, its world too cluttered, its orientation too veristic. Woolf and her generation, reacting against the Edwardians, would then figure as just one such return in a series starting with Cervantes' reaction against the chivalric epic (as Thomas Mann suggests), and ending provisionally with the reaction of New Novelists like Nathalie Sarraute against the behaviorism of the Hemingway school. This sketch of a spiral suggests that the "inward-turning" of the stream-of-consciousness novel is not nearly so singular a phenomenon, nor so radical a break with tradition as has been assumed, both by critics who applaud it (Edel, Daiches) and by critics who deplore it (Lukacs, Auerbach, Wolfgang Kayser). (p. 9)

But it is not only the cluttered world of fiction but also social and historical contexts that produce changes in consciousness. In his suggestive essay "The Distribution of Discourse," George Steiner observes that "interior language is subject to the influence of historical change. . . . The relations of proportion and intensity as between exterior and interior speech are subject to such change" (*Language and Silence*, pp. 55, 58). He goes on to note that "the shift in the balance of discourse since the seventeenth century has been outward" (p. 94): outer preferred to inner, and voiced preferred to silence in our culture. Indeed, he is tempted to define "crucial aspects of modernity in terms of the drastic reduction of internal language and of the concomitant inflation of public verbalization, of 'publicity' in the full sense of the term" (p. 58). In contrast, the transformation in literature, as Cohn has noted, is "inward," toward healing silence and the depths of contemplation—perhaps a modern literature that is in dialogue with the "outward" ruptures of the social and historical text.

Proust, Flaubert, and Joyce, along with Woolf, return literature to an inward matrix or, perhaps more accurately, to a condition of poetry. Woolf is constantly reaching for a condition of poetry or what she calls "saturation" or "essence" in her novels, and as Paul de Man states in his discussion of "presence" in *Blindness and Insight*: "The essence of poetry consists in stating the parousia, the absolute presence of Being" (p. 250). Julia Kristeva, in noting this quality, evaluates Woolf's narrative venture negatively when she states:

In women's writing, language seems to be seen from a foreign land; is it seen from the point of view of an asymbolic, spastic body? Virginia Woolf describes suspended states, subtle sensations and, above all, colors—green, blue—but she does not dissect language as Joyce does. Estranged from language, women are visionaries, dancers who suffer as they speak. ("Oscillation Between Power and Denial," p. 166)

Kristeva here reveals her preference for a "dissected" language, or what Woolf would describe as male-coded thought and language: "For if thought is like a keyboard of a piano, divided into so many notes, or like an alphabet is ranged in twenty-six letters all in order . . . he [Mr. Ramsay] had a splendid mind" (*To the Lighthouse*, p. 53). But Woolf's concept of poetry in the novel, announced in her essay "The Narrow Bridge of Art" published in 1927, theoretically breaks with traditional notions of the novel, and her practice as a writer, despite Makiko Minow-Pinkney's suggestive study, cannot be enclosed by Kristeva's theories, as will be demonstrated in Chapter 5.

IDEAS OF PRESENCE IN THE ENGLISH NOVEL

Ideas of "presence" in the novel have changed from the eighteenth to the twentieth century, preparing the way for Virginia Woolf's fictional explorations of the inner life. However, as Dorrit Cohn asserts, the narration of consciousness did not first appear in Woolf or on Joyce's fictional day in June. It is important to note that, though techniques for rendering consciousness may be new, developments in the novel are keyed to changes in notions of consciousness and presence. In the history of the novel, we could place Daniel Defoe at one end of the spectrum, with his focus on the external adventure, and Emily Brontë, with her liberation from the "facts" of the novel, approaching poetry, on the other. The moment when the "presence" of characters was taken out of the external world of action and adventure of Defoe, and was transposed within to a self-reflective consciousness, occurred gradually in English literature.

In "The Distribution of Discourse," George Steiner suggests that inwardness can be found in the soliloquies of characters of Shakespeare's plays, and it is no accident, as Lionel Trilling observes in *Sincerity and Authenticity*, that the difficulty of knowing and revealing the self arose in the Renaissance during an epoch of the theater when authors became more self-conscious about selves and roles. The sixteenth and seventeenth centuries were the classic age of the soliloquy, and this form of self-revelation, delivered offstage, was necessitated by the genre of the drama. Stage "presence" shifts, for example, in Shakespeare when a character is isolated to tell the audience everything it needs to know about ongoing events, hidden designs, or philosophical speculations. It is a shift in presentation of consciousness for a character to be revealed by speaking his thoughts aloud rather than through his relations with other characters in dialogue. This soliloquy can also be found in Robert Browning's dramatic monologues in the nineteenth century. He takes the techniques further than the Elizabethans in presenting the self in inner debate and, at the same time, revealing the less coherent, stray feelings and thoughts of a character. Observe the conversational voice and feeling in Browning's "My Last Dutchess":

> That's my last Dutchess painted on the wall,
> Looking as if she were alive. I call
> That piece a wonder, now: Fra Pandolf's hands
> Worked busily a day, and there she stands.
> Will't please you sit and look at her?
>
> (p. 349, ll. 1–5)

Browning here uses "quoted monologue," and, as mentioned earlier, this is a character's mental discourse, but it is bounded by the conventions of the dramatic monologue in that it is "voiced" and has the coherency of speech. Woolf, incorporating some of these forms of poetry in the novel, declares her interest in the silent soliloquy spoken in solitude. The new novel "will resemble poetry in this that it will give not only or mainly people's relations to each other and their activities together, as the novel has hitherto done, but it will give the relation of the mind to general ideas and its soliloquy in solitude" (*Granite and Rainbow*, pp. 18–19).

Thought or feeling or fantasy is generally signaled in Woolf, then, through certain conventions of fiction: reveries or daydreams during the day, or, as one approaches sleep, nightdreams or the fantasies of the mind in curious states. And though fiction has traditionally maintained a membrane between inward and outward, the advent of psychoanalysis—the speaking aloud of inner thoughts, the sounding of private speech—and the dramatic soliloquy and poetic sonnets of the Elizabethans, seventeenth-century meditative poetry, and nineteenth-century dramatic monologues have led to the narrative experimentation of Joyce and Woolf, who have pierced the membrane between inner and outer and introduced a subjective world into fiction. Indeed the sonnet and soliloquy tradition in Renaissance poetry and drama, seventeenth-century styles of meditation, and the dramatic monologue allowed for speaking inner thoughts aloud to an unseen audience (actual audience of the play, God as audience, other self as audience), for moving from overt to covert dramatization of self (from actual theater to "the theater of the brain"), and for initiating modern representations of subjectivity and multiple aspects of the self. See, for example, Bernard's soliloquy in *The Waves*, which is generally referred to as "interior monologue" and which not only reveals unstructured aspects of mind but also creates a "theater in the brain," a dramatic, inner representation of the stage of ideas: "But how to describe the world seen without a self? There are no words. Blue, red—even they distract, even they hide with thickness instead of letting the light through. How describe or say anything in articulate words again?—save that it fades, save that it undergoes a gradual transformation, becomes, even in the course of one short walk, habitual—this scene also" (p. 287). Woolf deflates the convention of coherency in soliloquy and the Romantic standard of sincerity in presenting the unvoiced aspects and disjunctions of the mind as above.

With the rise of the English novel in the eighteenth century, a genre appears that begins to record these solitudes, which existed in earlier poetic and dramatic forms. At the beginning of the eighteenth century, in a time when authors did not doubt that self and character were stable, Samuel Richardson explores the inner life of characters in his epistolary novels, *Pamela* and *Clarissa*, cast into third-person narrative. He introduces introspective narration through the epistolary form, though in Woolf's terms he was still, like other authors in the eighteenth century, "overt" not "covert." He proclaims himself merely an "editor" of Pamela's letters and creates the illusion of entering into the point of view of each character by capturing his thoughts and feelings in the process of being written. Richardson is not narrating through one female persona who insists she is writing her own story, like Defoe's Moll does in *Moll Flanders*, but he is distributing discourse to different characters in the form of letters, suggesting, even then, multiple perspectives on reality.

In Henry Fielding's *Tom Jones*, published in 1749, a multitude of characters and events appear and there are rapid shifts in time and place. But as Fielding narrates, though shifting his attention to the inner life, he avoids "inwardness." Note his description of Sophia's inner life: "A gentle sigh stole from Sophia at these words, which perhaps contributed to form a dream of no very pleasant kind; but she never revealed this dream to anyone, so the reader cannot expect to see it related here" (p. 527). Here the inner life is suggested, but narrated monologue conceals it. In *Vanity Fair*, William Thackeray begins to observe and reveal the inner life of his characters, but only as an opportunity to make general observations about human nature as an omniscient narrator. He, like Fielding, is still more interested in the social context than in the interior life. He stands at the borders of feeling as he describes Dobbin with ironic and knowing distance:

Mr. William Dobbin retreated to a remote outhouse in the playground, where he passed a half-holiday in the bitterest sadness and woe. Who amongst us is there that does not recollect similar hours of bitter, bitter, childish grief? Who feels injustice; who shrinks before a light; who has a sense of wrong so acute, and so glowing a gratitude for kindness, as a generous boy? And how many of those gentle souls do you degrade, estrange, torture, for the sake of a little loose arithmetic, and miserable dog-latin? (p. 53)

Here the author's narration is "about" a character's consciousness, reported feelings, and despite the narrator's direct address, "Dear Reader," we are only acquainted with Dobbin's feelings indirectly. However, though stylized, Thackeray does turn inward and refrains from presenting character, as in the picaresque models of the nineteenth century— Cervantes' *Don Quixote* or Smollett's *Roderick Random*—through external, outward adventures alone.

Both Fielding and Thackeray define "presence" of character in fiction mainly in terms of the external actions, gestures, and spoken thoughts and feelings of the character narrated in the third person—maintaining the omniscience and presence of the author—rather than from the viewpoint of the character himself, which develops as fiction evolves. The narrator in Thackeray's *Vanity Fair* is a performer and has difficulty entering the minds of his characters: they are viewed from the "outside" largely through the gaze of society.

Earlier, in the mid-eighteenth century, Laurence Sterne, influenced by Locke's concept of mind, "transfers our interest from the outer to the inner" (*Common Reader* 2, p. 81). He makes us "consult our own minds" as he moves us closer to the interior life of characters, cleverly revealing the unexpected associations and "hobby horses" of the mind of, for example, gentle Uncle Toby:

> Now, whether we observe it or no, continued my father, in every sound man's head, there is a regular succession of ideas of one sort or other, which follow each other in a train just like—a train of artillery? said my Uncle Toby—A train of a fiddle stick! quoth my father—which follow and succeed one another in our minds at certain distances, just like the images in the inside of a lanthorn turned round by the heat of a candle. (Sterne, pp. 190–91)

This spoken free-association is different from omniscient narration or what Dorrit Cohn labels "psycho-narration," illustrated above in the Thackeray passage. Sterne allows the blanks and lapses, the silence of the life of the mind, to appear on the page (see opposite), and Virginia Woolf says of Sterne that he "is singularly of our age." In this interest in silence rather than in speech, Sterne's black page calls attention to the materiality of the text. Silences are marked. This forerunner of Woolf, with his modern interest in silence—the blank spaces, the white and black pages, the typography (asterisks, ellipses, dashes, parentheses)—illuminates the unsaid in his time and place. The same desire to capture the materiality of silence—to embody the "emptiness"—informs Woolf's creation of a lexicon, metaphors, punctuation, and rhythms of silence to be described in Chapter 3. Admiring *Tristram Shandy*, Woolf notes that "it is a book full of poetry, but we never notice it" in its smooth transitions from the surface events to the depths of mood and mind (*Granite and Rainbow*, p. 21).

In the twentieth century, Henry James takes us even further into the inner life of characters by developing the technique of point of view suggested by Richardson's letters and Sterne's associationist thinking. The reader's angle on the story of *The Golden Bowl*, for example, consists of a series of reflecting minds—Maggie Verver, Charlotte, Colonel and Fanny Assingham—and through omniscient description of interior states, what Cohn labels "narrated monologue," James renders consciousness and reality. Woolf characterizes James's style in her *Reading*

Notebooks: "All these minds are reflecting each other indirectly—not Henry James' reflections. What people think—what they suspect—of something which we do not clearly see" (Silver, XIV, 12). James is not reporting consciousness and feelings as do nineteenth-century novelists like Thackeray, nor is he narrating consciousness in direct discourse as does Jane Austen. Rather, like Woolf and Joyce, he is engaged in "the splendour of the indirect," creating the illusion that he is inside the mind of the character and that the author has almost, but not quite—because he is syntactically marked in various ways—disappeared.

In the spirit of modernism, then, Woolf transposes "presence" in the English novel from the external world of action of Defoe, Fielding, and Thackeray to the inner life of mind, feeling, and sensation. What is "absent" in earlier novels—the exploration of subjectivity (aspects of mind, states of feeling, sensations)—becomes central, re-defining notions of "presence" in a novel.

WOOLF'S ENLIGHTENED ABSENCE

Derrida's concept of "différance" is important for this discourse about Woolf and is useful in structuring the seeming opposition of presence and absence, outside and inside, silence and talk or sound in her novels. Derrida's "différance" arises from the verb "to differ," which expresses both "difference as distinction . . . [and] the interposition of delay. [It is a structure, not a word or concept, that] precedes and sets up the opposition between passivity and activity . . . the origin or production of differences and the differences between differences, the play [jeu] of differences" (*Speech and Phenomena*, pp. 129, 130). "Différance" works by the very nature of language and plays beyond the control of the writer. Derrida continues:

The word assemblage seems more apt for suggesting that the kind of bringing together proposed here has the structure of an interlacing, a weaving, or a web, which would allow the different threads and different lines of sense or force to separate again, as well as being ready to bind others together. . . . Différance can refer to the whole complex of its meanings at once, for it is immediately and irreducibly multivalent. (Ibid., pp. 132, 137)

Woolf's silence is woven through the symbolic order of words and syntax as she traces the unconscious through the consciousness of a writer: she creates an enlightened absence, a silence, by marking its presence.

Silence as an idea, as a response to life, as a space for writing, as part of a narrative method is thus not an "emptiness" dependent on the notion of lack or absence. It is a presence to be acknowledged as Woolf's brilliant contribution to narration in the novel. We, as readers, are in the process of learning to read this moment.

It is by willed (and unwilled) performances of silence that Woolf gives "silence" an authority, a presence in her work. Edward Said claims that "presence and absence cease to be mere functions of our perception and become instead willed performance by the writer. Thus presence has to do with such matters as representation, incarnation, imitation, indication, expression whereas absence has to do with symbolism, connotation, underlying unconscious unity, structure" (p. 129). Though it may sometimes be hidden or inadvertent, silence is a constitutive element, part of the lexicon, theme, rhythm, and structure of her novels. And though conventionally perceived as "loss" or an "absence" in conversation or life, as will be demonstrated more fully in Chapter 2, it is important from the start to acknowledge "the restless play of difference" between presence and absence, words and silence, and men and women in Woolf's novels.

The structure of "différance" is in the root of the word "absent." Absent is derived from "esse" ("sum, esse, fui, futurus," the principal parts of the verb "to be") and "ab," a prefix meaning "not." Absence means "not being" and thus contains "presence" like the words "cipher" and "nul," which mean both something and nothing. Such a play of origins within a word complicates meaning and confirms Ferdinand de Saussure's principle of meaning: "in language, there are only differences without positive terms" (p. 121). We learn what absence is in Woolf because we know what she means by presence; we perceive presence because we know absence. In this book, absence and its meanings—everyday, historical, and unique—will be described in relation to ideas of presence; silence will always be described in relation to words and sounds. Meanings emerge from the "restless play of difference."

In *To the Lighthouse*, much of Virginia Woolf's narration can be seen as the ground on which the interplay of presence and absence takes place, and this interplay contributes to the alternating style of the novel, a technique reflecting a vision of life that will be described more fully in Chapter 5. This is not the same thing as a text that insists on "representing its own narrative ambivalence," which is Elizabeth Abel's claim ("Cam the Wicked," p. 171). Abel's choice of the word "ambivalence" rather than "alternation" suggests Woolf's psychological and narrative indecisiveness rather than a planned "alternation" of rhythm that is carefully structured into her text. In *To the Lighthouse*, we observe deliberate alternations: the musical play of presence and absence in the rhythm of words and silence in narration; the philosophical play of presence and absence in the juxtapositions of the ordinary "cotton-wool" of experience with timeless "moments of being"; the psychological play of the mind as Woolf "sinks" to the depths of consciousness or unconsciousness and then "surfaces" to the events and facts of life; and the structural play of presence and absence in the construction of the novel. For example, "The Window" section of the novel suggests a human presence and point of view, a framing or vision one sees from the window of a home; the "Time Passes" section takes on the "body" of time passing and thus creates silent "time" as a "thing" through the world of words. As Lacan states, "the concept, saving the duration of what passes by, engenders the thing" (*The Four Fundamental Concepts*, p. 39). This becomes a timeless perspective embodied in the structure: the thematic alternations of presence and absence in life-death, known-unknown, intelligible-obscure, and male-talk and female-silence.

Woolf's questions about women lead to her questions about life. Women in Woolf's novels are associated with the flux and shift; men, with the solid. Both metaphysical positions, the solid and the shifting, are elements necessary to Woolf's vision of life and techniques of narration. This is revealed in the original manuscript of *To the Lighthouse*, where Woolf's narration is omniscient and solid, whereas in her revision the narration shifts to multiple points of view. This confluence of social themes, life views, and narrative style is important, for in articulating Woolf's frequent association of women and silence in her novels, we note that narrative techniques reflect her vision of gender.

The alternation in the reading of men and women's minds—the known, coded, masculine alphabet and the silent, uncoded, feminine cuneiform—leads to differences in expression and language. Women are more often associated with the unspoken, the unsaid, and the unsayable, and men are more often associated with talk, in Woolf's novels. Mrs. Ramsay notes in a scene of silence involving Mr. Ramsay that:

He found talking so much easier than she did. He could say things—she never could. So naturally it was always he that said the things, and then for some reason he would mind this suddenly, and would reproach her. A heartless woman he called her; she never told him that she loved him. But it was not so—it was not so. It was only that she never could say what she felt. Was there no crumb on his coat? Nothing she could do for him. (*To the Lighthouse*, p. 185)

In the semiotics of silence, the unsaid, the gesture of brushing the crumb, is an expression of love. Her meditations continue:

Then knowing that he was watching her, instead of saying anything she turned, holding her stocking, and looked at him. And as she looked at him she began to smile, for though she had not said a word, he knew, of course he knew, that she loved him. He could not deny it. And smiling she looked out of the window and said (thinking to herself, Nothing on earth can equal this happiness)—"Yes, you were right. It's going to be wet tomorrow. You won't be able to go." And she looked at him smiling. For she had triumphed again. She had not said it: yet he knew. (Ibid., p. 186)

Women's silence here triumphs in its expressiveness.

Woolf's "being" as a writer and a woman incorporates presence and absence, silence as well as words, because she wants her novels to contain the indeterminacies of life, the suggestiveness of poetry, and women's apprehension of "reality." My next chapter will demonstrate that silence characterizes the inward discourse of women in a tradition of female authors: Jane Austen, Charlotte Brontë, and Virginia Woolf. Each author finds methods to convey the female characters' apprehension of reality through silent "rituals of truth."

If we then posit silence as "a determination and effect within a system which is no longer that of presence but that of différance" (Derrida, *Speech and Phenomena*, p. 147), then the mimetic "absence" of women's discourse as described by Xavière Gauthier and *l'écriture feminine* critics must be considered anew. An examination of the representation of men and women in Woolf's novels would lead us to discover "différance" in men and women's discourse and a new reading of "presence" in women's silences. Jeanne Kammer observes the nuance: "The use of silence in male artists is often characterized as an acknowledgment of the void, a falling-back in the face of chaos, nothing; for women, there appears more often a determination to enter that darkness, to use it, to illuminate it with individual presence" (p. 158). Woolf illuminates women's presence through various kinds of silence, and they are given a space in her writing. Some feminists view silence as only absence or a negation that Woolf is mimetically representing in her writing. Elaine Showalter views silence in women's writing only as an absence of women's voice in history, literature, and the main currents of life. She states that "women have been denied the full resources of language and have been forced into silence. . . . The holes in discourse, the blanks and gaps and silences, are not the spaces where female consciousness reveals itself but the blinds of a 'prison-house language'" (*New Feminist Criticism*, pp. 255–56). French feminists like Gauthier view the blank pages, gaps, borders, spaces and silence, and holes in discourse differently, suggesting that these rhetorical devices represent a new space for women. Although Gauthier claims that this is "the aspect of feminine writing which is the most difficult to verbalize because it becomes compromised, rationalized, masculinized as it explains itself" (p. 164), she nevertheless accepts it as a positive women's space, unlike many of the American critics. However, like Kristeva, she romanticizes this space, ignoring the narrative realities of marking and reading women's silence in a text and the social realities of the silence of exclusion.

Consequently, in dealing with the topic of silence, we cannot ignore Woolf's notion of a "woman's sentence." Locating her interest in this question "precisely in her textual practice," as Toril Moi urges, we discover in *A Room of One's Own* Woolf's call for "a woman's sentence": "The weight, the pace, the stride of a man's mind are too unlike her own for her to lift anything substantial from him successfully. . . . There was no common sentence ready for her use" (p. 79). The inclusion and patterning of lexical, syntactic, and structural silences in Woolf's elastic sentences, as well as the thematic association of women and silence to be developed in Chapter 2, conforms, to some degree, to Gilbert and Gubar's characterizations of a feminine text on a lexical, syntactic, rhythmic, and narrative level. It is a sentence that inscribes a rhythmic subtext consciously into the text. "Yet despite Woolf's ardor" Gilbert says, "no serious research into empirical linguistics has definitively disclosed what might be the special traits of 'a woman's sentence'" ("Woman's Sentence," p. 229) for those interested in the relationship between gender and writing. However, we can speculate. Although the notion is appealing, it is also difficult to establish what such a sentence might be without falling into essentialist definitions of women. Gilbert here, like Denis Donoghue in a review of *The Norton Anthology of Women*, mistakenly assumes "a" feminine sentence with universal traits, as Donoghue assumes "a" feminist "context of feeling" or "agenda": one unified criticism that would represent the perspective of all female critics. However, we must acknowledge for women what we do for men: there are multiple "women's sentences," styles of writing and criticism, that will develop out of different personal and historical contexts and ways of being "feminine."

To return to Woolf's question with sensitivity to its possible abuses by traditional or essentialist critics locked into realism: Is there such a thing as a woman's sentence? Woolf suggests that there is. And in studying this sentence, we must establish that there is no one feminine sentence or aesthetic for all women writers. My contribution toward such an aesthetic is that one of the traits of "a woman's sentence" as developed by Woolf is that it includes more "silence" than speech as empirically demonstrated in the lexicon of silence, punctuation of suspension, metaphors, themes, scenes of silence, and undercurrent of alternating rhythm in this book. It is a sentence that includes more techniques for poetically representing the various kinds of silence in women's psychic lives than sentences fashioned by other modernist writers. Words and silence alternate, capturing the rhythmic trace of mind as it moves from the conscious to the unconscious level: it goes beyond words to paralinguistically mark the energies that animate the psychic life of women in Woolf's time and place. The silence is represented by Woolf's lexicon of "gulfs, gaps, fissures, abysses, and cracks," which allow us to peer into previously unrepresented or hidden aspects of mind and experience. This is not the "snare of silence" that Hélène Cixous, a representative of *l'écriture feminine* school, writes of when she states that "It is by writing, from and toward women, and by taking up the challenge of speech . . . that women will confirm women in a place other than that which is reserved in and by the symbolic, that is, in a place other than silence" (p. 249). Rather, Virginia Woolf's representation of silence marks women's minds, feelings, and experience: woman is serenely absent and present, both at once, in Woolf's narration.

Silence is often, though not exclusively, associated with women, and it contributes to an alternating "up down" rhythm of a woman's mind, her participation in and absence from the conversation of the novel or, more broadly, the public and social conversation of the time and thus her outward and inward turnings. In her diary, Woolf makes "A note by way of advising other Virginias with other books that this is the way of the thing: up down up down" (4, p. 262). This may be her attempt, one of many, to capture what the open-ended, evolving "feminine" is.

Such an assertion is sure to provoke grumbles, not only among traditional critics who resist the foregrounding of gender as a critical or aesthetic category, but also among feminist critics who fear the question will lead to essentialist definitions of women and style. Although, at this stage of feminist criticism, authors like Judith Fetterly and Toril Moi urge us to be self-consciously "female" and "resisting" as we read and write texts, we must recognize that we venture into difficult critical territory. Not only do we add the category of gender to literary criticism, but, more important, we also challenge traditional assumptions about the way a literary critic thinks of him or her self as she or he writes. It

involves the critic in examining his or her own personal and cultural definitions of the terms "masculine" and "feminine" in grappling with the
rhetoric of Woolf's so-called feminine sentences. There is, among critics
in general, resistance to this exposure of one's categories even though
traditional critics have used gender categories seemingly unconsciously
for a long time. In discussing gender and reading in this way, we are
restoring, as Derrida does in his literary and philosophical works, the
complexities of reading to the dignity of a philosophical question, not
just a critical battle of the sexes. A feminist perspective, one of several
types of criticism employed in this book, contributes a new honesty to
the philosophical debate on reading now raging, based on the belief that
"the introduction of a neutral language of observations . . . is hopeless"
(Kuhn, p. 126).

One of the reasons for the controversy surrounding feminist readings is that, given the history of the profession, men have rendered the
judgments of qualities to be attributed to either sex and literary style.
Male and female critics now more conscious of themselves as male and
female readers have been reminded of their cultural constructions. The
gender label "feminine" when applied to literary style has traditionally
emerged from male associations, myths, fantasies, and dreams. Sometimes the feminine is defined by subject matter (home, family, housekeeping, flowers), qualities of perception (intuitive, instinctive, primitive),
tone (sweet, tender, sensitive, poetic), language (nuanced color terms,
emotional terms), or the body (pregnancy, motherhood, sexuality). Now
more female critics are limning the "feminine" from the inside as well
as the outside, but this concept is, as Virginia Woolf always asserts,
evolving.

However, there are critics representing a certain stage in feminist
thinking who are essentialist in their definitions of women. Feminist
readings of Woolf by Elaine Showalter, and Elizabeth Abel, and some
critics of *l'écriture feminine* school, have interpreted the narrative silences
under discussion, whether thematic or rhythmic, as a mimetic signal of
the exclusion of the female novelist, and of women in general, from
the social or the public domain. For example, in "Narrative Structures
and Female Development: The Case of Mrs. Dalloway," Abel hypothesizes that:

The fractured developmental plot reflects the encounter of gender with narrative form and adumbrates the psychoanalytic story of female development, a
story Freud and Woolf devised concurrently and separately, and published simultaneously in 1925. . . . The silences that punctuate *Mrs. Dalloway* reflect the

interruptions and enigmas of female experience and ally the novel with a recent trend in feminist aesthetics. (pp. 162–63, 184)

Such criticism, though useful in revealing the "facts" of women's lives, is what the feminist scholar Catherine Stimpson calls "vulgar mimesis." The correlation of the gaps and interruptions in women's lives with narrative style in the feminine *écriture* school, as well as in Abel's work, is a brand of social realism in which the silences that punctuate a work are viewed mimetically as a sign of women's linguistic shortcomings, absence from public life, and thus the absence of their voice in literary works. Although in a broad sense all literature is mimetic, all art a bricolage of life's pieces, viewing the gaps in narration as the result of gender ignores the importance of aesthetic transformations of raw experience. In paying attention to the silence that gives us access to the psychic life of women often omitted from novels, Woolf establishes a historical life of the mind for women in literature—she is not just mimetically marking its absence.

If, however, we build upon Abel's and Showalter's realist perspectives and view women's narrative silences, now infused with psychic life by Woolf, as imaginative transformations or poetic representations of "presence," we establish a new set of values. Women, in this view, are present in the silences we are learning to read, and they illuminate the "dark places of psychology" and the metaphysics of life because they embody the unspoken, the ineffable, the unfinished, and the unconscious. They are positioned in but not confined to the social realm where Showalter and Abel note their social "absence" and where Woolf, taking up the challenge of writing, imaginatively embodies their "presence." And if Woolf moves away from a certain notion of facts and reality in her novels, it is because, as Gillian Beer states, "she denies the claim of such ordering to be all inclusive" (p. 90). It is important to note that women do think about other things than just being women, and their silences include but are not limited to a critique of patriarchy. Silence also points to the limitations of language, in general, and Western notions of presence and absence, writing and knowledge, in particular.

Woolf's interest in fashioning an "elastic sentence" that could contain a woman's mind and its pace was piqued by Dorothy Richardson, who consciously worked on developing a feminine sentence. Woolf says of Richardson in her review of "Revolving Lights":

She has invented, or, if she has not invented, developed and applied to her own uses, a sentence which we might call the psychological sentence of the feminine gender. It is of a more elastic fibre than the old, capable of stretching to the extreme, of suspending the frailest particles, of enveloping the vaguest shapes. . . . It is a woman's sentence, but only in the sense that it is used to describe a woman's mind by a writer who is neither proud nor afraid of anything that she may discover in the psychology of her sex. (*Collected Essays* 3, p. 367)

The distinctions and qualifications here are important, for a woman's sentence is labeled as such "only in the sense that it is used to describe a woman's mind." Woolf suggests, then, that the adventurous woman writer can put language to her own uses and capture the traces of an enlightened absence, the psychic life of a woman formerly relegated to "dumbness" or "stupidity": nineteenth-century words that were often applied to women and animals and that contain "silence" in their roots. "Stupid" has the connotations "benumbed" and "dazed," which connects with "slow-witted"; "dumbness" implies "vexatious obtuseness" or "lack of intelligence." Such usage with traces in today's language—"dumb blonde"—connotes the subordinate and inferior position of women in society. However, if silence is read in a new way, we gain useful insights not only into a woman's sentence but also into a woman's mind and into more general problems of meaning in life and books. Woolf's "inward turning to convey the flow of mental experience" (Edel, p. 7) therefore involves the philosophical discourse of feminism as well as of modernism.

Woolf's narrative coup is to subvert the sexist tradition of the silent female by infusing her silence with a new being, a new psychic and narrative life. Through her marking of silence she shows that silence might express something other than an inferior and subordinate state of mind in women. Recognizing, then, that a social vision is the genesis of narrative in her novels, we see the relation between narration, speech, subjectivity, and gender, and the possibility of different models of textuality. Post-structuralist and feminist criticism has concentrated on explicating the role of the "speaking" subject in women's texts (Hélène Cixous), privileging the "symbolic" linguistic mode, and thus missing the subtlety of Woolf's interest in silence rather than speech. Like the philosopher Ludwig Wittgenstein, Woolf intuits that man or woman is not defined by having to speak to reveal his or her humanity. She marks a discourse of silence more often in women than in men, not as mimesis, a representation of their absence from society or the unattained "symbolic" modes of language, but as a sign of their self-presence and self-resistance: "a source of insight and power rather than merely of powerlessness" (Johnson, *Deconstruction*, p. 46). This is part of the strategy of the "split self" that Barbara Johnson describes: "[The woman's] ability to speak grows out of her ability not to mix inside with outside, not to pretend that there is no difference, but to assume and articulate the incompatible forces involved in her own division. The sign of an authentic voice is thus not self-identity but self-difference" (*The Critical Difference*, p. 164). A silent woman is a social "trace" in Derrida's sense of "the mark of the absence of a presence" (*Of Grammatology*, p. xvii). A woman cannot "be" and "mean" in a network of differences except in relation to men; we do not know how to decipher women's silence in Woolf's novels unless we understand the talk and "phrase-making" of men.

Woolf denies the silence of the position of a woman even as she expresses it by symbolically "sounding" or "marking" it through a lexicon, punctuation, rhythm, themes, and metaphors in her novels as a writer. In doing so, Woolf feminizes metaphors of mind. With an experimental stroke of great subtlety, the presentation of female body-mind-feeling states through visual images and the symbolic medium of words and rhythm, demonstrated below in Chapter 4, Woolf collapses, erases, and diffuses the "semiotic" and the "symbolic." In summoning silence into the text as language, as a presence, she resists Kristeva's metaphysical assignment of the feminine to the realm of semiotics or "nonverbal signifying systems."

CONFIGURATIONS OF SILENCE

Since the many kinds of silence to be discussed here present difficulties in articulation as well as audibility, we must make distinctions. Woolf heightens our awareness of silence in life, its varied types and functions, as she narrates its rich and complex nature in her novels. There is, after all, a certain ambiguity in silence as a communicative sign, it being more context-embedded than speech. In Woolf's novels, such ambiguity is explored, and in her first novel, *The Voyage Out*, silence often indicates unexpressed feeling, the unsaid; later, in *The Waves*, silence represents aspects of mind, life, and Nature, the ineffable; in *Between the Acts*, silence signifies what happens in the personal and historical spaces between the acts, the unspoken between the islands of speech.

Broadly, there are six configurations of silence that will take us within sight of the linguistically and philosophically intriguing subject of silence in Woolf's novels: psychological, social, historical, philosophical, rhythmic, and structural. Each of these kinds of silence is revealed in what shall be labeled "scenes of silence" in the novels, and, often, they intertwine.

This reading of narrative silence, however, is difficult because one of the assumptions about reading here is that "the reader brings to the surface a pattern or design that the work conceals; the reader fills gaps" (Culler, p. 37). This is an active, not a passive, reading of silence. However, since silence can mean many things, it poses problems of interpretation for the reader. As Deborah Tannen states in a sociolinguistic analysis of silence: "Silence is the extreme manifestation of indirectness. If indirectness is a matter of saying one thing and meaning another, silence can be a matter of saying nothing and meaning something" (Tannen and Saville-Troike, p. 97). Silence in a text may represent the unspoken, the unsaid, or an emotional loneliness or a pause as someone dips a pen in ink; silence can signal a question, a promise, or a denial; it can mean a warning, a deceit, a threat, or an insult, or even a request or command. It can denote indifference, absurdity, skepticism, or even selfishness; it may signal that someone is thinking or holding his peace, or waiting quietly, or being cut off or stifled; or it is something unsayable; it may even reveal something about human relationships, about gender or marriage.

For example, there are the wordless communications in marriage. In *To the Lighthouse*, Mr. and Mrs. Ramsay's "eyes met for a second but they did not want to speak to each other. They had nothing to say . . . something seemed to go from him to her" (p. 255). At another time, Lily silently observes Mr. and Mrs. Ramsay observing one of their children, and all communication is channeled into the visual: "So that is marriage, Lily thought, a man and a woman looking at a girl throwing a ball" (p. 110). On a narrative level, these scenes would be classified as a "continuous silence," a silence that completes a communication or thought between characters. Such silences will be distinguished from "discontinuous silences," which imply that communication between characters has been interrupted. When there is continuity of subjectivity between characters, the words and the silences result in a pattern of communication; when there is discontinuity in the thought as it moves between the space of two characters, there is a discontinuous silence, an interrupted communication, and usually a reflective or meditative state follows. For example, in *Between the Acts*, Mrs. Swithin begins to say something about going in to see Miss LaTrobe's play but then drifts off into another state of mind, illustrating a discontinuous silence where communication is interrupted: " 'It is time,' said Mrs. Swithin, 'to go and join—.' She left the sentence unfinished, as if she were of two minds, and they fluttered to right and to left, like pigeons rising from the grass" (p. 74). The narrator and character fuse in this psycho-narration as we are provided first with direct discourse, then the suspension of "talk" and the narrative observation, "She left the sentence unfinished." Then the visual metaphor of the fluttering image of birds captures the state of mind of an unfinished sentence and moves us into interiority. In admitting the drifting of mind or the surfacing of the unconscious aspects of self during conversation, Woolf presents the "moment" in life and narration and "all that it includes."

On a broad structural level, then, silence, representing interiority (both conscious and unconscious), occupies a space as important as that of talk on Woolf's narrative canvas. Its presence is not just a formalist preoccupation: it simultaneously reveals Woolf's social vision about the value of talk and silence as it relates to communication between the sexes, and to communication in general. Woolf's novels after *Jacob's Room* are "inaudible" or silent since they trace the unspoken life of her characters through a narration of silent observation and indirect discourse rather than exterior events. It is what interests her. Most of the communication in *Between the Acts*, her last novel and perhaps the "novel about silence" that Terence Hewet projects in *The Voyage Out*, is inaudible though it begins in sound. It is a novel that appreciates the contributions of silence to talk; indeed the whole novel is a kind of silence that prepares the reader for the last lines of the novel, where it is said of Isa and Giles: "They spoke."

Woolf structures many solitary scenes to create a narrative space for the exploration of psychological silences or interiority, and, consequently, the development of this discourse of silence. Such frequent marking of the narrative presence of silence is unique in Woolf among modernist writers, and it is her experimental contribution to the marking of subjectivity in writing, and more particularly female subjectivity. Words like "think, reflect, said nothing, not listening, observing, wish, suppose, know, intend, feel, hope, believe, silence, secrets, wordlessly, unsaid, unsayable" signal this interiority in Woolf. The solitary scenes capture the solitary activity or meditation of a character, most often a woman, or characters silently watching the behavior of others. For example, we note Lily's silence of determination, her effort to focus on her painting and not to give in to Mr. Ramsay's demand for pity after the death of Mrs. Ramsay:

Still she could *say nothing*; the whole horizon seemed *swept bare of objects to talk about*; *could only feel*, amazedly, as Mr. Ramsay stood there, how his gaze seemed to fall dolefully over the sunny grass and discolour it. . . . It was immensely to her discredit, sexually, to stand there *dumb*. One said—*what did one say?*—. . . . His immense self-pity, his demand for sympathy poured and spread itself in pools at her feet, and all she did, miserable sinner that she was, was to draw her skirts a little closer round her ankles, lest she should get wet. *In complete silence* she stood there, grasping her paint brush. (*To the Lighthouse*, pp. 227–28; my italics)

However, silence is not exclusive to solitary or meditative states. Woolf is also interested in capturing the silences and distortions of communication as well as the subjectivity of madness: Septimus in *Mrs. Dalloway* and the village idiot in *Between the Acts*. Who before Woolf in modern literature tries to capture the loneliness and thoughts of someone mad who "lose[s] communication with the world outside one's mind"? Septimus expresses this state: "I leant over the edge of the boat and fell down, he thought. I went under the sea. I have been dead, and yet am now alive, but let me rest still; he begged (he was talking to himself again—it was awful, awful!)" (p. 104). Here the scene of silence involves Rezia, Septimus's wife, and she can only feel powerless as she observes his solitude and lack of communication: "it was awful, awful!"

The solitude, the meditation, or the determination of some human beings is realized in silence, as others sit yearning for communication but do not achieve it. In *To the Lighthouse*, Mrs. Ramsay silently meditates about Mr. Ramsay's silence:

Slowly it came into her head, why is it then that one wants people to marry? What was the value, the meaning of things? (Every word they said now would be true). Do say something, she thought, wishing only to hear his voice. For the shadow, the thing folding them in was beginning, she felt, to close round her again. Say anything, she begged, looking at him, as if for help.

He was silent, swinging the compass on his watch-chain to and fro, and thinking of Scott's novels and Balzac's novels. But through the crepuscular walls of their intimacy, for they were drawing together, involuntarily, coming side by side, quite close, she could feel his mind like a raised hand shadowing her mind. (p. 184)

The married silence that joins, "the crepuscular walls of their intimacy," as well as the silence that separates, "his mind like a raised hand shadowing her mind," are both present here. Such a wonderful passage illuminates the silences of a man through the mind of a woman who suggests that his silence is one of abstraction, "thinking of Scott's novels and

Balzac's novels" (realists both), and she wishes to lure him into communication.

Later in the novel, after Mrs. Ramsay's death, we find a silent Mr. Ramsay again, but it is a shrouded and proud silence that reveals his inability to connect, this time with his children. "All the being and the doing" of Mrs. Ramsay's life, the coaxing of relationship, is gone, and Mr. Ramsay's children, Cam and James, both wish to ask him "What do you want? . . . Ask us anything and we will give it to you. But he did not ask them anything" (p. 318).

Mr. Ramsay keeps his silence here while Woolf breaks the silence of and about women's consciousness and life in her novels. Though concerned with the "unnatural silences" Tillie Olsen writes of in *Silences*—those silences of the inarticulate that relate to women's circumstances of class, color, the times, the opportunity for education, and the scope for public discourse—Woolf is equally concerned with the way silence has come to define women's voice and relationships in literature and life. Silence draws our attention to the way in which women relate to one another. Perhaps it reveals "the still hidden facts of our still unknown psychology" that women "are not so loose-lipped and fond of gossip as the tradition would have it" (*Three Guineas*, pp. 163, 73). Women, often "silent companions" to one another in Woolf's novels, seem to need words less than men. This is illustrated in a moment of being that Mrs. Ramsay and Lily share on the beach:

Mrs. Ramsay sat silent. She was glad, Lily thought, to rest in silence, uncommunicative; to rest in the extreme obscurity of human relationships. Who knows what we are, what we feel? Who knows even at the moment of intimacy, this is knowledge? (p. 256)

The silence of unexpressed feeling surfaces here as in an earlier scene with Lily and Mrs. Ramsay:

For it was not knowledge but unity that she desired, not inscriptions on tablets, nothing that could be written in any language known to men. . . . And yet, she knew knowledge and wisdom were stored up in Mrs. Ramsay's heart. How then, she had asked herself, did one know one thing or another thing about people, sealed as they were? (p. 79)

Silence marks a bond between women. Lily ruminates:

Aren't things spoilt then, Mrs. Ramsay may have asked (it seemed to have happened so often, this silence by her side) by saying them? Aren't we more expressive thus? The moment at least seemed extraordinarily fertile. (p. 256)

In *Mrs. Dalloway*, Lady Bruton invites Richard Dalloway and Hugh Whitbread but not Clarissa to lunch. Nevertheless, Lady Bruton's inquiry,

"How's Clarissa?" was known by women infallibly, to be a signal from a well-wisher, from an almost silent companion, whose utterances (half a dozen perhaps in the course of a lifetime) signified recognition of some feminine comradeship which went beneath masculine lunch parties and united Lady Bruton and Mrs. Dalloway, who seldom met, and appeared when they did meet indifferent and even hostile, in a singular bond. (pp. 160–61)

As Mrs. Ramsay says of women:

Don't we communicate better silently? Aren't we (women, at any rate) more expressively silently gliding high together, side by side, in the curious dumbness which is much more to our taste than speech? (p. 256)

And Mrs. Manresa in *Between the Acts* "ogled Isabella," for "always when she spoke to women, she veiled her eyes, for they, being conspirators, saw through it" (p. 41). Silence is here a marking of an enlightened presence and relationship. These are silences that signify not women's inferiority but their superiority, understanding as we do women's reasons for silence. Mrs. Ramsay "was silent always. She knew then—she knew never having learnt. Her simplicity fathomed what clever people falsified" (p. 46).

Many of the above silences "figure" interiority, but they are not signifiers that endlessly float in the "dark places of psychology." Rather, the silences are also "positioned," as Bakhtin would say, or "inscribed," as Derrida would term it, as social signifiers. Woolf also gives social silences their effect by textually marking in various ways the "pauses" between people's remarks that are, in her philosophy, as much a part of the conversation as the words. For example, in as early a story as "Kew Gardens," written in 1919, the narrator of the story notes:

Long pauses came between each of these remarks.
    "Lucky it isn't Friday," he observed.
    "Why? D'you believe in luck?"
    "They make you pay sixpence anyway. Isn't it worth sixpence?"
    "What's 'it'—what do you mean by 'it'?"
    "O anything—I mean—you know what I mean." (*Complete Shorter Fiction*, p. 88)

Both the framing narrative remark about "long pauses between" and the use of the dash create the presence of silences in conversation.

Her silences, then, are structured around not only solitary activity but also social conversation, custom, and belief. And it is here in society that Woolf continues to explore psychological states, not only the "unsaid" but also the "unspoken" not yet formulated and the "unsayable" based on the social taboos—the silences in company, between men and women, and between women concerning gender and sex. Communicative silences—some of which are continuous and complete communication; others, discontinuous because they interrupt it—occur at Mrs. Ramsay's dinner party in *To the Lighthouse*, at Mrs. Dalloway's party, and at the Pointz Hall luncheon in *Between the Acts*. For example, Mrs. Ramsay is captured in a narrative moment that Genette might describe as doubly silent: all conversation in the novel is arrested as Mrs. Ramsay retreats from the talk at her dinner party to a space that is silent: "Now she need not listen. It could not last, she knew, but at the moment her eyes were so clear that they [unveiled] these people . . . the sudden silent trout are all lit up hanging, trembling" (p. 160). Given the ambiguity of silence as a communicative sign, the social context sometimes helps to determine the interpretation.

There are also the silences of marriage. In the relationship between Mr. and Mrs. Ramsay, silence grows up between them from habit and is sometimes a marker of positive communication: "She had triumphed again. *She had not said it* yet he knew. . . . He found talking so much easier than she did. He could say things—she never could" (pp. 184–85; my italics). So in reading the kinds of silence present in this scene, a reader finds a psychological silence, Mrs. Ramsay's retreat from words; a social silence, Mrs. Ramsay's choice of being silent in her dialogue with Mr. Ramsay; perhaps a historical silence, in that there may be certain things that Mrs. Ramsay cannot say as a Victorian woman to a Victorian man; and perhaps a philosophical silence, as Mrs. Ramsay realizes that there are things one cannot express about life, something ineffable outside of human relations. Since the emphasis in this scene of silence is on the communication between Mr. and Mrs. Ramsay, it could broadly be labeled a social silence, but the other kinds of silence are implied also, and it is important to keep the multiplicity and flow in the experience of silence though struggling with the static as a critic. As was said of the lighthouse, "nothing was simply one thing" (p. 277).

Mr. and Mrs. Ramsay's relationship exemplifies both positive and negative silences. Although they experience wordless communications that signal their closeness, "That was typical of their relationship. Many things were left unsaid" (p. 263), there are also moments when "There was nothing to be said." This latter kind of silence, which Woolf refers to as a "gulf," is a separation between husband and wife that Clarissa Dalloway believes is necessary in marriage:

And there is a dignity in people; a solitude; even between husband and wife a gulf; and that one must respect, thought Clarissa, watching him [Richard] open the door; for one would not part with it oneself, or take it, against his will, from one's husband, without losing one's independence, one's self-respect— something, after all, priceless. (p. 283)

In *Between the Acts*, the relationship between Isa and Giles is also marked by an unspoken longing for intimacy, and they silently read each other's thoughts and communicate on a subjective level: "Isabella guessed the words that Giles had not spoken" (p. 48).

The unmarried state and courtship also has its silences. In *Night and Day*, Mary's silence is a response to Ralph's insincere speech: "There were two reasons that kept Mary very silent during this speech. . . . In the first place, Ralph made no mention of marriage; in the second, he was not speaking the truth" (p. 222). After Rachel and Terence fall in love in *The Voyage Out*, "Silence seemed to have fallen upon the world" (p. 271), and like lovers in a Shakespeare comedy, "Long silences came between their words" (p. 283).

In addition to psychological and social silences, which often intertwine in a Woolf novel, Woolf represents historical silences. These relate, in general, to human history, its brief moment in the universe, and sometimes its meaninglessness. In *The Waves*, Louis cautions: "But listen . . . to the world moving through abysses of infinite space. It roars; the lighted strip of history is past and our Kings and Queens; we are gone; our civilization; the Nile; and all life. Our separate drops are dissolved; we are extinct, lost in the abysses of time, in the darkness" (p. 225). This meaninglessness also relates to those on the margins of society: women, children, the obscure, the mad. In *Between the Acts*, for example, historical silences are represented in Miss LaTrobe's pageant. During the historical procession of scenes from English history, Woolf marks and then erases the presence of the working class by marching the villagers across the stage representing Chaucer's pilgrims: "All the time the villagers were passing in and out between the trees. They were singing; but only a word or two was audible '. . . wore ruts in the grass . . . built the house in the lane . . . .' The wind blew away the connecting words of their chant" (p. 80). Here the accomplishments of the pilgrims, the "ruts" and the "building" associated with the working class, are not memorialized or marked in history, but "the connecting words" of their story are blown away by the winds.

The silences of the working-class women whom Woolf taught at Morley College in 1905, and whom she wrote about in her introduction to Margaret Llewelyn Davies's *Life as We Have Always Known It*, are also represented in her novels in characters like the housekeeper, Mrs. McNab, in *To the Lighthouse*. In addition, Septimus, who is shell-shocked after witnessing the death of his friend and others in war, represents the damaged soldier of World War I. Silences that connect with the historical themes of the role of the working class, of women and of soldiers in World War I, appear.

Woolf knows that words have their limitations as well as their possibilities in capturing "what life is," and so she also creates philosophical silences to express this sense in her novels. In writing about *The Waves*, she states: "I am convinced that I am right to seek for a station whence I can set my people against time and the sea" (*Diary* 3, p. 264). This station is a philosophical one outside the space of human relations: "The sense of a world continuing without us" (*The Waves*, p. 122). This experimental intention to capture "something in the universe" in this novel stymies some critics who "underread" Woolf (rather than "overread," as the critic Nancy Miller suggests) in finding an affinity with only the psychological or social dimensions in this novel. Woolf's expression here of the ineffability of life is not an acknowledgment of "emptiness at the heart of life" and of her aesthetic as Mark Hussey suggests in *The Singing of the Real World* (pp. 39–40). Like the Western Inquirer in Martin Heidegger's work, critics sometimes confuse emptiness and nothingness. Heidegger makes a distinction between Western and Eastern views of silence and emptiness in an imaginary dialogue between a Western Inquirer and a Japanese philosopher:

> Inquirer: That emptiness then is the same thing as nothingness.
> Japanese: We marvel to this day how the European could lapse into interpreting as nihilistic the nothingness of which you speak in the lecture. To us, emptiness is the loftiest name for what you mean to say with the word "Being." (*On the Way to Language*, p. 19)

Hussey, in responding to Woolf's experimental novel, *The Waves*, as an "aesthetic failure" for being more about art than life—more about abstraction and pattern than human relations—misses the philosophical expressions of "being" in the novel. In her *Diary*, Woolf ruminates about her themes of "dawn, the shells on a beach" while working on an early

version of *The Waves*: "Well all this is of course the 'real life'; and nothingness only comes in the absence of this" (4, p. 236): "nothingness" here
is the "emptiness" or the "blankness" preceding creative expression. Or
"nothingness" can be a sublime state evoked by an Italian landscape of
"infinite emptiness, loneliness, silence" (4, p. 158); or being "overcome
with rigidity and nothingness" after an illness (4, p. 221); or the flatness
of feeling and fear of death during an air raid, lying in a field, fearing the
bomb will drop: "I thought, I think, of nothingness—flatness, my mood
being flat" (5, p. 311). Around the time that Woolf was writing *The
Waves*, she expressed her dissatisfaction with what she called "psychology" and spoke of her desire to break free from "personality" as the
focus of her fiction, realizing "how it is not oneself but something in the
universe that one is left with" (*Diary* 3, p. 113).

Philosophical silences in Woolf emanate, then, from her sense of
what we in the twentieth century would term the "ineffable" and what
she, at the turn of the century, marked as "dumb" or "inarticulate." She
wishes to capture in philosophical themes and silences the eternal and
the changeless in life, outside of human relations and the natural interest
that evokes in readers. She sometimes describes life from the perspective of being "inside" something and seeing through a film opaquely.
In "Modern Fiction" she asserts that "Life is not a series of gig-lamps
symmetrically arranged; but a luminous halo, a semi-transparent envelope surrounding us from the beginning of consciousness to the end"
(*Common Reader*, p. 154), and in "A Sketch of the Past" she describes
"the feeling . . . of lying in a grape and seeing through a film of semi-
transparent yellow" (*Moments of Being*, p. 65). Life is semi-transparent,
only partially knowable, and silence, a "floating signifier," marks this.
In *The Waves*, Bernard says "We felt enlarge itself round us the huge
blackness of what is outside us, of what we are not" (pp. 196–97), illuminating an awareness of being heightened by the recognition of "not
being" or death.

It is against this philosophical backdrop, present in all of her novels,
that Woolf poignantly conveys her perilous sense of life. After the death
of her mother when she was thirteen, of Stella Duckworth, her step-sister,
when she was fifteen, and of her brother Toby when she was twenty-four,
she states in her autobiographical writing: "So I came to think of life as
something of extreme reality. And this, of course, increased my feeling
of my own importance. Not in relation to human beings: in relation to
the force which had respected me sufficiently enough to make me feel
what was real" (*Moments of Being*, p. 118). This "force" of life heightens

her sense of "reality" and makes her feel vulnerable also. This feeling is captured in meditation in *The Waves*:

And, what is this moment of time, this particular day in which I have found myself caught? The growl of traffic might be any uproar—forest trees or the roar of wild beasts. Time has whizzed back an inch or two on its reel; our short progress has been cancelled. I think also that our bodies are in truth naked. We are only lightly covered with buttoned cloth; and beneath these pavements are skulls, bones, silence. (p. 81)

This image of life, reminiscent of an Edvard Munch engraving, is like "a strip of pavement over an abyss" (*Diary* 2, p. 73). The sense of it "being very dangerous to live even one day" (*Mrs. Dalloway*, p. 11) recurs in her writing. Sometimes, then, "emptiness" and "nothingness" signal an existential loneliness and a philosophical silence in the face of death. After her good friend Lytton Strachey's death, she notes her sense of emptiness in the world: "I wake in the night with the sense of being in an empty hall. Lytton dead and all those factories building" (*Diary* 4, p. 74). Does the death of God, as George Steiner argues in *Real Presences*, underpin this sense of absence and emptiness in Woolf's aesthetic vision and current theories of meaning? Woolf denies this in her essay "On Not Knowing Greek":

There is a sadness at the back of life which they [the Greeks] do not attempt to mitigate. Entirely aware of their own standing in the shadow, and yet alive to every tremor and gleam of existence, there they endure, and it is to the Greeks that we turn when we are sick of the vagueness, of the confusion, of the Christianity and its consolations, of our own age. (*Common Reader* 1, p. 39)

Rhoda in *The Waves* represents this Greek sense of loneliness in the universe, even leaping from a cliff to her death like Sappho. She lives outside conventional time in what Woolf describes as "the white spaces that lie between hour and hour"—the interludes. Her mind contains "whiteness," "emptiness," and "nothingness." Through Woolf's psycho-narration, we discover that Rhoda's "mind lodges in those white circles; it steps through those white loops into emptiness alone" (p. 22); "Alone," she says, "I often fall down into nothingness" (p. 44). All of these qualities and sensations—whiteness, emptiness, nothingness—are subjective qualities that relate to bodily and mental sensations.

But this space of "emptiness" can be a positive state that precedes creativity. Words like "vacancy" and "vapor" in Marivaux and of "lifelessness" in Mallarmé signal, on the contrary, a void. Even though these states may be connected to sleep or illness and may signal a retreat into oneself, they are linked in Woolf, as in other female artists, to creative power. Recently the performance artist Laurie Anderson created a work called "Empty Places," which stands, she says, for a big space: "The word 'empty' to me doesn't necessarily mean desolate. . . . An empty place is a place for potential. There's lots and lots of big skies in this performance and there's lots of things about the desire to leave. . . . Desire is the consciousness of a certain kind of emptiness that has to be filled" (p. 41). Like many female and non-Western artists, Anderson views emptiness as a presence, a space to be filled. "Emptiness" is a creative "absence."

Woolf intertwines three philosophical traditions to fill the canvas of silence and "emptiness" in her novels: the Oriental, the Romantic, and the meditative. She incorporates mystical elements of Oriental metaphysics, suggesting to the twentieth century the necessity of transcending language in Buddhism or Taoism, for example, and moving toward silence as illustrated in Sau Ling Wong's dissertation, "Virginia Woolf and the Chinese Point of View." In her sketch of Elizabeth Dalloway, Clarissa's daughter, who, like Percival in *The Waves*, does not speak in the novel, she includes details that suggest the influence of the East and the Orient on her character, which is largely unknown and unformed: "Elizabeth . . . was dark; had Chinese eyes in a pale face; and Oriental mystery; was gentle, considerate, still" (p. 186). Lily, too, possessing a name that embodies Oriental silence and far-seeing eyes in a puckered face, fixes the moment of illumination with her paintbrush.

Another philosophical tradition of the nineteenth century, Romanticism, also arrests moments in time and marks them with silence. However, this silent moment is not marked by a simple external gesture, as in the Oriental tradition, but is revealed as an inner "moment of being." Woolf is interested in intensities and qualities of being and experience; she removes certain moments in life from ordinary space and the limits associated with the physical world, and she marks them with silence. For example, Lily ruminates about such moments while painting:

illuminations, matches struck unexpectedly in the dark; here was one. This, that, and the other; herself and Charles Tansley and the breaking wave; Mrs. Ramsay bringing them together; Mrs. Ramsay bringing them together; Mrs. Ramsay saying, "Life stand still here"; Mrs. Ramsay making of the moment something permanent . . . this was of the nature of a revelation. In the midst of chaos there was shape. (*To the Lighthouse*, pp. 240–41)

This separation of a person or an object from its context in the ordinary world to prepare for a sudden illumination is a variation on the Romantic moment in which, as the critic Frank Kermode puts it, "chronos" suddenly becomes "kairos." M. H. Abrams, in his fascinating study of the Romantic tradition, *Natural Supernaturalism*, states that this Romantic separation and moment has a continuing literary life:

The illuminated phenomenal object, if transparent to a significance beyond itself, reappears as the symbol of the Symbolists, but if opaque, as the image of the Imagist; in both cases, however, the Romantic object is usually cut off from its context in the ordinary world in common experience and assigned an isolated existence in the self-limited and self-sufficing work of art. And the moment of consciousness, the abrupt illumination in an arrest of time, has become a familiar component in modern fiction. (pp. 418–19)

A third kind of philosophical silence in Woolf, meditative silence, develops perhaps from the seventeenth-century meditative tradition of dialogue with God about life, death, and salvation, but it is adapted to a psychological end, a movement discussed by Abrams. For example, Mrs. Ramsay in *To the Lighthouse* feels the need "to be silent; to be alone" (p. 95), like many of Woolf's female characters. The tone and movement inward suggest the meditative stance discernible in seventeenth-century poetry, the lives of the saints, and the voice of a silent inner teacher in religious revelations such as those described by St. Augustine in his *Confessions*. However, the retreat from words into silence relates more to an escape from selfhood or children or household and the burdens of ego into a philosophical state of being than to an escape from the temptations of "sin" as in the other genres of religious writing.

Woolf's novels, then, contain these many silences, limning the themes that are of interest to her—the woman's angle, the dark places of psychology, social customs, historical change, and the philosophical dimension of life. However, these silences are not categorically presented as in this chapter, but gracefully interwoven in her novels.

In 1932, Woolf suggestively labeled her novels "waves" after she completed *The Waves*: "And I want to write another 4 novels: Waves, I mean" (*Diary* 4, p. 63). Her novels continue to pulse and reverberate in us as readers, in the generous silence and gaps that she, more than any other modern novelist, leaves for us as readers. We learn through reading to become better "listeners" to the text: listeners who perform by silently reading a score. We receive "the pattern, however disconnected and incoherent in appearance which each sight or incident scores upon the consciousness" (*Common Reader* 1, p. 155). We experience these impressions not as "external stimuli" in the tradition of phenomenology, as Alex Zwerdling in *Virginia Woolf and the Real World* asserts, but in rhythmic partnership with the mind: giving, making, and creating perceptions. We "preserve" the work, as Paul de Man urges, in simply listening to it. We dwell, in a Virginia Woolf novel, in language and silence, twin houses of being.

As will be demonstrated in Chapter 2, women's silences can sometimes be a sign of resistance and, at other times, repression. But the "emptiness" that Woolf attempts to describe is, in many cases, a state of being that is a prelude to creativity. It is a silence, a space that needs to be filled: "For if life is a bowl that fills and fills," then, for Woolf the writer, so too is the sentence and the page a space that fills and fills with her twelve novels, two biographies, five volumes of diaries, five volumes of letters, four volumes of essays, and twenty-seven unpublished volumes of reading notebooks. And yet, beauty "was escaping all the time; one could only offer a thimble to a torrent that could fill baths, lakes" (*Death of the Moth*, p. 8).

2

Keeping and Breaking
the Silence

WOOLF RECOGNIZES the peripheral role that women have played in society and the transmission of a literary heritage. She acknowledges the poignant sense of her own exclusion from Oxbridge in *A Room of One's Own*:

And I thought of the organ booming in the chapel and of the shut doors of the library; and I thought how unpleasant it is to be locked out; and I thought how it is worse perhaps to be locked in; and, thinking of the safety and prosperity of one sex and of the poverty and insecurity of the other and of the effect of tradition and of the lack of tradition upon the mind of a writer. (p. 24)

Women, she acknowledges, lack a tradition and participate in reading and writing literature within an essentially male tradition. This tradition is a long one.

Beginning with *Genesis*, this tradition exiles women from symbolic activity: Eve is not permitted to "name" the animals in creation. Women are advised to "learn silence with all submissiveness: permit no woman to teach or have authority over man; she is to keep silent" (1 Timothy 2: 11–12). The silence of women, then, is a mark of their absence from or inability to participate in the intellectual, social, and public spheres of life. In keeping with this tradition, the Bishop of Puebla advises Sor Juana Inés de la Cruz, a learned seventeenth-century Mexican nun who wrote an effective critical attack on the sermon of a Portuguese Jesuit priest: "Women should be content to study for the love of learning, and not in order to teach." Sor Juana, publicly chastised by the publication of and remarks on her position paper, responds, and articulates her views of silence:

If I am to confess all the truth, I shall confess that I cast about for some manner by which I might flee the difficulty of a reply, and was sorely tempted to take refuge in silence. But as silence is a negative thing, though it explains a great deal through the very stress of not explaining, we must assign some meaning to it that we may understand what the silence is intended to say, for if not, silence will say nothing, as that is its very office: to say nothing. (p. 18)

Unable to deal with the institutional and personal pressures in the patriarchal church, Sor Juana does explain a great deal through "the very stress of not explaining" in her recently published writing. She is not unlike Silentius, a female character disguised as a male in a little-known Arthurian romance, *Le Roman de Silence*, in employing a strategy of silence. Written in the second half of the thirteenth century by a male poet, Heldris de Cornuaille, this romance tells the story of Silentius, a girl who is given a boy's name by her parents because of the king's law forbidding the inheritance of wealth or title through the female line. Silentius, disguised as a warrior, becomes entangled in embarrassing seductions and is pulled in different directions by nature and environment as she grows older. Like Sor Juana and many of her literary successors, she is culturally trained to bear the secrets of her sex silently.

Such social and literary positioning of women as silent and observing, rather than as speaking subjects of their own lives, has sometimes led to the romanticization or criticism of the nonspeaker in post-structuralist or feminist criticism. Women's silence, though at first viewed as the proper expression of intellectual and cultural "place," is now relegated to a mode of pre-verbal "semiotics" by theoreticians like Julia Kristeva, an intellectual romanticization of the social and metaphysical exile noted earlier. Such views confirm the paradigm of the silent, observing woman, part of what Foucault labels the fundamental code of our culture "governing its language, its schemas of perception, its exchanges, its techniques, its values, the hierarchy of its practices" (*The Order of Things*, p. xx).

But suppose we re-position this silent, seemingly passive, absent woman in literature and life as an active subject of the "look" or the "gaze," instead of its object. Suppose we view women who are keeping the silence, not as people who have nothing to say, but as individuals who possess a richness of being that is as yet undisclosed. Suppose we alter the hierarchy of our reading practices and read female characters with different schemas of perception. Can we go back, as Luce Irigaray urges, "through the masculine imagery" to interpret not only "the way it has reduced women to silence" (p. 164) but also to read and infuse the silences with new meaning?

Post-structuralist and feminist criticism has concentrated on explicating the role of the speaking subject in women's texts, criticizing women for their absence, and privileging the "symbolic" linguistic mode that, as Kristeva claims, is less accessible to women at this historical moment because of their position in our culture. Because language has been emphasized as a subject of analysis for post-structuralists and feminists and the Western tradition in general, there is the danger, as Barbara Johnson notes, "of losing self-resistance as a source of insight and power rather than merely of powerlessness" (*Deconstruction*, p. 46). Women's silence, though sometimes signaling exclusion, can also be read as resistance, as a ritual of truth, as a keeping of silence about something, and as a refusal to enact a subordinate position.

This preoccupation with silence and subjectivity, or other dimensions of being—what Foucault describes as "the true undertaking of thought . . . to bring it as close to itself as possible . . . thinking the unthought . . . of ending man's [and woman's!] alienation by reconciling him with his own essence" (*Foucault Reader*, p. 327)—can be discerned in women's texts from Austen to Woolf. In learning to read this historically positioned silent woman, it is not my intention to valorize the nonspeaker over the speaker. However, as will be demonstrated in this chapter, there is a female tradition that replaces the privilege of the speaking subject with the observing, perceiving, thinking subject— sometimes because women are socially forced into such positions, and sometimes because their silence on the margins of conversation is resistant, deconstructing the "talk" of men. It is an engendering silence that, in its way, communicates.

This discriminating, gazing female subject "sees" different things, as Martin Jay notes in a fascinating article on the gaze: "What is in fact 'seen' is not a given, objective reality open to an innocent eye. Rather it is an epistemic field, constructed as much linguistically as visually" (p. 182). Jay continues,

Language accounted the "noblest" of the senses, sight traditionally enjoyed a privileged role as the most discriminating and trustworthy of the sensual mediators between man and the world. Whether in terms of actual observation with the two eyes (often understood monocularly rather than in their true stereoscopic operations), or in those of internal mental speculation, vision has been accorded a special role in Western epistemology since the Greeks. Although at times more metaphorical than literal, the visual contribution to knowledge has been credited with far more importance than that of any other sense. (p. 176)

The woman, then, becomes the center of interiority in certain novels, the novel being a genre particularly suited for exploring the inner life. The quiet listening of Fanny Price in Jane Austen's *Mansfield Park* and of Anne Elliot in *Persuasion*, the meditative soliloquies of Jane Eyre in Charlotte Brontë's novel, and the psychological ruminations of Mrs. Ramsay in *To the Lighthouse* are feminine spaces created by the narrator in dialogue with the reader. That the silence is created in the text by these authors (the listening spaces, the meditative soliloquies, and the psychological ruminations) and is not just an indexing of women's social positioning is crucial to my argument about the importance of writing to silence. These narrative spaces are created in silent dialogue with the reader, who is expected to assume the same active and insightful position as the silent, observing female character in fiction.

SILENCE AS A RITUAL OF TRUTH

"Power," Foucault states, "is always interactional" despite the negative terms traditionally applied to its effects: "it 'excludes,' it 'represses,' it 'censors,' it 'abstracts,' it 'masks,' it 'conceals'" (*Discipline and Punish*, p. 194). Instead, he asserts, "Power produces; it produces reality; it produces domains of objects and rituals of truth" (ibid.). Thus there are at least two sides to any discourse of power: indeed, there are many discourses of power, not just one. There is a power in listening, as well as speaking, and women, who in certain times and cultures are brought up to "listen," then bring this quality of attentiveness to their representation of women's discourse in literature. This quality of attention or listening is marked in a narration with spaces of silence as well as words. Such spaces in Austen, Brontë, and Woolf are not an interruption or a "break" in narration with its overvaluation of the speaking subject, generally a man. Rather, the spaces of silence and talk, listening and speaking subjects, are part of a discourse of power, dependent on one another and structured textually and socially by Derrida's notion of "différance." In *The Years*, "talk" among some ladies is something that they engage in until the men arrive. Kitty notes: "They were chattering together. Yet animated as it sounded, to Kitty's ear the talk lacked substance. It was a battledore and shuttlecock talk, to be kept going until the door opened and the gentlemen came in. Then it would stop" (p. 258). Here the talk of the men is seemingly valued more than the women's. However, once the gentlemen do enter, there is a power in "listening" or "not listening," as the narrator in *The Voyage Out* points out: "Each of the ladies, being after the fashion of their sex, highly trained in promoting men's talk without listening to it, could think—about the education of the children, about the use of fog sirens in an opera—without betraying herself" (p. 17). Such rituals of silence in women are constituted from a certain doubleness: she is both an insider and outsider of culture at the same time, someone who is socially positioned to listen to men while creating a space to think for herself. The element of silence she supplies is as "productive," as much of a contribution, in discourse as talk.

That silent observation and listening is often a "ritual of truth" for women is a perspective advanced by Virginia Woolf. That there is power in this vantage point of an observing, thinking woman—an attentive listener, a receptive reader—is a perspective that is now evolving in the critics of consciousness: Martin Heidegger, Paul de Man, and Gaston Bachelard. Who could doubt it, reading Virginia Woolf reading Mrs. Ramsay reading her guests:

It could not last, she knew, but at the moment her eyes were so clear that they seemed to go round the table unveiling each of these people, and their thoughts and their feelings, without effort like a light stealing under water so that its ripples and the reeds in it and the minnows balancing themselves, and the sudden silent trout are all lit up hanging, trembling. So she saw them; she heard them; but whatever they said had also this quality, as if what they said was like the movement of a trout when, at the same time, one can see the ripple and the gravel, something to the right, something to the left; and the whole is held together; for whereas in active life she would be netting and separating one thing from another . . . she would be urging herself forward; now she said nothing. (*To the Lighthouse*, pp. 160–61)

The theory of mind suggested by the structure of the metaphors in this passage is one in which the mental processes of the observer are active and searching rather than inert and receptive: Mrs. Ramsay's "eyes . . . go round . . . unveiling . . . like a light stealing under water." We, as readers, perceive the illumination of the light of the mind in the act of silent observation. The mind is creating: it is a light, it is a lamp, it is almost an x-ray, extending the metaphorical tradition of mind of the Romantic tradition. Abrams, in his examination of Romantic theory and the critical tradition in *The Mirror and the Lamp*, reminds us that "In any period, the theory of mind and the theory of art tend to be integrally related and to turn upon similar analogues, explicit or submerged" (p. 69). The theory of art and mind presented in this passage by Woolf is an expressive one, suggesting process and movement in the mind of the observer: it is not a static theory of the observer and of imitation in which the woman is passive or the mind is merely a reflecting mirror.

If we are to properly perceive and value this silent, listening, observing woman, Mrs. Ramsay, and her precursors in the nineteenth century— including other observers like children, servants, colonials, minorities, the inarticulate, the creative—who have traditionally been submerged in literature, we must begin to develop different categories of discrimination and strategies for reading. "Mrs. Brown must be rescued, expressed" as Woolf said in her well-known essay, "Mr. Bennett and Mrs. Brown" (*Collected Essays* 1, p. 333). When Woolf observed in 1910 that "all human relations have shifted—those between masters and servant, husbands and wives, parents and children" (ibid., p. 321), she was noting also a change in politics and representation of "marginal" characters in literature. Therefore, this book is not intended to support a feminism that valorizes women or marginal characters as nonspeaking and observing subjects, but rather to suggest a critical transformation of the category of the silent observer as conventionally perceived and defined in literature and life in Woolf's time, and, sometimes, even today. Traditionally, an observer or a listener, often a woman, is someone obscure, powerless, and silent. But as Annette Kolodny reminds us: "Insofar as we are taught to read, what we engage are not texts but paradigms. . . . Insofar as literature is itself a social institution, so, too, reading is a highly socialized—or learned—activity" (p. 10). Bringing the paradigm of the observer into the open for scrutiny, first as a philosophical and social category, and then as a category of persons in the reading of literature, will place the observer in a revealing perspective for the reader.

The power in the role of the observer and the accompanying discourse of silence is revealed in Kierkegaard's fascinating philosophical novel, *Repetition: A Venture of Experimental Psychology*. This interest is marked in Kierkegaard's middle name, Silentius, coincidentally the name of the female character disguised as a male in the thirteenth-century Arthurian romance, *Le Roman de Silence*, mentioned earlier. Also, the author of *Fear and Trembling*, another work that is preoccupied with silence, is Johannes de Silentio, John of (or about) Silence: Kierkegaard's pseudonym. In this work Kierkegaard tries to account for Abraham's faith and keeping of silence about his purpose to kill Isaac before his family—Sarah, Eleazer, and Isaac. Thus we find anything but silence; rather, we find words, because Kierkegaard, John *of* Silence, keeps silence *about* Abraham's silence before God. He presents the paradox of divine and demoniac silence: "If I go further, then I stumble upon the paradox, either the divine or the demoniac, for silence is both. Silence is the snare of the demon, and the more one keeps silent, the more terrifying the demon becomes; but silence is also the mutual understanding between the Deity and the individual" (*Fear and Trembling*, p. 97). Amid such paradox and play of the divine and the demoniac, of male (Kierkegaard) and female (Heldris de Cornuaille) figures impersonating "Silentius," and of words and silence, this chapter will develop. It will explore both female and male and subject and object perspectives, and it will analyze presentations of silence in philosophy, psychology, and the English novel.

The form taken by Kierkegaard's philosophical novel, *Repetition*, is illuminating. Written in 1843, before Freud's articulation of the unconscious, this novel creates different ways for the narrator, Constantin Constantius, to see himself, much as psychoanalysis later dramatized aspects of the self through positioning a talking patient in relation to a listening, silent analyst. Using dramatization, letter-writing, and the technique of the double, Kierkegaard introduces into the philosophical discussion of repetition the story of a young poet in love with the idea but not the actuality of a woman. He seeks out Constantin, an older man, as a confidant and adviser in order to rationalize and end his relations with the woman. The double of Constantin is the young man, and we are presented with dualities: the young man and the older confidant; the teacher and the student; the writer and the reader; the actor and the observer; the master and the slave; words and silence. In part 1, we experience the young man as the young lover, the poet, the student, the listener; Constantin, by contrast, reports the story and is the controlling narrator, the master, the teacher, the advisor. In part 2, which takes the form of fragmentary letters from the young man to Constantin concerning his feelings about the woman and art, the relationship shifts. Addressing Constantin as "My Silent Confidant," the young man reveals the power in Constantin, categorically the observer's position. He writes to him of his dilemma with the girl, demanding silence and yet furious at his power to be silent, requesting no response and yet angry when Constantin does what he requests. Clearly, as in psychoanalytic theory, the best advisor is one who listens and whose silence urges one to say more, and to hear oneself more, and to clarify what one has said. However, the young man is rankled at the superiority of the stance of the observer, Constantin, and writes to him:

You hold me captive with a strange power. There is something indescribably salutary and alleviating in talking with you, for it seems as if one were talking with oneself or with an idea. Then upon finishing speaking and finding solace in this speaking out, when one suddenly looks at your impassive face and reflects that this is a human being standing before one, a prodigiously intelligent man with whom one has been speaking, one grows quite fearful. (p. 188)

Silence produces anxiety in the speaker, the young man:

The very next moment I despair over the superiority that inheres in knowing so much about everything that nothing is new or unfamiliar. . . . You have a demonic power that can tempt a person to want to risk everything, to want to have powers that he does not otherwise have and that he does not otherwise crave—just as long as you are gazing at him—that can tempt him to appear to be what he is not just in order to buy this approving smile and its ineffable reward. (p. 189)

The young man then goes on to describe his relationship with his reader, Constantin, and reveals the categorical power in the observer, a useful concept to apply to the roles of observers, mainly women, in literature:

Thus do you hold me captive with an indescribable power, and this same power makes me anxious; thus do I admire you, and yet at times I believe that you are mentally disordered. . . . Is it not mental disorder always to be alert like this, always conscious, never vague and dreamy! Right now I do not dare to see you, and yet I cannot get along without you. (ibid.)

The power of the observer and listener, and the necessity of his silence as a basis for talk, is thus philosophically established in Kierkegaard's novel.

If we project these categories of observer and listener, actor and speaker into the twentieth century, we find that they fit the analytic situation as described by Freud in his descriptions of psychoanalysis and power relations as depicted by Foucault and Kristeva.

In his *Introduction to Psychoanalysis*, Freud discusses the pact that the patient and analyst make, not unlike the relation between Kierkegaard's young man and his silent confidant: "The patient is required to put himself into a condition of calm self-observation, without trying to think of anything, and then to communicate everything [to the analyst] which he becomes inwardly aware of, feelings, thoughts, remembrances in the order in which they arise in his mind" (p. 253). The patient promises candor and puts all kinds of material influenced by the unconscious before the therapist. The unconscious, whose role is taken over by the analyst through transference, turns out in a successful therapy to be the ultimate narrator of the self. Silence in the analyst or in the listener is a response and provides the possibility for talk; ultimately, the unconscious, silent like the therapist at the beginning of therapeutic treatment, surfaces and talks. The power of the listener, the power of the talker, and the power of the listener in making the talker listen to himself, is, as Foucault suggests about power and discourse in general, "interactional." The therapist's listening is productive and creative; however, when a patient becomes silent, the resistance impedes communication until the therapist learns to "read" its meaning.

Foucault takes us further, outside the analyst's room in his discussions of discourse, knowledge, power, and institutions. Although he focuses on power struggles in the institution of the prison in his book *Discipline and Punish*, his assertion that those who are seemingly powerless in these discourses are as important to "the production of reality" as those who are in authority is a paradigm to apply to the discourse of sex and gender as well as race. "Capillaries of power" produce reality not only in institutional settings, but also in personal relations between the traditionally powerful man and the traditionally powerless woman. For example, when Mrs. Ramsay says in *To the Lighthouse* that "there was nothing to be said" to Mr. Ramsay when he "pursued the truth with such an astonishing lack of regard for other people's feelings," her "saying nothing" does not indicate abdication of self, but self-resistance. Although her stance of silence might seem to indicate acquiescence to Mr. Ramsay's position of not going to the lighthouse, it is actually her ritual of truth, her silence of reservation. It is an instance of what Woolf would call "insincere" relations, in which a woman suggests renunciation of her opinion but actually withholds agreement through silence. Foucault's paradigms of power can transform our perceptions of such discourse between men, often represented as the talkers or "phrasemakers" in a Woolf novel and, seemingly, in control of a situation, and women, silent observers, who are socially positioned as receptors. Instead of bewailing the "prison-house" views and language of women and other observers as so many current social theorists do, Foucault admits that power exists, that it will continue to exist, and that it is foolish to suggest that "renunciation of power is one of the conditions of knowledge" (*Discipline and Punish*, p. 27). In acknowledging that power is dialogical and interactional in society, a new kind of social knowledge is advanced: "Power produces knowledge; that power and knowledge directly imply one another; that there is no power relation without the correlative constitution of a field of knowledge, nor any knowledge that does not presuppose and constitute at the same time power relations" (ibid.). Foucault reminds us to analyze our own relationship to power, and to understand that the processes and struggles that make it up—both the talk and the silence—are what constitute the "domains of objects" and "rituals of truth."

Like Foucault, Kristeva in *Revolution in Poetic Language* incisively analyzes power relationships, but she focuses more particularly on the relations between the sexes. Ideologically, she shifts the social repression that women's silence may sometimes represent to one of "position" rather than "essence," and, like Foucault, she enables women and others "positioned" as observers and listeners to escape familiar social definitions. Studies on gender differences in the use of language, according to Belenky et al., reveal that "the world is commonly divided into two domains: speaking and listening. Studies repeatedly, but not always consistently, find that it is the men who do the talking and the women who do the listening" (p. 45). However, if we view women, as Kristeva does, as "sujet in procès . . . rejecting everything finite, definite, structured, loaded with meaning, in the existing state of society" ("Oscillation Between Power and Denial," p. 166), we arrive at Woolf's stance that the recognition of reality depends as much on the "disposition" of mind ("dis-" is operative here) as on "position" in society.

In the three paradigms above from the domains of philosophy, psychology, and politics—Kierkegaard, Freud, and Foucault and Kristeva—it is demonstrated that the silent observer or listener has an equal, and sometimes superior, position in relation to the talker, and has his or her own ritual of truth and discourse of silence. The listening Constantin, the listening analyst, those who are "positioned" as powerless in society, and the silent observer in the place of the speaking subject become the ultimate narrators of the story of the self, not, as might be expected, the speaking, conscious subject.

Through these models, we highlight a new kind of psychological, social, and philosophical knowledge. This analysis presents not the familiar, stereotyped view of the observer, but a new social, philosophical, and political paradigm that will affect the way we read the category of observers and listeners in literature. This includes many of the female characters depicted as observers and listeners by male and female novelists in the English novel.

KEEPING THE SILENCE: JANE AUSTEN, CHARLOTTE BRONTË, AND VIRGINIA WOOLF

In *A Room of One's Own*, Woolf observes that the imaginative capacity that flourished in Shakespeare's work produced only silence in his talented sister, Judith. She thinks about women's writing as an independent tradition, in the way that Elaine Showalter now urges, choosing to make comparisons among women writers in her literary reviews rather than between male and female writers. Following Woolf's lead, this section will survey touchstone English novels, examining first those written by women as a separate tradition (Austen, Brontë, Woolf) in which silence is a "ritual of truth"; the last section of the chapter will review women's silence as a "ritual of oppression" in novels written by men (Richardson, Meredith, Dickens, Hardy). This comparison throws into relief Woolf's narrative experiments and contributions to the genre of the novel with the background traditions of female and male writers of the eighteenth and nineteenth century.

This reading of eighteenth- and nineteenth-century novels also reveals that women novelists, despite the rigor with which society and men demand disclosure through talk, realize more fully than male authors that there is power in the vantage point of an observer and value in silence, largely because silence and observation are qualifications for inwardness and the exploration of, as well as the loss of, the "egotistical self" that Woolf criticizes. This may be the reason why female authors in the nineteenth century suggest incipient notions of the self and inwardness when male authors are still dealing with the overt, and why feminism is on the cutting edge of modernism. Jane Austen, Charlotte Brontë, and Virginia Woolf progressively develop methods for representing interiority because of their valorization of the inner life, a development in women prompted, perhaps, by social position, but transformed through the living of their lives. In turn, female authors creatively reflect and transform women's experience through writing, and they reveal through their narrative methodologies and worldviews that silence has its domains of objects and rituals of truth and can be a positive feature of women's experience and discourse. Indeed, unlike the male novelists of the eighteenth and nineteenth century, they include the metaphors of illumination and growth of the mind as well as concepts of power and superiority in relation to both the character and the position of observing women. Perhaps their motive for writing was, as Woolf said of other women novelists, "a desire to correct the current view of their sex expressed in so many volumes and for so many ages by male writers" (*Contemporary Writers*, p. 25). However, as Foucault notes, power is interactional, and women, as observers, may simply realize that they are in a dialogical position to reveal what is hidden because they have observed it from the sidelines so often.

Such a perspective does not condone female exclusion, socially or politically, or encourage female inhibition, nor does it advance a reactionary social stance, but it does suggest that critics have overlooked the fact that women writers often appreciate, use, and transform the category of silence and of the observer. Women observers and listeners become, as Kierkegaard claims of observers as a category, "secret agents," and perhaps, given "split" strategies of the self, "double agents": "And when an observer fulfills his duties well, he is to be regarded as a secret agent in a higher service, for the observer's art is to expose what is hidden" (p. 135). In a fictional and philosophical sense, women sometimes become the ultimate narrators of certain novels from which they are seemingly "absent" because they embody the repressed, the unconscious, the "unsaid" of society. Despite the authority and talk of men in Woolf's novels, it is the unconscious, often represented by the rich inner lives of female characters, that is the ultimate narrator of the story she has to tell.

However, the degree to which the unsaid or the unconscious is revealed through female characters in narration develops from the eighteenth to the twentieth century, as the novel develops from a genre that focuses on external adventure and action—the overt—to one that embraces interiority—the covert. In surveying touchstone novels with particular attention to the narration of the inner life of female characters and the function of doubling, one discovers that eighteenth- and nineteenth-century authors have difficulty entering the minds of women, in particular, and in capturing "consciousness" as we define it in the twentieth century, in general. Often an author will use the technique of "doubling" with female characters in order to capture both the "inner" and the "outer" aspects of women. For example, in Austen's *Mansfield Park*, we are presented with the outgoing, active, worldly character of Mary Crawford as well as the introverted, silent, observer Fanny Price, as aspects of self or categories of being: inner and outer. In Charlotte Brontë's *Jane Eyre*, we are presented with the social, scintillating Blanche Ingram as well as the plain, observing, retiring Jane Eyre. In Brontë's *Villette*, we find the coquette Ginevra Fanshawe as well as the observing Lucy. It is not until the twentieth century that characterizations develop which embrace both the social and reflective aspects of a woman in one character, as in Woolf's Lily Briscoe or Mrs. Ramsay.

Virginia Woolf

Woolf's interest in observers leads her to develop a narrative strategy that will enable her to give voice to those who are generally silent: silent in the traditional novel not only because observers are generally excluded from the arena of public discourse, but also because they have not found the appropriate language registers or forms of expression. Such characters are generally unrepresented in novels, not necessarily because they do not have words or ideas, but because authors do not believe they have anything of value to say or they do not have narrative methods to reveal them. Through the technique of "psycho-narration" (Cohn, p. 14) in which Woolf fuses with the consciousness she narrates, the inner worlds of those who are socially "inarticulate" or unrepresented in the dialogue of the novel are presented. Woolf, acutely aware of the "unsaid," the "unspoken," the "unsayable," and sometimes even the "unthought" in life and society, sought narrative methods to express the silent selves of observers or the moments that represent the loss of the "egotistical self." In *To the Lighthouse*, as Mitchell Leaska's informative study reveals, the views of women, children, and servants, observers and listeners in the traditional novel, dominate. Mrs. McNab, the housekeeper, and the omniscient narrator dominate the "Time Passes" section of the novel. Mrs. McNab, like the Victorian cook mentioned in "Mr. Bennett and Mrs. Brown," lived like a Leviathan in the depths, formidable, silent, obscure, inscrutable. And in parts 1 and 3, the consciousness of women and children prevail, as is revealed in Leaska's statistical study (p. 208) below:

PART	NARRATOR	PERCENT
1	Mrs. Ramsay	42
	Omniscient	17
	Lily Briscoe	13
	Mr. Ramsay	8
	Others (William Banks, Charles Tansley, Paul Rayley, Nancy Ramsay)	20
3	Lily Briscoe	61
	Cam Ramsay	11
	Omniscient	10
	James Ramsay	8
	Mr. Ramsay	5
	James and Cam	4
	Others	1

Disillusioned by the destruction and loss of lives in World War I, Woolf notes in her essay "Mr. Bennett and Mrs. Brown" that "In or about December 1910, human character changed" (*Collected Essays* 1, p. 320). Faith in human rationality and the amelioration of the human condition and progress diminishes, and multiple and inwardly shifting perspectives become increasingly important to Woolf in her socially and politically chaotic world. Accompanying this change in the view of human nature is a shift in sympathy, power, and confidence in authority that profoundly affects Woolf's view of the family and society as represented in her novels. She can no longer posit a fixed position, as the Edwardians do, from which to view people and life.

Woolf develops more of an interest in the inner life of those on the margins of society: Lady Bruton, a mother whose son died in the war, and the shell-shocked Septimus returned from the war in *Mrs. Dalloway*; the inarticulate servant, Mrs. McNab, and the "mute" Ramsay children in *To the Lighthouse*; and women, in general. These values affect her narrative strategies and uses of language and silence. Woolf develops (and this is her experimental gift to the genre of the novel) methods of indirection for saying the "unsaid," for saying the "unspeakable," for illuminating the minds of observers and listeners.

Woolf feminizes metaphors of mind. With an experimental stroke of great subtlety, the presentation of female body-mind states through the symbolic medium of words in *The Voyage Out*, *To the Lighthouse*, and *The Waves*, she collapses, erases, and diffuses the "semiotic" and the "symbolic" in summoning silence into the text as language, as a presence. Kristeva, in *Revolution in Poetic Language*, defines the semiotic as the pre-Oedipal, nonverbal signifying system that is related to vocal and kinetic rhythms; the symbolic is the social law given through the signifying process of language. Kristeva's distinction between the semiotic and symbolic is focused on a "speaking subject," a Cartesian conception of language "as an act by a subject" (p. 27). The "chora" and the "semiotic" in this scheme are equated with the feminine: the feminine that is "different" or "other" in relation to language; the "symbolic" is associated with masculine language and the "law." The "speaking subject," though "divided," once entering the "symbolic" order represses the semiotic or the "chora," defined by Kristeva as the pulsions, silences, absence, and disruptions associated with the feminine that pressure symbolic language (*Kristeva Reader*, p. 10). Like other post-structuralists, Kristeva concentrates mainly on the role of language in explicating the role of the "speaking subject" and relegates the feminine to the modality of the semiotic: this is an intellectual romanticization perhaps of women's linguistic, social, cultural, and metaphysical exile.

However, Woolf strongly resists Kristeva's metaphysical assignment of women to the realm of semiotics. Although Woolf is certainly concerned with description of states of mind and "chora," she is equally concerned with summoning and linguistically marking such subjectivity in her texts. Kristeva is unable to appreciate Woolf's use of the body as a metaphor for the mind (to be described in Chapter 4); instead, she reads the description of the body as estrangement from language. She states: "In women's writing, language seems to be seen from a foreign land; is it seen from the point of view of an asymbolic, spastic body? Virginia Woolf describes suspended states, subtle sensations and, above all, colors—green, blue—but she does not dissect language as Joyce does. Estranged from language, women are visionaries who suffer as they speak" ("Oscillation Between Power and Denial," p. 166). Kristeva is more of a structuralist than Woolf, and she prefers alphabets of dissection to Woolf's decodings of subjectivity. Woolf, firmly positioned in a feminine mind-body space is considerably more accepting, confident, and adventurous in her exploration of feminine states that "estrange" the scientist in Kristeva. With the creation of Rhoda of *The Waves*, a critical and fictional position mid-way between Kristeva's binary structuring of the semiotic and the symbolic is struck: she marks silent subjective states with symbolic language. Woolf, in attempting to capture Rhoda's dream states, makes her mind "transparent" through metaphors of the body, demonstrating that "The imagination is largely the child of the flesh" (*Life as We Have Known It*, p. xxi). Released from the body, the mind is free yet dependent on body metaphors for the imaging of mental voyaging. Woolf stakes out a feminine space here that is not always in the realm of consciousness but is, nevertheless, symbolic in its marking of states of body and mind through writing. And the "marking," the "stroke" of the symbolic pen, is a marking of metaphor of mind, not just a "spastic" bodily expression typical of women, as Kristeva claims. Woolf suspends the rational, linear movement of mind and plot, as do Jane Austen and Charlotte Brontë at times, arresting the narrative movement in the novel to focus on interior dream states: the feminine subjective.

Jane Austen

In the early part of the nineteenth century, Jane Austen creates two female observers in her later novels: Fanny Price of *Mansfield Park* and Anne Elliot of *Persuasion*. Marylea Meyersohn has written perceptively of Fanny Price as "a quiet auditor of the whole" and of her qualities as a listener and observer. Although in other novels Austen creates women like Elizabeth of *Pride and Prejudice* and Emma of *Emma*, who are shaped by talk, in *Mansfield Park* and *Persuasion* the inwardness of Fanny and Anne is created through their reflection as listeners and observers, usually in juxtaposition with a more social female character. They are characters who, interestingly, through their "listening" and "observing" what is "unsaid" in Austen's social world, herald a change in her heroines. J. F. Burrows, in his statistical analysis of the incidence of "speaking" and "thinking" in Austen's novels, reports that "In both *Mansfield Park* and *Persuasion*, the character narratives of the heroines are considerably larger than their spoken parts" (p. 166). His analysis reveals that Fanny of *Mansfield Park* speaks 6,117 words and thinks 15,418 words; Anne of *Persuasion* speaks 4,336 words and thinks 19,730 words; and Emma of *Emma* speaks 21,501 words and thinks 19,730 words. Such comparisons of conventional tags for external speaking or internal thinking of the heroines in Austen signal the change in Austen's interest in "reflection," "observation," and "thinking," from the "conversational" Emma to the plain, dominant heroines Anne Elliot and Fanny Price, who are actively "quiet." Fanny is described as a "quiet auditor of the whole"; Anne, similarly, as "a most attentive listener to the whole" (*Persuasion*, p. 34). As social observers rather than actors, they have an integrity and insight lacking in characters like Emma, with her blindness to other people's needs; Elizabeth, with her stubborn prejudice; and Mary Crawford, with her egotistical whims.

Moral goodness and perception in Austen's *Mansfield Park* and *Persuasion* are not allied with talkative and charming coquettes but with observing and listening females, belying Virginia Woolf's speculation that, "had Jane Austen lived beyond her forty-two years she would have trusted less to dialogue and more to reflection to give us a knowledge of her characters. . . . She would have devised a method, clear and composed as ever, but deeper and more suggestive, for conveying not only what people say, but what they leave unsaid; not only what they are but what life is" (*Common Reader* 1, pp. 148–49). In her novels, Austen disproves Woolf's assessment, and does indeed trust "reflection," beginning to devise a method for revealing the "unsaid" about society and life—though the difference lies in the quantitative relationship of narrated monologue and dialogue to inner monologue. The innovation of Woolf and the moderns was to express more intimate thoughts through the interior monologue or inward speech with a nod toward Austen's social conversation.

Austen, however, does create a category of women who are observers with a vantage that allows irony. In observing the "whole," Fanny Price and Anne Elliot reveal the distance between the conduct and the morality of nineteenth-century genteel society. Their ironic vantage point makes them into "secret agents in a higher service." And these women, like those in George Meredith's *The Egoist*, written 70 years later, embody the ironic spirit and become the social mirrors who civilize men.

Charlotte Brontë

Charlotte Brontë develops the inner life hinted at in Austen's novels by limiting the social conversation that sustains Austen's works. Through her characters' internal meditations in *Jane Eyre* and *Villette*, Brontë further develops the proportion of inner monologue to outer dialogue. Her characters do not learn the steps of the social dance to selfhood with the assistance of society, as Fanny Price and Anne Elliot do. They are placed in landscapes separate from society, reminding us of Piet Mondrian's paintings of lonely houses ensnared in webs of trees in bleak landscapes. Although Austen's characters may suffer temporary separation from the social world, they do not experience the ominous divisions of self and society that inform the characters of Jane Eyre and Lucy Snowe in Brontë's novels.

In Brontë, a female tradition of silence emerges that is not social or ironic, as in Austen or, later, George Meredith, but an offshoot of a different philosophical tradition: the seventeenth-century tradition of meditative silence and the soliloquy. Like Austen, Brontë tries out this method with orphan girls, Jane Eyre and Lucy Snowe, who are socially marginal, not part of the central social conversation, and so have reason to turn inward and reflect on their positions. They observe, listen, and watch more than other girls their age, and, therefore, the interiority of the novel develops. And they are more silent.

In Jane Eyre we encounter developed dialogues between the self and the soul, inner dialogues similar in tone to dialogues between self and God in autobiographical records of religious experience and in seventeenth-century metaphysical poetry. Jane Eyre's dialogue between the self and the soul, following a pattern of meditative, religious dialogue, is the beginning of narrative interiority in the nineteenth-century novel. It resembles dramatic soliloquy, a genre of self-dramatization that precedes psychoanalysis and stream-of-consciousness, as a way of presenting the hidden aspects of self. As Lionel Trilling states in *Sincerity and Authenticity*, "It is surely no accident that the idea of sincerity, of the known self and the difficulty of knowing and showing it, should have arisen to vex men's minds in the epoch that saw the sudden efflorescence of the theater" (p. 10).

Jane Eyre's soliloquies also reflect the tension between speaking and silence in the meditative tradition of the Quakers, a tradition that Virginia Woolf was familiar with, as argued in Jane Marcus's illuminating article "The Niece of a Nun: Virginia Woolf, Caroline Stephen, and the Cloistered Imagination" (*Virginia Woolf and the Languages of Patriarchy*). In Jane Eyre's soliloquy, she "turns traitor" on the traditional stance of man in relation to God. In drawing "aside" and meditating on her conflicts over Mr. Rochester, Jane thinks:

And while he spoke my very conscience and reason turned traitor against me, and charged me with crime in resisting him. They spoke almost as loud as Feeling: and that clamoured wildly. "Oh, comply!" it said. "Think of his misery; think of his danger—look at his state when left alone; remember his headlong nature; consider the recklessness following on despair—soothe him; save him; love him; tell him you love him and will be his. Who in the world cares for you? or who will be injured by what you do." Still indomitable was the reply—"I care for myself. . . . I will hold to the principles received by me when I was sane, and not mad—as I am now." (p. 319)

Here, it is my contention, a female tradition emerges: a transformation of seventeenth-century meditative poetry and religious colloquy that I shall call the female prayer. We are presented not with the traditional stance of man in embattled relation with God, but with a dialogue between a woman's self-interest indicated by "I care for myself" in conflict with "conscience" and "reason," which represent the interests of men and traditional religion. Notions of "conscience" and "reason" cloak social roles. As a part of this female prayer, the direct address to the reader—"Dear reader, may you never feel as I felt then," a convention of the nineteenth-century female writer—draws the female reader into the character's conspiracy of silence.

Later that night, Jane has a dream in which another dialogue between self and soul occurs—this time through a motherly intervention in a dream. A spirit addresses her: " 'My daughter, flee temptation!' 'Mother, I will' " (p. 322). This inner debate between feeling for the Other and the impulse toward self-preservation voiced by a motherly voice is echoed a century later when Lily Briscoe resists giving her sympathy to Charles Tansley at Mrs. Ramsay's dinner party:

There is a code of behaviour, she knew, whose seventh article (it may be) says that on occasions of this sort it behooves the woman, whatever her own occupation may be, to go to the help of the young man opposite so that he may expose and relieve the thigh bones, the ribs, of his vanity, of his urgent desire to assert himself. . . . But how would it be, she thought, if neither of us did either of these things? (*To the Lighthouse*, p. 137)

Concern for the Other in the Brontë and Woolf passages above shadows the women's psyches, but inner urgings toward protection of self rather than conformity to men's wishes or external standards of conduct and behavior are the focus of the meditations. This is a new "position" for women, and it is important to note its beginnings in the nineteenth century cloaked in a meditative dialogue with self.

Lucy Snowe of *Villette* also engages in inner dialogues, but they are even more clearly focused than Jane Eyre's on the social constructs of femininity. Lucy lacks resolution in her life and shrinks like a "snail into a shell" at the opportunity to teach and engage in a life of thought and reality, but she is determined to define her own voice and her own sense of being a woman. She does not yield to Mme. Beck's force or even M. Paul Emmanuel, the professor of literature, the "intelligent tiger" with whom she eventually falls in love. When M. Paul Emmanuel asks her to act the part of a man in a play, she firmly resists wearing a man's clothing. This incident, a woman establishing her own independence and identity without cloaking herself in a male role, reveals her reservations about Mme. Beck also. Lucy exclaims: "Nobody must meddle; these things must not be forced upon me. Just let me dress myself" (p. 124). The same word, "force," is applied to Mme. Beck in her urging Lucy to teach in her school. Mme. Beck is finely tuned in the art of watching, but Lucy observes that she "wore a man's aspect—not my kind of power" (p. 67). Lucy objects to acting or dressing "like a man"—not shrinking from the male "position" in Kristeva's terms, but from using male definitions of her female self. In the next century, Miriam Henderson in Dorothy Richardson's novel *Revolving Lights* will carry the metaphor of mannish clothes further and object to writing "with mannish cleverness," determined like Lucy to find her own feminine self and voice. Woolf will carry on the tradition and, like Richardson and Bathsheba in Hardy's *Far from the Madding Crowd*, bewail "having the feelings of a woman but only the language of men." But Woolf is unlike Brontë— freer, more playful, less vigilant and constricted—in creating her playful Orlando, who, unlike Lucy Snowe, found the costumes of men and the implications of changing gender quite exciting. Although at first Lucy is fearful of speaking or playing another role, she finds herself through acting in M. Paul Emmanuel's play:

That first speech was the difficulty; it revealed to me this fact, that it was not the crowd I feared so much as my own voice. Foreigners and strangers, the crowd were nothing to me. Nor did I think of them. When my tongue once got free, and my voice took its true pitch, and found its natural tone, I thought of nothing but the personage I represented—and of M. Paul, who was listening, watching, prompting in the side scenes. (p. 125)

Lucy lacks resolution but is determined to observe and define her own voice and her own sense of being a woman. Mme. Beck is also a vigilant observer, mainly of Lucy and her staff, but is more like a policewoman than a guardian of a secret life, as is Lucy Snowe.

Jane Austen's embodiment of silence and valorization of observation in her female characters Fanny Price and Anne Elliot, as well as similar qualities in Charlotte Brontë's Jane Eyre and Lucy Snowe, are a moral gesture toward the observing woman. The resistant silences of these characters as "rituals of truth" preserve their insight into themselves and society. However, though Austen and Brontë begin to reveal the uses of silence in female lives, it is left to Virginia Woolf to poetically narrate the fluency of women's inner lives. Male novelists of the eighteenth and nineteenth centuries, in contrast, more frequently represent women's exclusion and oppression in society through narrative absence, as will be demonstrated later. This, of course, raises for consideration "the very difficult question of the difference between the man's and the woman's view of what constitutes the importance of any subject. From this spring not only marked differences of plot and incident, but infinite differences in selection, method and style" (Woolf, *Contemporary Writers*, p. 27). What constitutes the importance of any subject? The distinction between the male and female points of view on silence is an important one and crucial to the thesis of this book. Female observers in Austen, Brontë, and Woolf's novels are viewed as producers of "domains of objects" and "rituals of truth," not just reflectors of social oppression or of men. Austen, Brontë, and Woolf embody differences in the selection and style of presenting silence. Observing women in this tradition turn inward rather than outward for the development or escape from their identities.

A positive view of observing, listening, silent women in literature is asserted here, moving further the feminist discourse on silent women in the recent writings of the French *l'écriture feminine* school, particularly Hélène Cixous and Luce Irigaray, and of American feminists like Elizabeth Abel and Elaine Showalter. In general, previous feminist scholars have viewed women's "silences" in literature as only "loss, lack, absence, darkness, negation." Female characters are viewed as social reflectors rather than producers or transformers of social and aesthetic reality. For example, Abel contends in her essay on *Mrs. Dalloway* that:

The silences that punctuate *Mrs. Dalloway* reflect the interruptions and enigmas of female experience and ally the novel with a recent trend in feminist aesthetics. The paradoxical goal of representing women's absence from culture has fostered an emphasis on "blank pages, gaps, borders, spaces and silence, holes in discourse" as the distinctive features of a self-consciously female writing. Since narrative forms normally sanction the patterns of male experience, the woman novelist might signal her exclusion most succinctly by disrupting continuity, accentuating gaps between sequences. Can the female self be expressed through plot or must it be conceived in resistance to plot? Must it lodge between the facts? ("Narrative Structures," pp. 184–85)

Although Woolf is aware of the gaps and "unnatural silences" in women's lives, the kind that Tillie Olsen writes of in *Silences* and that Abel suggests—"women's absence from culture"—she is also aware of their "presence" and of other kinds of silence in women's discourse that these critics do not name. Those writers who engage in "self-consciously female writing" may try to mimetically represent women's social absence through certain narrative methodologies of gap and silence. However, the social order is only one order of reality; there are others. Contradictions emerge from the different definitions of "reality" offered by feminist critics. As Rachel Bowlby perceptively states in her recent book, *Virginia Woolf: Feminist Destinations*:

One strand of feminist criticism takes its cue from this model, positing women's writing as the principal locus of the undermining of realist conventions identified as masculine. Another strand, working with broadly "realist" assumptions, takes "women's writing" to describe a female experience hitherto devalorized, if not wholly banished, by the institutional or more general constraints implied by a patriarchal society. (p. 12)

Depending, then, on the definition of "reality," silences woven into the fabric of a woman's text are an absence or a presence. If a feminist critic accepts the social order of "reality" as "masculine," then women's silences in literature and life are an "absence." Showalter, in her essay "Feminist Critics in the Wilderness," takes women's writing as mimetic of their devalued social positions or as lacking the full resources of the language—signs of absence: "Women have been denied the full resources of language and have been forced into silence. . . . The holes in discourse, the blanks and gaps and silences, are not the spaces where female consciousness reveals itself but the blinds of a 'prison-house language' " (*New Feminist Criticism*, p. 255).

If, however, the woman's experience is taken as the standard based on orders of experience other than the social, as in *l'écriture feminine*, then women's writing is viewed as capturing this "reality"—its gaps and silences—as a "presence." Differing from both of these feminist positions (dualist and essentialist in nature), the "reality" of Woolf and, consequently, of this interpretation is grounded in a structure of "différance." Meaning and reality emerge from a network of differences that involve not either/or but both masculine and feminine definitions of experience.

Silence in Woolf's narration is the space where female consciousness does reveal itself; she fills the silence with a positive narration of presence that male authors assign to women as oppressive. Her themes and narrative techniques continually remind us that the recognition of reality depends as much on the disposition of mind as one's position in the social world: women are not just political and social mirrors—they have kaleidoscopic selves. Some females in life and literature turn their observant silence to personal and social advantage; others cannot or do not and, therefore, experience various kinds of oppressed silence. And although the historical, material, and psychological conditions do not always allow women's development, and although we must, of course, work to better these conditions, it is important that writers like Woolf remind women through a politics of narration, through the narration of inwardness, that they can transform and control their experiences as women—sometimes through thought or a community of feeling, and sometimes through writing. Ideologically, we are trapped if we cannot shift the social repression of women, as Kristeva urges, from one of "essence" to one of "position."

BREAKING THE SILENCE: SAMUEL RICHARDSON, CHARLES DICKENS, GEORGE MEREDITH, AND THOMAS HARDY

In establishing a tradition of female novelists, we have discovered that silences in Austen, Brontë, and Woolf's novels often represent a narrative space for the dreaming, thinking, feeling, listening, and questioning woman: they represent women's silence as rituals of truth developed from an inner stance of self-resistance. Male novelists, in contrast, do not ignore the feminine silences but acknowledge their "otherness" and their silence in disparaging or reductive ways. Certain male novelists more frequently represent women's silences as a sign of intellectual inferiority and exclusion from society through narrative absence. The silences and stammerings of women in selected eighteenth- and nineteenth-century novels written by Samuel Richardson, Charles Dickens, George Meredith, and

Thomas Hardy are framed as "rituals of oppression": women defined from the "outside" in relation to social facts, women as lovely and usually silent cameos.

Samuel Richardson

"Black transaction," the unrepresented rape in the eighteenth-century novel *Clarissa*, is the taboo or "hole in discourse" of which Foucault and the *feminine écriture* critics write. Samuel Richardson's novel, written in 1747–48, is marked by a rape in the center of the novel, implied in a narrative silence. After her drugged rape by Lovelace, Clarissa's writing and speaking, with its spurts and stops, represents a kind of silence that she must assume as an eighteenth-century bourgeoise when her views as a woman cry out to be revealed. Lovelace, fired by Clarissa's haughty beauty and fascinated, as Terry Eagleton suggests, by the "integrity of the human person" which is "fanatically" preserved (*Rape of Clarissa*, p. 88), uses insidious stratagems to subdue her. His "linguistic lawlessness" enables him, as Eagleton so aptly states, "to unfix a sign as deftly as he can break a hymen" (p. 84), and he constructs a snare from which Clarissa cannot escape. Her rape, however, is "unspeakable" and "unnameable" in her social and historical context; sexuality is one of the categories of excluded language, as described by Foucault.

Immediately after the rape, Lovelace writes a brief note to his friend, John Belford, marking the event: "The affair is over. Clarissa lives." There is an italicized authorial intrusion, a form that usually confines the author to the viewpoints of the characters. The narrator states: "The whole of this black transaction is given by the injured lady to Miss Howe, in her subsequent letters, dated Thursday, July 6" (p. 305).

In the shadow of Lovelace and the rape, Clarissa is utterly unable to "fix" her own signs, and she utters only "broken sentences," not unlike the mythic Philomel whose tongue is cut out after her rape by Tereus and so must weave a tapestry of her story. At a later stage of the dessication of objectivity in modernism, these "broken sentences" transform into "broken syllables." Clarissa's silence is presented, then, through the multiple viewpoints of Richardson's epistolary style. Lovelace represents his account of the rape, including Clarissa's ruptured utterances:

At last, with a heart-breaking sob, I see, I see, Mr. Lovelace, in broken sentences she spoke, I see, I see—that at last—at last—I am ruined! Ruined, if your pity— let me implore your pity! And down on her bosom, like a half-broken-stalked lily, top-heavy with the overcharging dews of the morning, sunk her head with a sigh that went to my heart. (p. 304)

Later Clarissa herself attempts to put pen to paper to produce what Virginia Woolf would call almost two centuries later "scraps, orts and fragments." Clarissa's note contains the "semiotics" of grief and distraction: what she writes she tears, and throws the paper in fragments under the table.

> *Paper 1 (Torn in two pieces)*
> My Dearest Miss Howe,—O what dreadful, dreadful things I have to tell you! But yet I cannot tell you neither. (p. 308)

Through the epistolary form, Richardson opens the way to the revelation of Clarissa's inner life and shows the "sentiments"—the moral views—that inform Clarissa's psychology, but he does not, as twentieth-century authors do, explore the subjective feelings, the mind, of Clarissa. Nevertheless, his focus on the "injury" to a woman's soul and body allows an incipient treatment of interiority that differs from Defoe's earlier treatment of a woman in *Moll Flanders*, where the narrative focuses only on the adverse external circumstances in a woman's life. Clarissa is a character developed in the gaze of society, and individual feelings separate from that society are unnameable, perhaps unthinkable, for a character in an eighteenth-century novel. She is the center of the novel, yet marked by silence; consequently, the reality of women's lives produced by "domains of objects" and "rituals of truth" related to their bodies and sexuality remains unrepresented in this novel.

Charles Dickens

Charles Dickens's novel of realities, *Hard Times*, also contains the oppressed silences of a woman without an "-ology." Mrs. Gradgrind is sketched as a woman of mental and bodily feebleness, "a pink-eyed bundle of shawls," with no "fancy" about her. She lives with Mr. Gradgrind, an egoist, who has an "-ology" of utilitarianism that does not include her registers of expression. On her deathbed, Mrs. Gradgrind calls out to Louisa, her daughter, to explain her silences, why she has "long left off saying anything" to the bullying Mr. Gradgrind: "You must remember, my dear, that whenever I have said anything, on any subject, I have never heard the last of it, and, consequently, that I have long left off saying anything" (p. 199). She also speaks of broken connections:

You learnt a great deal, Louisa, and so did your brother. Ologies of all kinds from morning to night. . . . But there is something—not an ology at all—that your father has missed or forgotten, Louisa. I don't know what it is. I have often sat with Sissy near me, and thought about it. I shall never get its name now. But your father may. It makes me restless. I want to write to him, to find out, for God's sake, what it is. Give me a pen, give me a pen. (Ibid.)

Here Mrs. Gradgrind, like many women before and after her, denies herself as a speaking subject: "I don't know what it is. . . . I shall never get its name now."

Cam, Nancy, and Minta in *To the Lighthouse* also lack the ability to name things. Cam often says nothing (p. 253), and Nancy and Minta refer to "things without names" (p. 112), suggesting that women can visualize but not designate: things remain unsaid and have yet to evolve into language. However, it is Mrs. Ramsay who reminds us of Mrs. Gradgrind, because she also feels that her husband, the philosophy professor, has missed something in life. She will state that Mr. Ramsay "could always say things . . . I never could." However, in Mrs. Gradgrind's case the refusal of speech connects with a fear of ideology, whereas Mrs. Ramsay's "not saying things" is a resistant stance of silence that she adopts as superior to men's "talk." Mrs. Gradgrind's feebleness of voice and "broken sounds" are not only those of one dying but also yet another representation of a woman unsure of herself and her capacity for discourse even in the private sphere of her own home. Her "broken sounds" are even less audible than Clarissa's "broken syllables" spoken after her rape or Woolf's later "broken sentence": a linguistic and intellectual progression in the representation of women's voice and mind from phonemes to morphemes to sentences. However, when Lily Briscoe in *To the Lighthouse* exclaims that "one could say nothing to nobody" (p. 265), complaining of "the little words that broke up thought," she is not repressing language but acknowledging its limitations.

The sense of rupture in women's ways of being, knowing, and talking is revealed in these broken utterances from the eighteenth century to the twentieth, but the linguistic consciousness of the male and female authors that informs the utterances differs. From "broken sentences" to "spurts" to "stops" to "strange stammerings" to "blanks in thought" to "broken syllables" in the male novelists in this sample, and then to "the little words that broke up thought," in Woolf's Lily Briscoe, there is a refusal of language in the feminine condition. However, Mrs. Ramsay and Lily adopt silence rather than words as a metaphysical stance, not because they do not have the "names" to express their thoughts but because, as reflective women, they realize the limitations of female speech in Victorian society as well as the metaphysical limitations of language. They have a sense, like Kristeva, that "the feminine" is a "position" that is constantly changing rather than an "essence": "In 'woman' I see something that cannot be represented, something that is not said, something above and beyond nomenclatures and ideologies" ("Women Can Never Be Defined," p. 137).

Mrs. Gradgrind, on the other hand, is not "above" and "beyond" ideologies, she is "without" them. She realizes that she cannot "name" her own "ology" in the repressive, utilitarian world of facts that Mr. Gradgrind has constructed around her like Gunnar in Ibsen's *A Doll's House*. Interestingly, she is reminded of what Mr. Gradgrind has missed when she is in the company of another woman. She tells Louisa, "I have often sat with Sissy near me, and thought about it," suggesting like Mrs. Ramsay that "being" with another woman is a "silent companionship," indeed a "conspiracy." However, she forgets this moment of being with another woman and reverts to her subordinate role in asking for a pen to write to her husband, who dominates her even in his absence from her deathbed. She piteously asks to write to him to ask him to name what he has "missed or forgotten" in life, something that she intuits but cannot articulate. She, like Mrs. Ramsay, "could feel his mind like a raised hand shadowing her mind" (*To the Lighthouse*, p. 19). Mrs. Gradgrind drops the pen, and the voice of the narrator continues: "It matters little what figures of wonderful no meaning she began to trace upon her wrappers. The hand soon stopped in the midst of them; the light that had always been feeble and dim behind the weak transparency, went out" (pp. 199–200).

The irony of the narrator's comment suggests that the "figures of wonderful no meaning" may matter, but not in this utilitarian world. We, in the twentieth century, cannot miss the suggestiveness of Dickens's words "trace," reminding us of the layers of language of which Derrida speaks, and "figure," which Genette describes as the "gap" between a sign and its meaning, the inner space of language. We interpret the "gap" between Mrs. Gradgrind's feeble tracing of figures on her quilt and their meaning in her inhuman utilitarian world. Nevertheless, yet another female character dies with her own "-ology," her own inwardness unarticulated, unsaid. However, her vague feelings are "figured" by Louisa in confrontation with her father at the end of the novel: "Where are the graces of my soul? Where are the sentiments of my heart? What have you done, oh Father, what have you done, with the garden that should have bloomed once, in this great wildness here?" (p. 215). Here then in this deathbed scene, Dickens presents four kinds of female silence: the oppressed silence of a woman living with an egoist who has "long left off saying anything"; the preservation of silence—the silent feelings of the heart—through the companionship of another woman, Sissy Jupe, and her relationship with Louisa; the silence of Louisa, who, though she can articulate the questions that her mother could not ask, remains in the shadow of her father's philosophy; and the unnamed something, intuited by a woman, that is not an "-ology" that dies in the nineteenth-century social and political climate of utilitarianism—the lost trace of Mrs. Gradgrind on her wrapper, a semiotic pattern.

Mrs. Gradgrind's sense of what is lost, like Clarissa's rage and madness after her rape, is left a blank. The dearth of signs does not even take us into the realm of semiotics, let alone the symbolic order of words that Jacques Lacan describes.

George Meredith

Whatever that "something" is that Mrs. Gradgrind seeks is preserved in Meredith's novel, *The Egoist*. Clara Middleton, an honest and sensible woman, poses an ordeal for Sir Willoughby when she rebels against her engagement to him. But she is bound, like Jane Austen's women, to the social conventions of an engagement that her father, the humorous Mr. Middleton, insists she honor. It is in this conflict of the individual woman with society, now thinkable after Austen, that women begin to express themselves on formerly taboo topics, albeit through halting and fragmented language. She is spirited and intelligent, a typical Meredith heroine, unlike the vulnerable Clarissa of Richardson's novel but not unlike Elizabeth of Austen's *Pride and Prejudice*, whose ironic stance civilizes men. At the beginning of *The Egoist*, Clara is "an attentive listener to Sir Willoughby" (p. 52) but "finds in the word 'egoist' her medical herb, her illuminating lamp, the key of him" (p. 115). Before long she cannot bear being controlled by him and richly exclaims, "My mind is my own, married or not" (p. 88). It is left to her to strip Sir Willoughby, who frequently straightens "his whole figure to the erectness of the letter 'I'" (p. 19), of all pretences and to show that "Through very love of self himself he slew." This egotistical self is reminiscent of the male "I,I,I" in Woolf's *A Room of One's Own* or the "arid scimitar" that throws its phallic shadow across the pages of *To the Lighthouse*.

Although Sir Willoughby has no luck with Clara, he does find a listening, gazing woman in Laetitia Dale, a woman "with a romantic tale on her eyelashes." Looking into Laetitia's eyes he "found the man he sought there, squeezed him passionately and let her go." Meredith's irony points to Willoughby's foolish egotism. Later, when asking Laetitia to marry him, he exclaims "You were a precious cameo, still gazing!

And I was the object" (p. 487); he reflects that marriage with Laetitia is "marriage with a mirror, with an echo" (p. 464).

Cleverly styled, static portraits of women are typical of Meredith—cameos—but in Woolf's *Reading Notebooks* she says of him "That his optimism is wrong. That his optimism comes from his bristly egotism. He wouldn't be so optimistic if he could listen instead of talking. The hammer of his phrases scaring all sorts of small things away. Did not let [   ] filter in" (Silver, XLVI, B10). Woolf, influenced by Meredith and aware that women have historically served as looking-glasses, "reflecting men at twice their size," allows her women to be "lamps" and magic lanterns who emit multiple perspectives and patterns. This perspective is possible because she devises methods to capture women's inner lives, thinking, and reflections. However, the issues of propriety and doing things "without a name" still induce social silences in Meredith, as the "wonderful figures of no meaning" that Mrs. Gradgrind traces upon her wrapper do in Dickens. Mrs. Mountstuart, who is critical of Clara's behavior and is part of Meredith's chorus of society, chimes "But to break and bounce away from an unhappy gentleman at the church door is either madness or it's one of the things without a name" (p. 430). Clara realizes that Sir Willoughby, the egoist, and the conforming society around her will not acknowledge what is visible enough in the strife of this relationship. She reflects, "And if I marry, and then—Where will honor be then? I marry him; to be true to my word of honor, and if then—An intolerable languor caused her to sigh profoundly. It is written as she thought it; she thought in blanks, as girls do, and some women. A shadow of the male egoist is in the chamber of their brains overawing them" (p. 114).

This notion of male presence shutting out the view, cutting off the possibility, causing blanks, and overawing women's speech—also evidenced earlier in Mrs. Gradgrind—has been written about in Sandra Gilbert and Susan Gubar's "Milton's Bogey: Patriarchal Poetry and Women Readers" (*The Madwoman in the Attic*), and it is realized in Woolf's Mrs. Ramsay, who sometimes feels Mr. Ramsay's mind, the phallic shadow that represents men's position in society, overshadowing her.

Thomas Hardy

In *The Mayor of Casterbridge*, Thomas Hardy introduces another kind of silence into the novel, a cosmic silence that emanates from a Greek sense of tragedy. In this novel, Hardy is like Virginia Woolf in that he leaves "a description of reality more and more out of [his] . . .

stories, taking a knowledge of it for granted as the Greeks did?" (*Collected Essays*). The larger tragic vision absorbs his characters in the working out of Fate, and this vision is often embodied in the female characters in a Hardy novel—in this case, Mrs. Susan Henchard and her daughter, Elizabeth-Jane. Early in *The Mayor of Casterbridge*, published in 1896, seventeen years after Meredith's *The Egoist*, we are presented with another headstrong male egoist, Michael Henchard, who is impulsive and made of "unruly volcanic stuff." He is engaged in the selling of his wife, Susan, a practice not uncommon, as recorded in rural records in England at the time. Susan Henchard is presented as "stupid," in the nineteenth-century sense of being without speech, meek, simple, and "silently thinking." She possesses "sub-speciae aeternitatis," "the expression of one who deems anything possible at the hands of Time" (p. 5), as she is sold by her drunken husband to a stranger, Donald Farfrae. For twenty years after this act of auctioning off his wife, Henchard abstains from drink and becomes the mayor of Casterbridge, though this secret from the past haunts him. When Susan finds him again, he vows to make amends to her and Elizabeth-Jane, his alleged daughter. She, like her mother, is a model of patience and self-effacement: a "dumb, deep feeling, great-eyed creature" (p. 168). However, though she has learned her mother's lessons of renunciation, she is silent because she has, according to Henchard, become "an observing woman." Initially he labels her ignorant, but he misreads her silence. Hers is not as oppressive a silence as her mother's; she reads much and is preoccupied with the "inner chamber of ideas" (p. 123). But both female characters embody a sense of the cosmic silences that Woolf captures in *The Waves*, and death acts as a tragic backdrop to the mutability of life.

CONCLUSION

This sample of eighteenth- and nineteenth-century male novelists reveals their focus on the "domains of objects" and "rituals of truth" of male rather than female characters, the viewing of women from the "outside," the inability to perceive the power in the vantage point of an "observing woman," the fragmentation or absence of women's discourse on taboo subjects in the narration, and, in general, the absence of a narrative methodology to capture a woman's inwardness. This stance reveals Foucault's rules of exclusion in language:

We know perfectly well that we are not free to say just anything, that we cannot simply speak of anything when we like or where we like; not just anyone, finally, may speak of just anything . . . [for] the production of discourse is at once controlled, selected, organized and re-distributed according to a certain number of procedures, whose role is to avert its powers and its dangers, to cope with chance events, to evade its ponderous, awesome materiality. ("The Discourse on Language," p. 217)

The "materiality" of women's language as it relates to the body, sex, politics, and madness is a domain that has its "dangers" and where language exclusion operates.

The power of women's silences is averted in narration. The pattern of female silence or stammering, with all of its spurts, stops, and hesitancies, that is represented in the sample of male novelists in this chapter reveals that women are sketched from the "outside," capturing only their stammering, public voices. This is realized through a certain rhythm of incomplete sentences. Dashes and ellipses are a pattern in women's sentences that occurs again and again in novels of the nineteenth and twentieth century. As the anthropologist Shirley Ardener claims:

Because the arena of public discourse tends to be characteristically male-dominated and the appropriate language registers have been "encoded" by males, women may be at a disadvantage when wishing to express matters of particular concern to them. Unless their views are presented in a form acceptable to men, and to women brought up in the male idiom, they will not be given a proper hearing. If this is so, it is possible to speculate further and wonder whether, because of the absence of a suitable code and because of a necessary indirectness rather than spontaneity of expression, women, more often than may be the case with men, might sometimes lack the facility to raise to conscious level their unconscious thoughts. (*Perceiving Women*, pp. viii–ix)

Certainly the representation of women's language written by male novelists before the twentieth century illustrates this, and recent theoretical works by Carol Gilligan and by Mary Belenky, Blythe Clinchy, Nancy Goldberger, and Jill Tarule address this.

Just as Ardener speculates about the effect of "the absence of a suitable code" and "a necessary indirectness" on women's "facility to raise to conscious level their unconscious thoughts," so too do Belenky, Clinchy, Goldberger, and Tarule. In their fascinating interviews with 135 women, they discover women of silence, "deaf and dumb" with "no words that suggest an awareness of mental acts, consciousness, or introspection" (p. 25), reminding us of Clarissa, Mrs. Gradgrind, Laetitia Dale, and Susan Henchard. Undoubtedly, the lack of confidence in these women and their inability to rely more on their own experience and less on the "authority" of men influence their ability to find expression.

However, it must not be forgotten that these women inhabit what Maria DiBattista argues is a "specifically female domain, the domain of the clandestine" (p. 284). Just as Carol Gilligan's *In a Different Voice* reveals the differences in language and registers of expression in men and women—women investing common words like "moral" with different meanings from men—so too might the working-class women in the Belenky study have difficulty with the language of consciousness sometimes used in the interviews, the context of conversation, and the mode of self-questioning. Lower-middle-class and working-class women who are not used to self-reflective language (though not necessarily self-reflection) and who are not familiar with the therapeutic mode are understandably concrete in response when asked: "How would you describe yourself to yourself?" Yes, reflective words are lacking perhaps because, as the authors suggest, the thoughts are unformulated, but also because these women cannot yet find the right language register for these academic interviewers, or for the language "encoded by males" to which Ardener and Woolf refer.

These issues with language, methodology, and definitions of voice and self make us pause in assuming "voicelessness" in women whose language has not yet been formulated or revealed by current social science methodologies, or whose semiotics (gestures and other signs) we have not yet learned to read. If there are other ways of telling, as Belenky et al. posit, then we must try other ways of "hearing," as Lillian Rubin so poignantly urges in her study of working-class families, *Worlds of Pain*. These women want to talk about their concerns and their unpredictable and chaotic lives, but, like the female characters discussed in the novels above, they must be heard from within, "standing in their own shoes" (Belenky et al., p. 32). An understanding will emerge from a semiotics of silence as well as an understanding of the use of common words with new resonances. Gaining "voice" and "self" is an evolving process in women, not a stage that is reached where "voice" is either present or absent. As one of the working-class women in *Women's Ways of Knowing* reminds us: "One doesn't have to be told in words. That's the point. That's the thing that's very hard for word people to believe—that there are other ways of telling" (ibid., p. 75). It was Woolf, literary daughter of the upper-middle class, who said, "There's no doubt in my mind that I have found out how to begin (at 40) to say something in my own voice; and that interests me so that I feel I can go ahead without praise" (*Diary 2*, p. 186).

Woolf states in "Women and Fiction" that "The extraordinary

woman depends on the ordinary woman. . . . It is only when we can measure the way of life and the experiences of life made possible to the ordinary woman that we can account for the success or failure of the extraordinary woman as a writer" (*Collected Essays* 2, p. 142). Woolf, the extraordinary woman writer, relies on and represents in her writing the evolving inner lives of ordinary women: it is this that her rhetoric of silence reveals.

DiBattista argues that "other ways of telling" occur in a specifically female space of silence. Her view of Marguerite Duras's female characters as developed in "The Clandestine Fictions of Marguerite Duras" could arguably be extended to Woolf's strategies in recording the underground life of female characters: "Duras thus recuperates the clandestine as the domain (assigned or preferred?) of women's literature, the literature of an unknown and as yet unformulated language, the 'silence of women'" (DiBattista, p. 289). This belief that women in particular times and cultures are linguistically (and perhaps intellectually) inhibited or unable to raise unconscious thoughts to a conscious level, as described above, of course affects the representation of women in novels. Woolf presents silent women because:

Not only do women submit less readily to observation than men, but their lives are far less tested and examined by the ordinary processes of life. Often nothing tangible remains of a woman's day. The food that has been cooked is eaten. . . . Her life has an anonymous character which is baffling and puzzling in the extreme. For the first time, this dark country is beginning to be explored in fiction and at the same moment a woman has also to record the changes in women's minds and habits which the opening of the professions has introduced. She has to observe how their lives are ceasing to run underground. (*Collected Essays* 2, p. 146)

Most of this book deals with the "dark country" of women's minds that Woolf is exploring at the beginning of the twentieth century, and not the changes in women's minds and habits that are more fully revealed in fiction today. Clarissa, who speaks in "broken sentences" after her rape; Mrs. Gradgrind, who traces "wonderful figures of no meaning"; Clara, who "thinks in blanks" when men are near; and Susan Henchard, who is "dumb" in the face of her fate—all of these eighteenth- and nineteenth-century women undoubtedly have lives and language that run underground but that are unrepresented in the fiction of male writers. Such "absence" of women can then be attributed to law and custom, women's inherent "inferiority" according to the prevailing beliefs of the time, male authors' lack of "interest" or lack of knowledge about women's lives, or the lack of narrative methodology or the genre requirements of the time. Some feminists, as discussed earlier, attribute the lack to women in presenting the mimetic theory as explanation for the absence: women's silences in literature reflect their own lack of language in life. Woolf and this book suggest another hypothesis: that male and sometimes female authors, in not valuing or believing in the evolving inner lives of women and the semiotics of their expression, do not seek to find, as Woolf did, the narrative methodologies to express them. Narrative methodologies and experiments in the novel, therefore, emerge from personal and social values and vision, as well as from the genre formulations of the time.

Since women's expression has often been socially inhibited in private arenas and sometimes excluded from public discourse, we have no way of knowing about "facility" in generating ideas. We have no way of knowing unless, as Shirley Ardener, who studied Bakweri women in the Cameroons, suggests, we learn to recognize forms of expression other than direct speech as a way of understanding women's ideas and models of the world. Similarly, Julia Kristeva urges the study of semiotics, the "chora" of women's discourse, to understand the discourse of sex and gender, one of many that comprise the individual.

Austen, Brontë, and Woolf view women from the "inside." In this narrative space, they free themselves from dependence on social "facts," and through writing they create a lightening of the social and political facts of women's being. They sound woman's voice, and though it is often an inner voice not yet public in its resonance, it is an insightful and resistant, not a stammering, voice. Brontë creates a plain-speaking, meditative voice in the character of Jane Eyre; Austen creates a socially scintillating voice in Emma and a reflective one in Fanny Price; and Woolf creates a fluent inner voice in Mrs. Ramsay. Moreover, Woolf not only gives her female characters more opportunity for expression of the inner life than earlier novelists, but, because of her inventive narrative methods for capturing the inner life, she also gives them fluency—a kind of expression rare for women in the English novel.

3

The Reading and Writing of
Silence in Woolf's Novels

THE READING OF SILENCE

THE PARADOX OF READING SILENCE, or "reading the unreadable" (Felman, p. 187), requires a faculty of attention perhaps dormant in this age of speech and noise. Derrida's concept of "différance" is helpful in understanding Virginia Woolf's notions of such a reader as expressed in her essays, letters, and novels, where traditional oppositions between reading and writing are dissolved. From Woolf's perspective, outlined in her early essay "How One Should Read a Book," meaning is no longer produced solely by the reader or the writer. Woolf advises: "Do not dictate to your author; try to become him" (*Collected Essays* 2, p. 2). In "The Reader," one of the last essays she wrote before her death in 1941, she asserts the birth of the modern reader at the end of the Elizabethan period, when the book takes the place of the play:

Now the reader is completely in being. He can pause; he can ponder; he can compare; he can draw back from the page to see behind it a man sitting alone in a labyrinth of words in a college room thinking of success. He can read what is on the page, or, drawing aside read what is not written. There is a long drawn continuity in the book that the play has not. It gives a different pace to the mind. We are in a world where nothing is concluded. (Silver, "The Reader," p. 429)

"Nothing is concluded" in the book because meaning lives on in the reader. "Heaven," for Woolf, "is one long unexhausted read," and reading gives "a different pace to the mind." The act of reading, like writing, has its own rhythms.

Reader and writer are dialogical in Woolf. When we ask what silence is in the experience of the reader, we are simultaneously asking what it is in the experience of the writer. This is not to say, as Roland Barthes does, that you write the book you read, but the process of reading and writing, in reading Woolf, is to be understood as reciprocal. A participatory reader, whom modern female novelists like Margaret Drabble now take for granted, was posited by Woolf in the 1920's. Gérard Genette captures this intertwining of the reader and the writer:

The text is that Moebius strip in which the inner and outer sides, the signifying and the signified sides, the side of writing and the side of reading, ceaselessly turn and cross over, in which writing is constantly read, in which reading is constantly written and inscribed. The critic must also enter the interplay of this strange reversible circuit and thus become, as Proust says, and like every true reader, "one's own reader." (*Figures of Literary Discourse*, p. 70)

Woolf writes of the participation of the audience in the act of creation in "Notes on an Elizabethan Play," and this reciprocal relation is established long before Reader-Response critics claim the field. She writes in her 1924 version of "Mr. Bennett and Mrs. Brown":

Mrs. Brown . . . is just as visible to you who remain silent as to us who tell stories about her. . . . In your modesty you seem to consider that writers are of different blood and bone from yourselves; that they know more of Mrs. Brown than you do. Never was there a more fatal mistake. It is this division between reader and writer, this humility on your part, these professional airs and graces of ours, that corrupt and emasculate the books which should be the healthy offspring of a close and equal alliance between us. (*Collected Essays* I, p. 336)

Metaphors of gender reveal "healthy" and "corrupt" ways of reading and, at the same time, open up the act of reading to the creation of a community of minds—more than an issue of gender. "Corrupt" objective divisions of the reader and writer are allied with "emasculated" habits of reading, while "healthy" reading is the feminine "offspring" of a close alliance between reader and writer. A feminine way of perceiving and reading, a feminine narratology that springs from images of the body—"offspring"—is suggested here, a topic to be explored further in Chapter 4.

One of Derrida's main concerns as a literary critic and philosopher is to restore the complexities of reading to the dignity of a philosophical question—just as Woolf poses philosophical and pragmatic questions about the nature of the reader and the writer and about language and interpretation, in general, in her novels. Her historical recognition that "the theater must be replaced by the theater of the brain" (Silver, "Anon," p. 398) and that Anon, the artist, is dead, creates this new role for the reader. The spaces in her novels for the reader are the silences of the writer whose conception of writing is to allow the reader's emotions and responses a place to grow in the generous spaces of ellipses, dashes, and a lexicon and scenes of silence. When reading a Woolf novel, "we are in a world where nothing is concluded" (Silver, "The Reader," p. 429).

Proceeding through a lexicon and metaphors of silence, and by ellipses, dashes, and parentheses—a punctuation of suspension—to be illustrated later in this chapter, Woolf's concept of this world "where nothing is concluded" changes. In *The Voyage Out*, silence is a space for personal feeling and unexpressed emotion; in *To the Lighthouse*, the "veil of silence" is torn to allow space for the reader's sense of a philosophical silence of time, time passing, and death; in *The Waves*, silence represents the unconscious aspects of mind and of the life of nature outside man; in *Between the Acts*, perhaps the novel that Terence Hewet foretold, a silent meta-conversation is created between characters who "say nothing."

Woolf's fluid and exploratory prose style invites the reader's participation to fill in the suggestive silences, which represent her sense of the uncertainties and gaps in life that are incorporated, as even a traditionalist like György Lukács says they must, in the form of the novel. Woolf compositionally marks a place for the reader's active understanding. In sympathy with Bakhtin's notions of the dialogic imagination, she too knows that "responsive understanding is a fundamental force, one that participates in the formulation of discourse, and it is moreover an *active* understanding, one that discourse senses as resistance or support enriching the discourse" (*The Dialogic Imagination*, pp. 280–81).

Woolf's appreciation of these uncertainties, changing states of mind, and the role of chance in life, almost in the Greek sense that Thomas Hardy hints at in his novels, is realized in various kinds of silence. She renews our knowledge that the "self" that is reading as well as the "self" that is writing is in flux, and in her essays, letters, and diary she invites us to question how we make interpretations, in general; her novels do no less. Through the use of lexical, syntactic, metaphorical, thematic, and structural silences, including the rhythm of, perhaps, a "feminine sentence," Woolf creates opportunities to let the reader "into" her sentences, novels, and characters' consciousnesses in new ways. And these opportunities, as Harvena Richter asserts in her excellent book on Woolf's subjectivity,

are not artificial techniques imposed from without, but the actual processes which, when rendered through the medium of language, tend to make the act of reading approximate to the experience itself. . . . The reader, placed within the mind of the character, becomes to some extent that mind, receiving certain of the emotional stimuli and sharing in its response. (pp. vii, x)

Woolf created a different method to narrate life as experienced not in the speech but in the consciousness of a character.

By incorporating this vision of irresoluteness in her style, Woolf invites the reader to enter and to clarify himself, to complete the text. As Mary Ann Caws has demonstrated in her essay on *The Waves* in *Reading Frames in Modern Fiction*, "the reader must add to what is not said, in order to read it and frame it" (p. 243), a participation that Woolf encourages more than other modernist writers. We are left always in Woolf with the sentence, perhaps a feminine one, that pulsates beyond the periods—so many of which Leonard Woolf and editors like Susan Dick and Mitchell Leaska inserted for clarity's sake. To achieve fullness of meaning, as George Steiner states, one must punctuate and arrest interpretation. Woolf's liberal use of the semi-colon (a semi-stop), as any cursory review of her holographs reveals, and of the deletion transformation resists this full stop, the period, in punctuation and philosophy.

One of the things that Woolf refuses to end-stop is the meaning of "being a woman." She avoids essentialist definitions such as those advanced by feminist realists who define the new "content" or roles of womanhood in old forms. Woolf admits in *A Room of One's Own* that she has "shirked the duty of coming to a conclusion upon . . . the true nature of women" (p. 131), and again she asks: "But what is 'herself' . . . what is a woman? I assure you, I don't know; I do not believe that you know; I do not believe that anybody can know until she has expressed herself in all the arts and professions open to human skill" (ibid.).

Both Barbara Johnson, in articulating the difficulties of reading complex texts, and Jacques Derrida, in restoring questions of reading to the dignity of a philosophical question, formalize the "indeterminacies" of language and life that Virginia Woolf embodies in the silence and language of her novels. Deconstruction, along with structuralism and feminism, inform my critical vision and provide a way of making these silences "readable" while they slip through the nets of other more totalizing critical perspectives and vocabularies like, for example, New Criticism. Though there is analysis of "scenes of silence" in this book, in accord with the methodology of New Criticism, the critical stance of making all aspects of a text "mean" and "fit" a certain interpretation ignoring narrative anomalies is rejected. The kind of reading of silence proceeds from claims such as Johnson's in "Rigorous Unreliability." Deconstruction, she states,

confer[s] a new kind of readability on those elements in a text that readers have traditionally been trained to disregard, overcome, explain away, or edit out— contradictions, obscurities, ambiguities, incoherences, discontinuities, ellipses, interruptions, repetitions, and plays of the signifier. . . . As a critique of a certain Western conception of the nature of signification, deconstruction focuses on the functioning of claim-making and claim-subverting structures within texts. A deconstructive reading is an attempt to show how the conspicuously foregrounded statements in a text are systematically related to discordant signifying elements that the text has thrown into its shadows or margins; it is an attempt both to recover what is lost and to analyze what happens when a text is read solely in function of intentionality, meaningfulness, and representivity. (p. 279)

As Steiner states in a seminal essay, "On Difficulty," a frontier topic like this one can seek only to clarify "the state of art at a crucial point of difficulty. The assertiveness is provisional" (p. 18). The exploration of interiority and silence presents particular difficulty in two methodological categories for the critic as outlined by Steiner. First, the modal difficulty is a difficulty in the beholder of a text who has to learn the idiom and the orders of apprehension of other times, the philology. In dealing with Woolf's lexicon and apprehension of "reality," self and language and silence, I am reminded that there is no neutral observation (Kuhn, p. 42) for an American critic in the 1980's. One must, as far as possible, enter into her consciousness, her language, her worldview— and what I term her rhetoric of silence, a model that suits a unique representation of consciousness. This difficulty has been broached in this book by the establishment of a working lexicon of silence, developed later in this chapter, as gleaned from Woolf's novels and consultation with James Haule and Philip Smith's concordance to the novels. Second, Steiner reminds us of the ontological difficulty, and it is one that forces us as critics to confront the "blank question of the nature of human speech" or language.

Other Readers of Silence: Woolf Critics

This formal concern with silence in Virginia Woolf's novels—or in modern literature in general—is still an uncharted field. Of those critics who do address issues related to silence in Woolf, as in Lucio Ruotolo's *The Interrupted Moment*, more attention is given to the theme than the narrative strategy of silence in different novels. Ruotolo, in focusing on the historical and political dimension of "interruption," asserts that interruption is central to all of Woolf's thinking, "heralding change, and the growing expectation that society is on the verge of radical transformation" (p. 16). However, Woolf breaks the mold of the novel and ventures into the field of silence, varying her experimental intention with each new novel and expressing the nuances of silence with a lexicon of "pause, nothingness, emptiness, blanks, abyss, absence, gulfs" as well as a particular kind of silence, "interruption," which Ruotolo explicates. Sometimes the concepts of silence express harmony, as in the word "pause"; at other times, words like "gap," "rupture," or "interruption" express disjunction. The discontinuous, fragmented succession of thought and silence that Woolf captures in *The Years* and *Between the Acts* is a part of "capturing the moment whole," since the values of words and silence are juggled to show, as Samuel Beckett would say, "Total Object, complete with missing parts, instead of partial object" (*Proust and Three Dialogues*, p. 101). Contrary to Ruotolo's assessment that the spurts and stops are "interruptions," Woolf sometimes views them as part of the "whole" representing both the conscious and unconscious levels of language, character, and history. The "interruptions" in a Woolf novel represented by a certain lexicon of silence or punctuation, such as parentheses, brackets, ellipses, or dashes, are not only "occasions for inventive impulses," as Ruotolo claims, but also part of "capturing the moment whole." The seeming opposition between notions of "totality" and "fragmentation" is collapsed in Woolf's narrative techniques, and, to use George Poulet's modern notion, "On the one hand, everything becomes suspense, fragmentary arrangement, with alternation and opposite terms; on the other hand, everything contributes to the total rhythm" (p. 274). And it is this total rhythm, its alternations and irresolutions in theme and narration, that so many critics of Woolf miss or ignore as anomaly or ambivalence rather than conscious design.

Alex Zwerdling, who has written an informative book on Woolf's social vision, *Virginia Woolf and the Real World*, reflects this humanist desire for a noncontradictory, unified view of the world and, in a sometimes reductive fashion, tries to lock her ideas into structuralist, binary oppositions. Those who focus on Woolf as a political or social thinker become ensnared in this trap of polarities because "real world" resolution is sought in Woolf's fictional flux. For example, Zwerdling, in his criticism of *To the Lighthouse*, finds that "The continuous presence in Part III of . . . compromised rebellious gestures finally makes it impossible to see Woolf's novel as a liberation fable" (p. 200); equally, she does not write a sentimental novel of Victorian family life. Liberation fable or conventional Victorian family plot? Zwerdling's questions turn on the oppositions of a social thinker. One can sense his exasperation. Why can't she make up her mind? Along with Elaine Showalter, Zwerdling fails to find a "fit" for Woolf because he denies orders of mind other than the social. He forgets what Genette reminds us of—that literature "breathes new life into the world, freeing it from the pressure of social meaning, which is named meaning, and therefore dead meaning, maintaining as long as possible that opening, that uncertainty of signs, which allows one to breathe" (p. 41). Such criticism of Woolf topples with its social-realist frame.

Deconstruction, in contrast, operates with a working principle that fits Woolf's sense of flux in life and narration, and it can embrace Woolf's style, which turns on oppositions like liberation tale/Victorian restraints; inside/outside; male/female; I/not I; conscious/unconscious. Deconstruction accounts for the alternating rhythms in theme and style in *To the Lighthouse* (see Chapter 5), not as oppositions but as differences that can turn into one another. As Johnson states in "Nothing Fails Like Success": "The very word 'deconstruction' is meant to undermine the either/or logic of the opposition construction/destruction" (pp. 9–10). With this perspective, Woolf need not resolve multiple or shifting points of view into a reductive program of social action for the Victorian family or binary categories: she rests easy with the ambiguities and contradictions. Zwerdling's either/or tendency, his desire to have Woolf choose, assert, decide—perhaps as part of his own definition of effective writing or in the creation of a political and social Procrustean bed—is revealed in his observations of *To the Lighthouse*. He labels the alternation of viewpoints and syntax a "mannerism of style" (p. 205). Yet if we locate, as Toril Moi urges, "the politics of Woolf's writing precisely in her textual practice" (p. 16), we perceive that alternation not as a "mannerism," not as "narrative ambivalence" as Elizabeth Abel claims, but as the essence and embodiment of Woolf's vision of life. "One wanted fifty pairs of eyes to see with," sighs Lily Briscoe in *To the Lighthouse*. Woolf's worldview is marked in the fluctuating narrative style and themes of her novels: she turns events and people and life around and around, adjusting the narrative distance, creating different scenes, viewing life as through a kaleidoscope with her "fifty pairs of eyes." That this narrative practice is also a social vision is often overlooked by critics intent on unifying or accounting for what is unaccountable in Woolf.

Makiko Minow-Pinkney, in *Virginia Woolf and the Problem of the Subject*, is more sensitive to "the unaccountable" in female discourse on deeper, more structural levels, and she seeks to radicalize the reading of Woolf's texts by bringing contemporary critical theory to bear on her readings. She views Woolf's experiments in the novel as "feminist subversion of the deepest formal principles—of the very definitions of narrative, writing, the subject—of a patriarchal social order" (p. x). That these narrative orders also represent Western notions of the alphabet and writing is neglected; nevertheless, Minow-Pinkney's use of Julia Kristeva's work in her discussions of feminine language is suggestive, employing as it does Kristeva's notion of a "sujet in procès."

Rachel Bowlby, in her recent book *Virginia Woolf: Feminist Destinations*, acknowledges readings such as Minow-Pinkney's in which Woolf is viewed as subverting "masculine modes" of writing; however, she also animates other opposing critical perspectives of Woolf as a realist in support of a feminine cause or a modernist in her attention to formalism. Bowlby presents the paradoxes of contemporary Woolf criticism in a style of dash and hurry, and she leaves us, like Woolf, questioning the differences. She states: "The demand to pin her [Woolf] down to a definite position closes off just those questions which Woolf's texts never do determine once and for all, insisting contrary to many warnings on the part of her narrator and her character that she be this or that. . . . Instead she keeps open many lines as a response" (p. 81).

THE WRITING OF SILENCE: THE FRAMING OF THE INNER LIFE

A reader might, at first, find silence everywhere in a Virginia Woolf novel because the narration of the unsaid, the unspoken, and the unsayable interests her more than speech. Although modern dramatists like Harold Pinter, quick to see the complexity and ambiguity of silence, find conversational silences most intriguing, such silences play a less prominent role in Woolf's novels. Interior silences intrigue her; in fact, much of the communication that takes place among characters in her novels after *Jacob's Room*, published in 1923, is not voiced or audible. The interest in the unsaid and the unspoken for the moderns, as she states in "Modern Fiction," is in the "dark places of psychology" and, as she comes to believe in later life, the ineffable. Within this broad understanding of Woolf's narration of the unspoken, different themes and techniques for narrating or writing silence will be considered below. It will provide an overview of Woolf's methods of writing silence—its varied types and functions.

Silence disturbs narration, for it is one of "the signs by which literature draws attention to itself and points out its mask" (Genette, p. 29). What is literature's mask? Language. In literary studies, the attention to silence signals the new preoccupation with metalinguistics: linguistic anomalies, indeterminacy of meaning, the limitations of interpretation, and questions of narration that lie beneath or above the written language. Or as Steiner marks this modernist phase in *Real Presences*: "after the Word."

Theoretical issues occasioned by this interest in silence—its nature, its meanings, and its uses—are also revealed in other disciplines. In linguistics, for example, silence has traditionally been ignored except as a boundary-marking function, determining the beginning and ending of utterances. As Muriel Saville-Troike asserts, "The tradition has been to define it negatively as merely the absence of speech" (p. 3). In psychoanalytic theory, silence has often been interpreted as resistance; in communication studies, as passivity or absence, and this "perceptual bias has led researchers to attend to more readily noticeable behaviors while treating silence as merely background" (Saville-Troike, p. 14). Similarly, the fields of sociology and anthropology, until recently, have viewed the absence of the poor or the oppressed from certain social roles as a part of their silence, their inferiority or enactment of subordinate status. Only recently is there an appreciation that different voices and ways of being and knowing exist, as demonstrated by Carol Gilligan's study of women's moral stances, *In a Different Voice*; by Belenky, Clinchy, Goldberger, and Tarule's study of self, voice, and mind in *Women's Ways of Knowing*; and by Clifford Geertz's notions of anthropology in *Works and Lives*.

Cultural and sexual biases have led literary critics to attend to more readily noticeable behaviors, talk, and words, treating silence as background or inaction, and thus the important position of silence in human communication and literature has sometimes been overlooked. As Ron Scollon perceptively states in "The Machine Stops: Silence in the Metaphor of Malfunction," the metaphors that generate these ways of thinking about silence in different disciplines are important. In his own research on the stereotyping of the "Silent Indian" in education, legal affairs, politics, and social services, and in research by Feldstein, Alberti, and BenDebba (in Tannen and Saville-Troike) on college women with different patterns of pausing in conversation, it appears that for our society "a slower pace in exchanging turns is a highly negative quality" (p. 25). Scollon states,

Conversational silence appears to be a very negative quality. . . . In my view, these researchers have chosen to suggest this direction of causation on the basis of a generative metaphor. This generative metaphor is the foundation of this research and, in fact, of modern industrial society. It is the metaphor of the machine. If one assumes the engine should be running, the silences will indicate failures. Smooth talk is taken as the natural state of the smoothly running cognitive and interactional machine. (pp. 25–26)

However, in the field of religion and philosophy, unlike the disciplines mentioned above, silence has always had its valued place. Joseph Mazzeo, in "St. Augustine's Rhetoric of Silence," shows that though classical rhetorical tradition tried to join wisdom and eloquence, St. Augustine introduced a distinction between eternal and temporal wisdom, and equated the eternal with "silent," internal words. The voice of the silent, inner teacher, the voice of revelation, moves from Logos or speech into silence in Augustine's schema. This religious tradition in which silence is valued above speech is also discussed in Jane Marcus's article on the Quakers and their influence on Woolf, "The Niece of a Nun: Virginia Woolf, Caroline Stephen, and the Cloistered Imagination" (*Virginia Woolf and the Languages of Patriarchy*). In this view, silence is not a passive act but a space within which God can work and reveal eternal "truths." Similarly, a branch of Hinduism recognizes four distinct forms and stages of sound, which originate in different parts of the body, only one of which has an auditory realization in the mouth. The other stages of sound, originating in the heart, navel, and lower abdomen, are not audible. In Woolf, this silent space of the body or mind represents unconscious aspects of mind rather than spirituality: the theological transformed into the psychological.

Woolf's style expresses this meditative tradition as well as Romantic and Oriental philosophical perspectives. She changes the metaphor of silence and thus changes its meaning. It becomes a part of the rhythm of the whole, and thus the metaphor that generates absence or the sign of a malfunctioning machine is discarded. In making silence a positive and constituent part of narration as well as a valued stance toward life, Woolf is marking ambiguity and uncertainty about states of mind, about life, and about narration.

There has been much critical activity surrounding the term narration, beginning with Käte Hamburger's *The Logic of Literature* in 1957.

Sometimes narration is defined as "story," as the signified or narrative content; "narrative" is defined as the signifier, the discourse, the narrative text itself; "narrating" or "narrativity," according to Roland Barthes, is the act of narrating or producing taken in itself. Silence, then, is a "narration" of presence in that themes of silence—psychological, social, historical, and philosophical—are presented as content; the methods of writing silence are the discourse, the "narrative"; and since silence is a questioning presence that points to the limitations of language, its "narrativity" is also an issue.

The remainder of this chapter will engage the various meanings of "narration" and locate the kinds of silences by identifying "scenes of silence" in selected Woolf novels. The focus is on "scenes" because "story" is slight in Woolf's novels: little happens externally, and she concedes in her diary, "I can make up situations, but I cannot make up plots" (3, p. 160). Both a lexicon of silence—a semantic network of related words—and certain tense shifts, punctuation, and rhythms frame her "scenes of silence." Using markers that frame the inner life is a linguistic strategy discussed by Mary Ann Caws in her fresh look at fiction in *Reading Frames in Modern Fiction* and applied here. The first type of scene involves various forms of self-address ranging from the flotsam of word or sentence to defined, focused inner monologue. The second, communicative silences between characters that structure communication (pauses, lulls, interruptions, repetitions) but do not convey propositional content (false starts, deviation from rules, changes of plan, pauses, afterthoughts, repetitions); communicative silences that do carry propositional content, and analysis of a communicative event, such as genre, topic, function, setting, participants' status, and role relationship. The third type of scene contains moments of being, fixed philosophical moments, marked by silence in arrested conversation.

Silence in narration is, of course, verbal and unvoiced. What is left obscure, open-ended, and incomplete—Woolf's sense of what life is— is reflected then in her use of a lexicon of silence, punctuation, tense shifts, repetition, and a rhythm—techniques to be elaborated below. The "narrative" of silence will be examined on the levels of semantics, syntax, chapter divisions, and the novel's structure as revealed in a lexicon, punctuation, rhythm, spacing, metaphors, themes, and structures.

It is crucial to first distinguish between marked and unmarked silences in the text: those linguistically marked and those that the text allows but are not required. In *To the Lighthouse*, for example, Mrs. Ramsay, in exasperation with Mr. Ramsay's ignoring of people's feelings, notes in a marked silence that "There was nothing to be said" (p. 51). Later Lily, in an unmarked silence, watches Mrs. Ramsay "drifting into that strange no-man's land . . . follow[ing] them with her eyes as one follows a fading ship until the sails have sunk beneath the horizon." Her silence is suggested by a metaphor.

Some silences are filled and others are unfilled. In a filled silence, no room is left for the listener to complete the meaning: it is a silence of impotence, stultification, suffocation, or ineffability. For example, when Lily, feeling the loss of Mrs. Ramsay, thinks that words about death are impotent: "Little words that broke up the thought and dismembered it said nothing. About life, about death; about Mrs. Ramsay—no, she thought, one could say nothing to nobody" (p. 265).

Scenes of Silence

Thought has its psychological, philosophical, spatial, rhythmic, and temporal dimensions, and Woolf seeks to capture these elements in new metaphoric structures of mind in her novels. Focusing on "scenes of silence" that point to unrevealed aspects of character or life, Woolf explores sensations, feelings, and aspects of mind through certain techniques. Silence is not everywhere—between letters, words, and sentences—as certain deconstructionist critics might claim, but is embodied in a syntax and a narrative lexicon: pauses, gaps, blanks, trances, abysses, crevices, cracks, emptiness, nothingness, interruptions, gulfs, and absences. These are the formal devices of "silence" that mark changes in narrative gear and emotional tone and scene in Woolf's novels. They generally mark a suspension of narrative movement by arresting all human speech and, with the vocabulary and sensation of "sinking," move the character and the reader from external reality to internal thoughts. For example, in a scene with Mrs. Ramsay, we experience as readers two different strata of mind:

[Stratum 1: surface] For now she need not think about anybody. She could be herself, by herself. And that was what now she often felt the need of—to think; well, not even to think. To be silent; to be alone. All the being and the doing, expansive; glittering; vocal, evaporated.

[Stratum 2: deep level] And one "shrunk," with a sense of solemnity, to being oneself, a wedge-shaped core of darkness, something invisible to others. Although she continued to knit, and sat upright, it was thus that she felt herself; . . . and this self having shed its attachments was free for the strangest adventures. When life "sank" down for a moment, the range of experience seemed limitless. (pp. 96–97)

Pauses or suspensions occur when a character stops speaking and contracts ("shrunk," "sank") in order to "listen" (as urged by Martin Heidegger and Paul de Man) to the inner or outer world.

And Woolf moves the mind—the fret and hurry of surface events—to the deep moments to give "a great edge to both realities—this contrast" (*Diary* 4, p. 152). After finishing *Orlando* in 1928, she comments:

> Orlando has done well. . . . People say it was so spontaneous, so natural. And I would like to keep those qualities if I could without losing the others. They came of writing exteriorly; and if I dig, must I not lose them? And what is my own position toward the inner and the outer? I think a kind of ease and dash are good—yes: I think externality is good; some combination of them ought to be possible. (*Diary* 3, p. 209)

The inner and the outer, the surface and the depths, the exterior and the interior: these are recurring dimensions of Woolf's narrative dilemma. Again, while working on *The Pargiters* in 1933, Woolf comments on this problem, questioning the use of static language to describe the process of two strata of the mind—the upper and the under: "At present I think the run of events is too fluid and too free. It reads thin: but lively. How am I to get the depth without becoming static?" (*Diary* 4, p. 152). The "depths" are connected with the underside of the mind: the unconscious, the unsayable, the unknowable, the inaudible—the silence. Woolf's concern with surface and depths, dimensions that continue to interest artists and critics like Jean Baudrillard, leads her eventually to collapse these two concepts into a style of texture and pattern. The chart below maps her concern with the separation of "realities" and the structures she creates to textually signal the "narrative distance"—a lexicon, punctuation, and metaphors of "silence." This structural analysis reveals the "iron bolts" beneath the feathery and evanescent surface of her style. And it is the "zone of art," her writing, that acts as the buffer between the realities of the "surface" of everyday life and the "depths" of consciousness.

SURFACE (outer, speak, upper)

ZONE OF ART
Punctuation of suspension
Lexicon of silence
Metaphors of silence

DEPTH (inner, think, under)

The narration of Jane Austen and Virginia Woolf is interesting to compare in relation to the incidence of words and acts relating to these surfaces and depths of life. Anchored in society and the stable ego of "character," Austen trusts talk and dialogue in her novels; Woolf, on the other hand, is distrustful of external "facts" and moves toward an exploration of consciousness and silence. It is no surprise, then, when J. F. Burrows, in his fascinating study of Jane Austen's style, *Computation into Criticism*, notes that in *Emma* her heroine speaks 21,501 words and thinks 19,730 words. In Austen's other novels, when she trusts more to reflection, the proportion of "speaking" and "thinking" words shifts somewhat. "In both *Mansfield Park* and *Persuasion*, the character narratives of the heroines are considerably larger than their spoken parts" (p. 166): Fanny of *Mansfield Park* speaks 6,117 words and thinks 15,418 words; Anne of *Persuasion* speaks 4,336 words and thinks 19,730 words.

In Woolf's novel *To the Lighthouse*, published in 1927, Woolf uses variations on "say" less frequently than verbs of inner action ("think, reflect, remember, knew, seem, sense, look, feel"), as revealed in a review of Haule and Smith's concordance to this novel. It is the reverse in her social novel about a Victorian family, *The Years*, published in 1937: say (says, said, saying, speaks, speaking, spoke) is used 2,136 times; think (thinks, thinking, thought, thoughts) is used 758 times. Such changes in the frequency of speaking or thinking verbs reveal the different experimental intentions in Woolf's novels.

However, a reader must be cautious in his or her interpretation of frequency tables. The word "think" is often used in an incantatory way in Woolf's novels: a lexical cue to scenes of silence and the introduction of the inner life or the "other," which, as Freud has taught us, is sometimes just another aspect of self. Such shifts of narrative gear from outer to inner through the uses of lexical cues suspend the outward speech of the novel.

Adjusting the Scene: Narrative Distance

Woolf's "adjustment" and pivoting of the scene is important to the narration in her novels because "Reality [is] something . . . put at different distances" (*Diary* 3, p. 50). In *The Years*, Eleanor ruminates after spending an active day doing errands: "She felt a little 'spun round' as she put it to herself. What did you spin things round on? she wondered, helping herself to bread sauce—a pivot? The scene had changed so often that morning and every scene required a different adjustment; bringing this to the front; sinking that to the depths" (p. 104). Spoken discourse and

silent thought will be paired in this volume according to Genette's concept of "narrative distance": "Narrative 'representation,' or more exactly,
narrative information has its degrees: the narrative can furnish the reader
with more or fewer details, and in a more or less direct way, and can
thus seem (to adopt a common and convenient spatial metaphor, which
is not to be taken literally) to keep it at a greater or lesser distance from
what it tells"(p. 162).

Silence connects with Woolf's adjustments of the scene, her narrative
distance for the telling of certain subjects. For example, the narrative distance in *The Waves*, dealing with philosophical themes, is greater than in
To the Lighthouse, which attends more to human relations. The greater
narrative distance created by the almost ego-less narrator of *The Waves*
leads some readers to feel less comfortable with Woolf's narrative experimentation in this novel. A lexicon of silence arises from the "depths" of
Woolf's style while words skirt the surface events and actions. We hear a
range of sound and silence that reveals the "narrative distance": spoken
discourse to "hums" to "murmurs" to "muffled sounds" to "muteness"
to "silence."

This idea of narrative distance could be further developed using a
spatial instead of an auditory metaphor, for it is important to note that
she often describes life from the perspective of being "inside" something
that is semi-transparent. In "Modern Fiction," life is described as "a
luminous halo, a semi-transparent envelope surrounding us from the beginning of consciousness to the end" (*Common Reader* 1, p. 154). And
in *A Sketch of the Past* she recalls a childhood memory of Cornwall
"lying in a grape and seeing through a film of semi-transparent yellow"
(*Moments of Being*, p. 65). Life in these passages lacks clear outline and
suggests Genette's concept of narrative distance, narrative adjustment,
and narrative degrees, which is useful in describing what I term Woolf's
alternating style. This style reflects Woolf's distance from "reality" as
a narrator, and it is evident in a passage from *The Years* when Sally
remembers one of North's letters riding in a cab:

> It was a treat to take a hansom. . . . For a minute her mind was completely
> vacant. She enjoyed the peace, the silence, the rest from exertion as she sat there
> in the corner of the cab. She felt detached, a spectator, as it trotted along. The
> morning had been a rush; one thing on top of another. Now, until she reached
> the Law Courts, she could sit and do nothing. . . . She half shut her eyes, and
> then, involuntarily, she saw her own hand take a letter from the hall table. When?
> That very morning. What had she done with it? Put it in her bag? Yes. There it
> was, unopened; a letter from Martin in India. She would read it as they drove
> along. . . . "We started at dawn," she read. (pp. 107–8)

This greater or lesser "narrative distance" has to do with the character's consciousness and connection with outward events, the outside "surface" of life, and the submerged part of events, the unconscious, unspoken aspects of life that relate to the "depths." Silence, whether represented by auditory or by spatial metaphors, relates to Woolf's adjustment of a scene, her narrative distance.

If actuality is glimpsed through a window (as in the first section of *To the Lighthouse*) or reflected in a mirror (when the actors hold them up to the audience in *Between the Acts*), an "interior distance" is created by Woolf that protects or shields from contact. The creation of this zone of silence through the use of physical and fictional devices preoccupies Woolf from the beginning of her career. In "Slater's Pins Have No Points," written in 1926, she creates silence around characters living in a "cool glassy world of Bach fugues" (*Complete Shorter Fiction*, p. 103) who cannot break the pane of glass separating them from other people, from the world.

In *To the Lighthouse*, structural silences are visible in the form of the novel. Life is viewed in the first section, "The Window," through a pane of glass. The "Time Passes" section of the novel is a silent indeterminate middle in between "The Window" and "To the Lighthouse," more definite ends. In *Between the Acts*, silence moves into the realm of doubleness, reflection, and repetition through the use of glass "mirrors." Miss LaTrobe's play is separated from and yet reflects the audience in a mirror when the actors hold up mirrors in the last act of the play. Using these devices of imagery, theme, and structure, Woolf creates what Poulet would term an "interior distance" to separate one reality from another and what some might call a shield from contact. Woolf is well aware from personal temperament as well as experience in fiction that "we are no longer in a world where everything touches everything else" (Poulet, p. 92). These images of glass or mirrors provide a visual and emotional shield from contact; just as punctuation, like parentheses, ellipses, and brackets, will provide a temporal remoteness and syntactic framing; just as the lexicon of silence provides a semantic buffer; and just as repetitions, echoes, and reverberations provide an auditory distancing.

Woolf often pairs the color blue with space and silence, patterning blocks of color on the canvas of her text. In her diary, she refers to "the deep blue quiet space" when she emerges from her depression (5, p. 78); she speaks of "that feeling" which "slipped between the spaces that separate one word from another; like a blue flower between two stones" (*Pointz Hall*, p. 5); and on the night that Dora Carrington, companion of

Lytton Strachey, kills herself, Woolf refers to "walking along that silent blue street with the scaffolding" with Leonard, seeing "all the violence and unreason crossing in the air" (*Diary* 4, p. 176). Blue, a color abstracted from an emotion, suggests coolness, distance, sky, and silence. Such a device is used to undercut externality in Woolf's novels and to create a narrative space between the external and internal world.

In the above passages from *The Years* and *To the Lighthouse*, Sally and Mrs. Ramsay travel an interior distance and apprehend "reality" not in its actuality, but in the reflective distance of mind that Poulet describes as:

> The state in which an author breaks the sensuous enchantment and enchainment, turns aside from the actual, [to] establish . . . what he has felt, what he is going to think, or interior distance, a zone of calm, of reserve, and of silence, in which the seed of thought will find the ground and time necessary, over a long period, in which to take shape. He must space his words, his sentences, his thoughts. First of all, one must create an open space, a place, a spot. (p. 77)

This "interior distance" is the "zone of art" in the middle of every art that Woolf speaks of in her essay on Walter Sickert (*Collected Essays* 2): it is a domain for both Woolf and her characters that is removed from the actual, the political, the historical. It is an intellectual or artistic space or zone that widens between reality and consciousness and the place where, as Poulet says, "the mind discovers the powers to evolve, where without risk of running afoul of matter and being trapped in the actual, it can 'travel open spaces.' Space is freedom of mind" (p. 72). It is in these spaces of silence located in Woolf's narration that she creates for herself as an artist, and for the reader, the space to explore the inner life of her characters and life. These spaces also arouse creative and inventive impulses, as Ruotolo perceptively argues in *The Interrupted Moment*.

Silence is related more frequently to this interiority, but not exclusively. Woolf, more than other modern novelists, uses silence to mark a shift in narrative gear leading to a separation of "realities" and a suspension of "time": a way of representing the inner life. This then frees her to explore through her characters "the obscure places of psychology" and the limitations of language in expressing the conscious and unconscious mind.

The Separation of Realities: Outer and Inner

In this fictional category of the unspoken, Dorrit Cohn in *Transparent Minds* identifies three types of fictional presentation of consciousness that offer useful distinctions in this discussion of fictional minds in fictional texts: first, psycho-narration, which he describes as the narrative discourse about a character's consciousness intertwining narrator and character; second, quoted interior monologue, which is a character's mental discourse; and third, narrated monologue, which is a character's monologue in the guise of the narrator's discourse (p. 14). Psycho-narration is a handy label for one of Woolf's favorite techniques for rendering the inner lives of her characters because the narrator often fuses with the consciousness she narrates. Psycho-narration and psycho-analogies mark the presence of the author in narration through a method that does not clearly distinguish between the character and the author. In *To the Lighthouse*, the narrator's presence can be observed in the metaphor which states that Mrs. Ramsay's vision was "like a light stealing under water," a metaphor provided by the narrator, and in the past-tense comment, "so she saw them." Woolf uses psycho-narration and Joyce and Lawrence use narrated monologues in preference to quoted or interior monologues. These techniques offer more control over the language and presentation of the inner life of the character, representing a character's mental discourse blended with the narrator's discourse. For example, as Eleanor silently reads a letter from Martin in *The Years*, we perceive her direct associations of thinking and feeling, yet the narrator is always present in ways that are almost imperceptible:

"I had lost my way; and the sun was sinking," she read. "The sun was sinking . . ." Eleanor repeated, *glancing ahead of her down Oxford Street*. The sun shone on dresses in a window. A jungle was a very thick wood, *she supposed*; made of stunted little trees; dark green in colour. Martin was in the jungle alone, and the sun was sinking. What happened next? "I thought it better to stay where I was." So he stood in the midst of little trees alone, in the jungle; and the sun was sinking. *The street before her lost its detail.* (pp. 107–8; my italics, to indicate narrative presence)

In this psycho-narration, Woolf explores Eleanor's thinking ("A jungle was a very thick wood, she supposed"); her feeling ("So he stood in the midst of little trees alone"); her perceptions ("The sun shone on dresses in a window"); and the living moment ("The street before her lost its detail"). This interiority is externalized through Woolf's techniques for exploring "silence."

In *Mrs. Dalloway*, Woolf uses a metaphor or, to use Cohn's term, a psycho-analogy to describe Mrs. Dalloway's unhappy state of mind: "But-but-why did she suddenly feel, unhappy? As a person who has dropped some grain of pearl or diamond into the grass and parts the tall blades very carefully, this way and that, and searches here and there vainly, and at last spies it there at the roots, so she went through one thing and another" (pp. 182–83). Woolf compares Mrs. Dalloway's unhappy moment to the state of mind of a person who has lost something and searches for it. Quoted monologue would confine her to the language and perception of the character alone, since quoted interior monologue, as Cohn notes, is a rendering of a character's mental discourse, with the narrator's presence unmarked by analytical terms, reportorial indirection, or metaphors. Woolf's presentation of the inner life generally lacks demarcation between the character and the narrator, and it is her contribution to the modern novel to "trace the pattern, however disconnected and incoherent in appearance which each sight or incident scores upon the consciousness" (*Common Reader* 1, p. 155).

The shift in narrative gear and adjustments of the scene described above mark the separation of realities and thus a "scene of silence" in a Woolf novel. Woolf is always in search of a form that will embody what experience is, and she creates zones of silence around particular events and characters, isolating them, separating them, using new forms of punctuation, characterization, and structure in a novel. The separation of realities, the outer life from the inner, the daily life from the moment of vision, is safeguarded by Woolf's formal use of silence. The following sections of this chapter will deal with Woolf's formal techniques in creating a "narrative" of silence. Broadly, we could characterize these techniques as structures of silence: the punctuation, lexicon, metaphors, and larger structures of silence. The rhythms of silence, another structure, will be developed in Chapter 5.

The Punctuation of Suspension

Some silences offer possibility and infinite room for the reader's feelings and interpretation. Through the use of punctuation, particularly the ellipses—a Greek term meaning "to fall short" or "to leave out"—Woolf expresses this incompleteness or, perhaps, suspension. The ellipsis is a device that Woolf uses more frequently as she develops as a writer, and it offers the reader the possibilities discussed earlier in this chapter of continuing and participating more fully in Woolf's narration. In her essay "The Reader" (quoted at the beginning of this chapter), she states that, with a book, "one can read what is on the page, or, drawing aside read what is not written."

Ellipses, too, invite us to "read what is not written," the silences in the text. In *Three Guineas*, Woolf comments on her use of ellipses: "But . . . here again, in those dots, doubts and hesitations assert themselves (p. 88). Later, she speaks of the fear that makes concealment necessary between people: ". . . Again there are three dots; again they represent a gulf—of silence this time, of silence inspired by fear" (p. 184). The dots are a device, as she states in her review of Laurence Sterne, "part of an artistic system" that prevails in his novels as well as her own and that invites the reader to be open to the fugitive wanderings of his own mind as well as the author's.

In a scene from *Mrs. Dalloway*, Richard and Clarissa Dalloway sit down for a few minutes to chat: he, wordlessly expressing his admiration for her; she, thinking of Peter Walsh, her old boyfriend: "It all looked so empty. All the chairs were against the wall. What had they been doing? Oh, it was for the party; no, he had not forgotten, the party. Peter Walsh was back. Oh yes; she had had him. And he was going to get a divorce; and he was in love with some woman out there. And he hadn't changed in the slightest. There she was mending her dress . . ." (p. 179). These ellipses invite the reader to fill in the details of Clarissa's state of mind as she and her husband talk; they call into being her memories and past relationship with Peter before she became Mrs. Dalloway—the unspoken.

The three dots also represent the silences of women inspired by fear as recounted in *Three Guineas*: "But . . . those three dots mark a precipice, a gulf so deeply cut between us that for three years and more I have been sitting on my side of it wondering whether it is any use trying to speak across it" (p. 5). As Woolf states in "Women and Fiction": "Law and custom were of course largely responsible for these strange interruptions of silence and speech" (*Collected Essays* 2, p. 142). Law and custom dictate Woolf's use of ellipses, particularly in relation to women and sex. Ellipses in Woolf's novels and other works of the time mark the silences of a culture about sex—both heterosexual and homosexual. Like the asterisks so generously sprinkled throughout Sterne's *Tristram Shandy*, ellipses mark the areas of repressed discourse. In *The Years*, Lady Warburton, likening her niece to her grandmother who was a "famous beauty," begins to tell her what she was like. But she deletes certain stories from her account: "The old lady began making a selection from her memories; it was only a selection; an edition with asterisks; for it was a story that could hardly be told to a girl in white satin" (pp. 259–60). This is like Isak Dinesen's storyteller in "The Blank Page," who asks: "Who then . . . tells a finer tale than any of us? Silence does. And where does one read a deeper tale than upon the most perfectly printed page of the most precious book? Upon the blank page" (*Last Tales*, p. 100).

Lady Warburton, like many women before her, presents a "blank page" inscribed with a cultural message to the young women.

The dash is another device that invites the reader's participation; it is a riddle in the story only to be filled in as the reader understands the meaning of silences. Neville in *The Waves*, the novel that is a mosaic of voice, speaks of "Words and words and words, how they gallop—how they lash their long manes and tails, but for some fault in me I cannot give myself to their backs; I cannot fly with them, scattering women and string bags. There is some flaw in me—some fatal hesitancy, which, if I pass it over, turns to foam and falsity" (p. 83). The dashes contain the gallop of words, their racing ahead of Neville, yet their inadequacy, their hesitancy, Neville's hesitancy. The dash also contains haste, a theme about lack of time, which is a favorite in the twentieth century.

Punctuation is used to provide a separation of the outer and the inner, for example, in *Between the Acts*. Note the separations of inner and outer in the narration of the audience's thoughts during an intermission of Miss LaTrobe's play: "When we wake (some were thinking) the day breaks us with its hard mallet blows"; "The office (some were thinking) compels disparity" (p. 119). Thoughts here, not dialogue, are presented in quotation marks, externalizing the internal. The narrator's comments in parentheses intertwine with the character's thoughts, and we find ourselves as readers within two orders of mind. Similarly, in *To the Lighthouse*, we read a novel about the inner life of the characters, but we are provided with simultaneous brackets of external action, as when Mrs. Ramsay dies:

[Mr. Ramsay, stumbling along a passage one dark morning, stretched his arms out, but Mrs. Ramsay having died rather suddenly the night before, his arms, though stretched out, remained empty.] (p. 194)

This visual bracket turns out to be the only textual marker of the novel's pivotal event, the death of Mrs. Ramsay. Shortly after there is a ten-year passage of "silence" entitled "Time Passes," which records Mrs. Ramsay's presence through "absence," and the "nameless spirit" that hovers over the "empty" house is, perhaps, we, the readers. We remain nameless because we continue the passing of time and yet we too are replaced by other readers who fill in the blank of time in this chapter and life: the unspoken feelings following the death of the mother of this family. Similarly, Prue's marriage and death, the external story line, occur in brackets, and the presence of society is marked by the incantation "people said," a repetition that carries its own kind of silence:

[Prue Ramsay, leaning on her father's arm, was given in marriage. What, people said, could have been more fitting? And they added how beautiful she looked!] (p. 198)

[Prue Ramsay died that summer in some illness connected with childbirth, which was indeed a tragedy, people said, everything, they said, had promised so well.] (p. 199)

As Jeanne Schulkind notes in her introduction to *Moments of Being*, Woolf's punctuation is idiosyncratic and highly expressive. In *The Waves*, we find Woolf using parentheses not for external events but for Rhoda's secret selves. Even in the domain of syntax, we find her using the illusion of print to modulate and mark her private voice, freeing it from the traditional conventions of punctuation.

If for Edmund Husserl, the phenomenologist, objects exist independently of ourselves in the external world, and anything beyond our immediate experience is "bracketed"—then for Woolf it is the opposite. In her unique treatment of the outward and the inward, "the march of events" is relegated to brackets (with the exception of *The Waves*) while the inner discourse of characters is center stage. In bracketing externality, Woolf separates realities, suspends events, draws the reader's attention, and captures the simultaneity or counterpoint of outer events and inner thoughts and feelings. She breaks the membrane between inner and outer speech through the unconventional use of brackets, parentheses, and quotation marks. She signals her disregard for the "facts" of language just as she more overtly rejects "the novel of fact." In undermining the current fictional, linguistic, and philosophical "reality," she sloughs off her dependence on convention, free to explore the inner life through new narrative methods. Characters are projected mainly through their inner lives, and externality is "bracketed," asserting the reality and valorization of the inner life and the simultaneity of the two strata of experience. What is traditionally considered "inside" subjective consciousness is presented outside in the flow of words in a sentence, sometimes in quotation marks, which generally apply to spoken language; what is traditionally considered "outside" is enclosed within parentheses or brackets. Woolf's punctuation reveals a layer of consciousness represented by black dots — ... ( ) [ ] on a page. The dash has its haste; the ellipses, a sense of possibility and suspension; the parentheses and brackets, a sense of simultaneity with the other action in the sentence. These marks of punctuation (ellipses, dashes, dot-dashes, parentheses, brackets) correlate with Woolf's lexicon of silence, words like "gaps, gulf, silence, pause, abyss," to express her sense of the indeterminacies, the irresoluteness of life and language.

Her punctuation, then, separates "facts" from "the inner life" and the flow of words in time from the suspension of the silences. Woolf captures two strata of time and mind, and, like Emily Brontë whom she admired, with her punctuation of suspension, she "could free life from its dependence on facts."

The Lexicon of Silence

Woolf's changes in narrative gear are also signaled by a lexicon of silence. The use of structural semantics—a concept developed by linguists in the 1920's for a branch of linguistics that classifies word meanings—makes it possible to approach Woolf's formal use of "silence" in narration in a new way. Lexical and structural analysis can take us within sight of what is at stake when we attempt to locate silence in a Woolf novel, for the lexicon of silence is far from being a narrow linguistic methodology but is bound with narrative structures. Through this methodology we can develop an awareness of the larger implications of the psychological and social themes of silence and the peculiarities of incidence that come to define Woolf's "style." Burrows, in his use of computational methods in criticism, states that "The style of a discourse is the message carried by the frequency-distribution and the transitional probabilities of its linguistic features, especially as they differ from those of the same features in 'the language as a whole' " (p. 181).

Although Woolf's use of the word "silence" itself deserves close scrutiny, it is important to establish the whole penumbra of meaning related to silence in the novels to be examined: *The Voyage Out, To the Lighthouse, The Waves,* and *Between the Acts.* In order to establish this meaning, mechanical theme or word-hunts have been eschewed to establish a network of words related to silence based on Ferdinand de Saussure's brilliant observations about the important principle of meaning in language: "In language there are no positive terms" (p. 120), and "Language is a system of interdependent terms in which the value of each term results solely from the simultaneous presence of others" (p. 114). In establishing a preliminary lexicon as part of my identification of scenes where silence is marked, I have found that Woolf rarely or never uses words like "absence, inertia, non-being, rupture, vacuity," words that appear often in the poetry of Mallarmé, nor does she ever use Joyce's word "paralysis" to describe interior states. However, she does use categories of words listed below for temporal, spatial, bodily, psychological, and philosophical silences in her novels. She also uses different frequencies of the word "silent" (silence, silences): in *To the Lighthouse* (1927), 41 times; in *The Waves* (1931), 48 times; in *The Years* (1937), 121 times; and in *Between the Acts* (1941), 27 times.

These different frequencies do not suggest a developmental view of silence in her novels; rather, they suggest that her experimental intentions vary in different novels, and here we explore the different directions of silence. *The Years* concerns a Victorian family that is often pargeting (plastering over or whitewashing) its conduct, and so the frequency appears greater here, whereas *Between the Acts* is characterized less by social silence than by staccato rhythms of plot and dialogue marked by interruptions, gaps, and fragments, and so a different vocabulary of silence, more psychological, appears. In the listing below I have avoided binary distinctions and, wherever possible, indicated progressions and degrees of sound and silence. Careful reading of the novels and the use of Haule and Smith's concordance to these works reveal a network and sometimes a progression of related sensations, feelings, and thoughts, a lexicon of silence, which consequently helps to locate scenes of silence:

I. *Silence and Time*: relates to the auditory, including music, repetition, rhythm, and movement (these are further developed in Chapter 5).
   A. Harmony: silence, pause, quiet, rest;
   B. Disharmony: interruption, gaps, gulfs, broken syllables, rupture, fragments, scraps;
   C. Suspension (relates to simultaneity): suspend, fixed moment, tranced, moment of being;
   D. Repetition: incantation, echoes, simultaneity;
   E. Degrees of auditory silence: mute, silent, quiet pauses, interruptions, gaps, gulfs muffled, murmur, hum;
   F. Punctuation: use of ellipses and dashes to present incompletion, haste, and hurry as a theme or aspect of voice.
II. *Silence and Space*: relates to the visual, the spatialization of thought, and the body (these are further developed in Chapter 4).
   A. Degrees of spatial silence: night, absence, emptiness, nothingness, blank, blank space, white space, void / abyss, crack, fissure, crevice, gap / fading, flickering / veil, membrane / sign, shape, scaffolding, structure;
   B. Movement in space (duration):
      1. Positive: surface, rise, up;
      2. Negative: sink, fall, thud, drop, down, deep;
   C. Visual repetition: mirror, shadows, simultaneity;
   D. Punctuation: ..., —, ( ), [ ], " ";

E. Body silence: paralysis, immobility, sleep, illness, disease, inertia, peace, rest, still, quiet.

This spatial and temporal lexicon of silence helps to identify textually a scene of silence rather than rely on thematic pointers or a mystical sense, and, in time, the metaphors of mind and body of each domain of silence—temporal (auditory metaphors) and spatial (visual metaphors)—will be collapsed into a pattern as they evolve in Woolf's style. In Woolf's writing, time and space, believed by structuralist thinkers to constitute a major binary opposition, are deconstructed.

The method of locating a "scene of silence" can be illustrated in *To the Lighthouse*. Here we note a scene of silent observation involving Lily and Charles Tansley. The passage begins with a suspension of time, a concept of temporal silence that is marked in the first sentence by the word "suspended": "Lily Briscoe knew all that. . . . Could she not see, as in an x-ray photograph, the ribs and thigh bones of the young man's desire to impress himself, lying dark in the mist of his flesh—that thin mist which convention had laid over his burning desire to break into the conversation? But, she thought, screwing up her Chinese eyes, and remembering how he sneered at women, 'can't paint, can't write,' why should I help him to relieve himself?" (p. 137). Here we note that the narrator supplies the mind-stuff that Lily cannot see. In training her fictional eye on something that had never been as visible or audible before—the inner life—Woolf sees "into the life of things" with a different optical instrument. She separates this moment from ordinary reality, and the moment of vision is silent. This scene illustrates that the location of silence leads inevitably to an examination of Woolf's narrative style. Although the identification of silence begins with structural analysis and semantic networks, it is by no means limited to the type of linguistic analysis introduced in the 1960's that accustoms us to a new type of objectivity in examining language. Indeed, "silence" in all of its forms in Woolf's novels "outplays the codes on which she seems to rely" (Culler, p. 26), and silence always relates to psychological, social, and philosophical worldviews.

The Metaphors of Silence

Woolf was searching for a language of the mind in the midst of changing concepts of mind in the early twentieth century. If, as Michael Kearns asserts, the "mind as entity" metaphor—mind impressed by the external world—"which was shared by all writers on the mind, gave way to the metaphor 'sentience as life,' which was advocated by psychologists after the middle of the nineteenth century" (p. 2), so too was this metaphor implemented by novelists like Virginia Woolf. The emphasis on the figure of consciousness as sentient relations, vibrations, reverberations, and flickerings is reflected in Woolf's metaphoric structures of mind. The above lexicon reflects the flickering "sentience" of the conscious and the unconscious mind, not a mind that is "impressed" with external stimuli. And if we accept Lacan's notion that the unconscious is a form of writing (in Derrida's broad sense of "sign") and that all meaning is not necessarily linguistic ("Of Structure as an Intermixing of Otherness," in *The Four Fundamental Concepts*, p. 188), we can read the "sentience of life" concept of mind in her metaphors. We note her favorite and repeated metaphors of a "fish world," "stroke," and "pause" as poetic renderings of thought, writing, and silence, respectively.

As Freud and Lacan have demonstrated, the unconscious is by no means a dimension that is closed to investigation: we can infer its meanings from symbols, metaphors, dreams, fantasies, images, and lacunae in Woolf's narrated monologue, psycho-narration, or in the narrative attempt to shape the psychology of the moment with a metaphor or psycho-analogy. After all, Woolf the writer is not interested in clinical transcriptions of "mind stuff"—but in language and metaphor. Her exploration or creation is of underwater landscapes of the mind, not the accurate recording of the "stream" of the mind (if such were possible) or each "fish" or thought in the "stream." In looking within to the life of the mind, both conscious and unconscious, instead of outside events, Woolf begins her search for a method, any method: "and . . . nothing—no 'method,' no experiment, even of the wildest—is forbidden, but only falsity and pretence" ("Modern Fiction," p. 158). To achieve this interiority, Woolf uses "narrated monologue" and "psycho-analogies," and this decisively shapes her act of narration and distinguishes her from other writers.

Woolf often refers to her thoughts and consciousness in her autobiographical writings and fiction, "as a fish in a stream; deflected; held in place; but cannot describe the stream" (*Moments of Being*, p. 80). She uses the metaphor of a "fish world" or "the pool" to represent the fluidity of sensation, feeling, thought—consciousness—and imagination; "light" or "light beams" represent the searching, creative mind; "strokes" or "marks" or "notes" are the metaphors for art—painting or writing; and "pauses" are the silence that is part of her sense of mind, language, and life. Thoughts, words, and silence are thus part of the pattern she is creating in her novels in order to capture the moment "whole." Woolf is not seeking to abandon plot or character or structure in the novel, as many of her critics contend, but, like Mallarmé, to multiply "the forces at work in the field of which that structure is a part" (Johnson, *The Critical Difference*, p. 71). By focusing on the unconscious as well as the conscious, the silence and pauses as well as the sounds and the words, the inward as well as the outward, she multiplies the forces at work in the field of the novel. Only Proust and Joyce before Woolf in the field of the European novel attempt this.

In her essay "Professions for Women," she presents the unconscious state of mind of the novelist, particularly the female novelist, exploring underwater depths as she asks the reader to "imagine me writing a novel in a state of trance":

I want you to figure to yourselves a girl sitting with a pen in her hand, which for minutes, and indeed for hours, she never dips into the inkpot. The image that comes to my mind when I think of this girl is the image of a fisherman lying sunk in dreams on the verge of a deep lake with a rod held out over the water. She was letting her imagination sweep unchecked round every rock and cranny of the world that lies submerged in the depths of our unconscious being. Now came the experience, the experience that I believe to be far commoner with women writers than with men. The line raced through the girl's fingers. Her imagination had rushed away. It had sought the pools, the depths, the dark place where the largest fish slumber. (*Death of the Moth*, p. 240)

The experience, "far commoner with women writers than with men," of exploring the depths of being in the slumbering unconscious, "the obscure places of psychology," is established here.

In *To the Lighthouse*, Woolf again compares the flickering, multi-colored, evanescent quality of fish in their underwater environment to a world of unconscious thought in a passage where Mrs. Ramsay retreats from the active, conversational life of her dinner party to observe her guests in silence:

Now she need not listen. It could not last, she knew, but at the moment her eyes were so clear that they seemed to go round the table unveiling each of these people, and their thoughts and their feelings, without effort like a light stealing under water so that its ripples and the reeds in it and the minnows balancing themselves, and the sudden silent trout are all lit up hanging, trembling. So she saw them; she heard them; but whatever they said had also this quality, as if what they said was like the movement of a trout when, at the same time, one can see the ripple and the gravel, something to the right, something to the left; and the whole is held together. (p. 160)

The fluidity of the underwater vision of Mrs. Ramsay "like a light stealing underwater," suggests the clear eyebeam of a lighthouse, and this metaphor reveals the inner life of the other guests at the table. We also have a sense of the slumbering unconscious of Mrs. Ramsay with its feelings, sudden dartings, and discoveries.

The Greek God Momus, who was said to have blamed Vulcan because in his creation of the human form he had not formed a window in the breast so that whatever was thought or felt could be brought to life, would delight in Woolf's narrative technique of "narrated monologue" that here blends the perspectives of the author and the character. Mrs. Ramsay, herself "suspended" in a silent moment of vision by Woolf's narration, is not unlike the "silent trout," the guests, she observes. Thought is suspended while Woolf creates the psycho-analogy of deep-water fish and darting "sentient" thought familiar to us also from *A Room of One's Own.* Thought, "However small it was, it had, nevertheless, the mysterious property of its kind—put back into the mind, it became at once very exciting, and important; and as it darted and sank, and flashed hither and thither, set up such a wash and tumult of ideas that it was impossible to sit still" (p. 5).

Woolf places increasing emphasis on subjective experience of all kinds in her writing. In historical perspective, one notes that an eighteenth-century author like Daniel Defoe is concerned with the external imprint of "things" on the mind in *Moll Flanders*, reflecting the "mind as entity" concept: "These things," says Moll, "oppressed my mind" (p. 41). In the next century, in Austen's novel *Emma*, the narrator comments that "It would be impossible to say . . . which of all [Emma's] unpleasant sensations was uppermost" (p. 131); in Charlotte Brontë's *Jane Eyre*, the "soul" is repeatedly presented, incipient but unanalyzed inner life. However, it is not until Virginia Woolf that vivid metaphors of mind give compact expression to the historical "silence" of the mind in the English novel.

Woolf has to grapple not only with the sentience of the mind— the fluidity and obscurity of thoughts and feelings—but also with the conventions of writing and the alphabet. More than other modernists, Woolf *writes* her sensations, feelings, and thoughts about life and about writing (both Occidental and Oriental) by spatializing and temporalizing thought in new ways. Curiously, she is also conscious of the production of writing or the act of writing itself, and, liking certain kinds of pen and ink, mentions in her diary that "pauses" are sometimes the mechanical result of having to dip her pen in ink—certainly, a blot on all these observations.

Nevertheless, she marks the thinking and feeling of fictional minds in fictional texts. But how does an author capture process, the fluidity of life and the mind with static marks on a page? In analyzing Woolf's metaphors, we discover recurrent images that represent mind, language, and silence. If the "fish world" or a "pool" represents, at times, Woolf's notion of the fluid world of the mind, then the "stroke" and sometimes "marks" and "notes" are her metaphors for art and, more particularly, writing; her musical "pauses" are a metaphor for the spaces between "strokes," the silences. For example, the strokes and pauses of Lily Briscoe's paintbrush in *To the Lighthouse* establish a metaphor of the relationship among thought, writing, and silence:

> With a curious physical sensation, as if she were urged forward and at the same time must hold herself back, she made her first quick decisive stroke. The brush descended. It flickered brown over the white canvas; it left a running mark. A second time she did it—a third time. And so pausing and so flickering, she attained a dancing rhythmical movement, as if the pauses were one part of the rhythm and the stroke another, and all were related; and so, lightly and swiftly pausing, striking, she scored her canvas with brown running nervous lines which had no sooner settled there than they enclosed (she felt it looming out at her) a space. (p. 235)

The "space" that Lily encloses on her canvas is both musical and visual. "Pausing," "striking," and "scoring" have meaning in both domains, and Woolf creates a curious synesthesia in her novels. In the word "stroke," Woolf merges Lily's paint *stroke*, the light-beam *stroke* of the lighthouse, the *stroke* of the oars (the Ramsays' trip to the lighthouse), the *stroke* of a clock, and the beat of words and of music: each use of "stroke" comes from a different domain—art, the world of action, life, music— and attempts to communicate the incommunicable through a metaphor.

The strokes of Woolf's pen not only mark the alphabet but also suggest, at times, other codes of writing: hieroglyphics. Lily, sitting next to Mrs. Ramsay, imagines "how in the chambers of the mind and heart of the woman who was, physically, touching her, were stood, like the treasures in the tombs of kings, tablets bearing sacred inscriptions, which if one could spell them out, would teach one everything, but they would never be offered openly, never made public" (p. 79). Mrs. Ramsay's being is later referred to as a "wedge-shaped core of darkness" (p. 95), suggesting cuneiform, with all of its mysterious connotations. Woolf toys with notions of Egyptian writing as a form of writing able to express orders of mind and feeling not captured by the Western alphabet. Lacan and his notion come to mind,

That the dream has the structure of a sentence, or, rather to stick to the letter of the work, of a rebus; that is to say, it has the structure of a form of writing, of which the child's dream represents the primordial ideography and which, in the adult, reproduces the simultaneously phonetic and symbolic use of signifying elements, which can also be found both in the hieroglyphs of ancient Egypt and the characters still used in China. (*The Language of the Self*, p. 30)

The "strokes" of writing in Woolf reverberate beyond the Western alphabet as she reminds us of other forms of writing in her characterizations.

The act of writing for Woolf is an act of self-preservation, "a stake," as she says near the end of her life, "against oblivion": a way to "overcome desolation" (Silver, "'Anon' and 'The Reader,'" p. 403). Through writing, she overcomes the "emptiness" of Being and depression that she sometimes refers to in her diary, and by putting "two and two together, two pencil strokes, two written words" (ibid.), she fills the form of the sentence, an emotional as well as narrative space—just as Lily fills the space of her canvas. She thinks of "something very profound about the synthesis of my . . . being: how only writing composes it: how nothing makes a whole unless I . . . am writing" (*Diary* 4, p. 161). Her diary reflects the difficulty of filling this narrative space as she plans *To the Lighthouse*: "I cannot make it out—here is the most difficult abstract piece of writing—I have to give an empty house, no people's characters, the passage of time, all eyeless and featureless with nothing to cling to" (*Diary* 3, p. 76).

"Emptiness" is a state that interests Woolf, and it figures in her art because it figures in her feelings. Sometimes it represents a hollow emotional center, embodied in Peter Walsh in *Mrs. Dalloway*:

As a cloud crosses the sun, silence falls on London; and falls on the mind. Effort ceases. Time flaps on the mast. There we stop; there we stand. Rigid, the skeleton of habit alone upholds the frame. Where there is nothing, Peter Walsh, said to himself; feeling hollowed out, utterly empty within. Clarissa refused me, he thought. He stood there thinking, Clarissa refused me. (p. 55)

Such feelings of emptiness cannot be conveyed directly; consequently, Woolf must find spatial metaphors, empty places, to figure it. In the holograph of *Between the Acts*, the narrator notes "there was a silence in the dining room," revealing Woolf's interest in empty places as a metaphor for the emptiness she sometimes feels. Similarly, Lily ruminates about empty places in *To the Lighthouse*, longing for Mrs. Ramsay, now dead: "For how could one express in words these emotions of the body? express that emptiness there? (She was looking at the drawing-room steps; they looked extraordinarily empty.) It was one's body feeling, not one's mind" (p. 265). As this book argues, Woolf is preoccupied with structuring "emptiness" or "absence" into her art: "The thing that exists when we aren't there" (*Diary* 3, p. 114); the description of the dining room at Pointz Hall, "Empty, empty, empty; silent, silent, silent. The room was a shell, singing of what was before time was, a vase stood in the heart of the house, alabaster, smooth, cold, holding the still, distilled essence of emptiness, silence" (*Between the Acts*, p. 47). Woolf is preoccupied with the "presence" of "absence" discussed in Chapter 1: other people, other times, dead people, other lives lived in the same rooms, earlier lines of poetry and literature. Woolf wants to convey something about life that contains knowledge "behind the eyes," suggesting the kind of knowing represented by Milton's *Samson Agonistes*, "eyeless in Gaza" or Tiresias, the blind seer. Such knowledge or views are beyond the human observer, as suggested in *The Waves*, "a mystical eyeless book," and in *To the Lighthouse*, where "distant views seem to outlast by a million years (Lily thought) the gazer" (pp. 36–37). "Rooms" in houses as well as "distant views" of Nature outlast the observer, and their "emptiness" contains other lives of other times that a writer can construct: a writer can fill the "vacancy and silence somewhere in the machine" (*Diary* 3, p. 260) in the same way that he fills the empty form of the sentence. Filling "emptiness" is a creative act.

"But how to describe the world seen without a self? There are no words" (*The Waves*, p. 204). Woolf approaches the feelings of "emptiness" that suggest the non-being from which "being" arises by indirection and constructs spaces in her novels—empty rooms, empty steps— to suggest depression, desolation, the sense of strangeness about being in the world or the silence before creativity. And because this space of being is ineffable—"I have not really laid hands on the emptiness after all" (*Diary* 3, p. 260)—it must be apprehended by the participation of the reader as discussed earlier in this chapter.

The Rhythms of Silence

Alternating rhythm, this time of sounds and rests from the auditory domain, rather than strokes and pauses from the spatial domain of painting or writing, is presented in *Mrs. Dalloway*. Septimus ruminates: "Sounds made harmonies with premeditation; the spaces between them were as significant as the sounds. A child cried. Rightly far away a horn sounded. All taken together meant the birth of a new religion" (p. 33). The use of the word "space" here is both visual and musical. Also, Bernard, in considering his literary style in *The Waves*, begins with observations of Byron's style, and remarks: "Now I am getting his beat into my brain (the rhythm is the main thing in writing). Now without pausing I will begin, the very lilt of the stroke" (p. 79).

The "pauses" in the above passages are one of Virginia Woolf's uses of silence, and, in this instance, part of the alternating rhythm of thought and experience as represented in her art, which is both visual and musical at times. Often, in a scene of silence, the surface level of mind slumbers or drowses, is "suspended," and then a "pause" occurs just before the mind "sinks" to unconscious depths or before a subject gains clear outlines. In terms of "narrative distance," a concept of Gérard Genette's discussed earlier, there is a "veil," "fog," or "mist" that obscures the subject, then a "pause," a "silence," and the veil lifts and a subject emerges with clarity and simplicity. The narrator begins to see the subject with clear outlines as the "narrative distance" decreases. Through these examples, we observe that rhythm is another technique (to be developed more fully in Chapter 5), along with metaphors, a lexicon of silence, and a punctuation of suspension, that signals activity of mind in fiction.

The Larger Structures of Silence

The last narrative technique to be discussed in this chapter is the structures of silence. Since Woolf's novels often begin with formal concerns as well as a feeling, critical analysis of plot and character seem unresponsive to her experimental concerns. In fact, several of her novels, as can be discerned in her diary, begin with ideas of structure and form rather than theme. In her early designs of *To the Lighthouse*, for example, she draws two blocks connected by a corridor of time:

Or the beginnings of *Flush* in 1933: "I visualize this book now as a curiously uneven time sequence—a series of great balloons, linked by straight narrow passages of narrative" (*Diary* 4, p. 142). And one visualizes:

————◆————

CHAP. XL.

I AM now beginning to get fairly into my work ; and, by the help of a vegetable diet, with a few of the cold seeds, I make no doubt but I shall be able to go on with my uncle Toby's story, and my own, in a tolerable straight line.
Now,

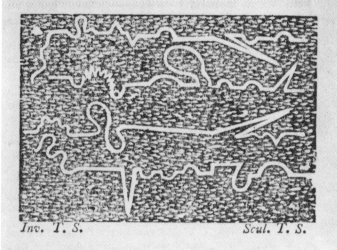

Inv. T. S.   *Scul. T. S.*

These were the four lines I moved in through my first, second, third, and fourth volumes——

In the fifth volume, I have been very good,— the precise line I have described in it being thus :

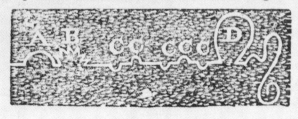

1.   Laurence Sterne, story lines in *The Works of Tristram Shandy* (1804).
Reproduction courtesy of the New York Public Library.

This delineation of form reminds us of Laurence Sterne's sketches of his zig-zag story line in *Tristram Shandy*, an author Woolf named the "fore-runner of the moderns" because of his interest in silence. His structurings are also a figuration of silence (Illustration 1). Such initial designs are illustrations of structural "silences": themes and emotions charted into the novel in relation to one another. Silence is carefully structured into the text through various forms discussed in this book: parentheses, brackets, the "Time Passes" section of *To the Lighthouse*, the "Interludes" of *The Waves*, the interpolations between the acts of Miss LaTrobe's play in *Between the Acts*, and the physical spaces in the text of *Mrs. Dalloway*. Such notions of form are not just formalist concerns but "emotion put in the right relations" (*Letters* 3, p. 133). As this chapter suggests, it is a form of silence that we must learn to read.

4

Escaping the Alphabet

DECODING THE BODY AND THE MIND
IN 'THE VOYAGE OUT' AND 'THE WAVES'

IN LEARNING TO READ the narration of silence, in general, and the silence of women in eighteenth- and nineteenth-century novels, in particular, we gain a useful historical perspective on Virginia Woolf's narration of silence in the twentieth century. We discover, in addition to other forms of silence, Woolf's expression of the mind through the body. The bodies of Rachel in *The Voyage Out* and Rhoda in *The Waves* become the loci of techniques for keeping silence as well as for expression. Bodily gestures and images are the means by which silence becomes externalized and visible to others: silence is embodied in women.

In Woolf's novels, the materiality of the body is posited as the origin of thought and narratology in women, spiraling from a "Sentio ergo sum" rather than "cogito ergo sum." For example, after Mrs. Ramsay's death in *To the Lighthouse*, Lily thinks, "For how could one express in words these emotions of the body" (p. 266). In illness and in health, Woolf's thought and writing spring out of a sensory mold and poetic correlatives for the sensations of body and mind, not social representations, of women. Although Lacan and Kristeva theorize that this impulse originates in women's denial of or exclusion from the symbolic realm, Woolf posits that it is indeed "a difference of view." "The book," according to Woolf, "has somehow to be adapted to the body" (*A Room of One's Own*, p. 81)—the woman's body.

In creating the characters of Rhoda in *The Waves* and Rachel in *The Voyage Out*, Woolf adds to our cultural definitions of women, fashioning new modes of subjectivity in which we, as readers, are invited "to consult our own minds." She creates ways in which we can see, feel, think, and experience "Woman Dreaming," particularly in the character of Rhoda. It is a new interest and contrasts with the preoccupation of Emerson and other male authors who cast men in the traditional role of the "delegated intellect . . . Man Thinking" ("The American Scholar," *Essays*, p. 85). In portraying the dreaming mind of a woman, Woolf begins to dissolve the boundaries that enforce oppressive hierarchies like that of "Man Thinking" and defining what woman is. In Rhoda, the visionary woman, Woolf writes a woman's body into the text, a body that is participating in the experience of perceiving and thinking. In a stroke of "différance," she "disembodies" Rhoda in freeing her from her ordinary body for spatial-sensory ventures and, at the same time, "embodies" her dreams and thoughts by giving them a material form through bodily metaphors. This dreaming mind is glimpsed in Rachel in *The Voyage Out* during her period of delirium, when "she was completely cut off, and unable to communicate with the rest of the world, isolated alone with her body" (p. 330). By the time Woolf writes *The Waves* in 1931, she has developed psychological and narrative techniques that place the reader in the mind and body of the character, Rhoda.

Such expression of mind and body joins a long philosophical tradition that has grappled with distinctions between body and mind: what is external to us, what is external to our minds, and what is internal. Woolf collapses the categories of G. E. Moore, her contemporary, who in his *Proof of an External World* distinguishes internal—"things presented in space" such as images we see with our mind's eye—from external—"things to be met with in space" that can be perceived by others as well as one's self. In her narrative representations of body and mind, she collapses the internal and external and creates new definitions of "self." During Rhoda's dream state in *The Waves*, she exclaims:

Oh, to awake from dreaming! . . . Let me pull myself out of these waters. But they heap themselves on me; they sweep me between their great shoulders; I am turned; I am tumbled; I am stretched, among these long lights, these long waves, these endless paths. (p. 28)

Compare this state to Rachel's in Woolf's first novel, *The Voyage Out*, in which she describes how the eye-mind-body experiences delirium:

The sights were all concerned in some plot, some adventure, some escape. . . . Now they were on the sea; now they were on the tops of high towers; now they jumped; now they flew. But just as the crisis was about to happen, something invariably slipped in her brain, so that the whole effort had to begin again. The heat was suffocating. At last the faces went further away; she fell into a deep pool of sticky water, which eventually closed over her head. She saw nothing and heard nothing but a faint booming sound, which was the sound of the sea rolling over her head . . . all her tormenters thought that she was dead. (p. 341)

"It is this emphasis," as Harvena Richter observes, "on the subject's experience of the object which separates Virginia Woolf most clearly from her contemporaries" (p. viii). This detailed image of a woman's subjective state limned with words of pain and sensation—waters that heap and sweep and close over her head, in which she is suspended, turned, tumbled, stretched, and tormented—could be compared to Josef Breuer's description of Bertha Pappenheim in *Studies in Hysteria*:

In the afternoons she would fall into a somnolent state which lasted till about an hour after sunset. She would then wake up and complain that something was tormenting her—or rather, she would keep repeating in the impersonal form "tormenting, tormenting" . . . and during the climax of the illness, when the contractures had extended to the left side of her body. . . . There were extremely rapid changes of mood leading to excessive but quite temporary high spirits, and at other times severe anxiety . . . and frightening hallucinations. (p. 24)

Max Ernst's collages of women in *Une Semaine de Bonté* depict a similar state of body and mind (Illustrations 2–4).

We can observe similar disjunctions of body and mind expressed in terms of spatial form in the representation of women in Woolf's novels, Freud's and Breuer's case studies of hysteria, and Max Ernst's surrealist collages. This has been historically coded as feminine space, beginning with Charcot, then Freud's fascination with female hysterics and the sur-realists' preoccupation with the hysteric's bodily gestures, and leading up to Lacan's present rewriting of Freud's psychoanalytic theory in terms of language. Such comparisons help to establish the new "rhetoric of silence" that Genette claims will include the semiotics of all discourses: literary, anthropological, visual, and psychological—and the feminist view represented by Kristeva that there is something about women which escapes discourse. Woolf, Freud, Breuer, and Ernst treat the silent phe-nomenon of delirium and hysteria in women as a "supreme means of expression" as well as a pathology, and similar silent gestures—bodily, verbal, and visual—are repeated in varying forms in each.

Like Mary Ann Caws and Jane Gallop, I want to juxtapose literary, psychological, and artistic representations of women to reveal a cultural "intertextuality" concerning women's dream states and hysteria. Such

2.   Max Ernst, *Une Semaine de Bonté.* Reprinted by permission of the
Print Collection, Miriam and Ira D. Wallach Division of Art, Prints, and Photographs,
the New York Public Library, Astor, Lenox, and Tilden Foundations.

juxtaposition reveals that a literary structure, such as Woolf's construction of Rachel in *The Voyage Out* or Rhoda in *The Waves*, "does not
simply exist but is generated in relation to another structure" in the culture (Kristeva, *Desire in Language*, p. 64). Rachel and Rhoda, sketched
by Woolf in 1916 and 1931, Dora and Anna O., analyzed by Freud and
Breuer in 1895 and 1905, respectively, and the collages of Charcot's hys-

terical women constructed by Max Ernst in *Une Semaine de Bonté* in 1930 create a discourse on hysteria and the "silence" of bodily expression. "Any text," Kristeva states, "is a mosaic of quotations; any text is the absorption and transformation of another" (ibid.).

However, though the gestures of dream and hysteria are shared, different cultural readings—the reading of women's bodies, minds, and silence, yet once more—are possible. As discussed in Chapter 2, the

3.   Max Ernst, *Une Semaine de Bonté.* Reprinted by permission of the Print Collection, Miriam and Ira D. Wallach Division of Art, Prints, and Photographs, the New York Public Library, Astor, Lenox, and Tilden Foundations.

4.   Max Ernst, *Une Semaine de Bonté*. Reprinted by permission of the Print Collection, Miriam and Ira D. Wallach Division of Art, Prints, and Photographs, the New York Public Library, Astor, Lenox, and Tilden Foundations.

female is a silent subject rather than a "speaking subject"—given the psychological, social, and historical position of women. The mute states of dream, delirium, and hysteria invite specular rather than auditory interpretation because bodily and mental expressions of unspoken disturbance must be read visually. Charcot, a major French theorist of hysteria at the turn of the century, is described by Freud as a "visuel," a seer, because his approach to psychiatric interpretation is so strongly visual. This can be glimpsed in his *Iconographie Photographique de la Salpêtrière*, voluminous photographs of his patients in various stages of hysteria. Woolf, in representing Rachel and Rhoda's pain, dreams, and illness as an expression of their misalignment with the social order, differs from other thinkers and artists in terms of belief and focus. Charcot recognized the importance of hysterical states of women in his observations at the Salpêtrière clinic, but he nevertheless believed that female hysterics were often exaggerating their pain and paid little attention to what they were saying. This extraordinary visual focus and the development of a vocabulary of movement was recently captured in a visual drama and dance created by Dianne Hunter, Lenora Champagne, and Judy Dworin, "Dr. Charcot's Hysteria Show."

Foucault has written of the importance of the visual and sight in constituting medical knowledge and "the sovereign power of the empirical gaze" in *The Birth of the Clinic*. Charcot's photographs and the Dianne Hunter visualization indeed suggest the sovereignty of the gaze. His photographs and other artistic representations of female hysterics reveal, as Martin Jay perceptively notes, that "What is in fact 'seen' is not a given, objective reality open to an innocent eye. Rather, it is an epistemic field, constructed as much linguistically as visually" (p. 182). The bodily distortions and exaggerated behavior fixed in Charcot's gaze make visible the invisible disturbances of women's minds. In André Brouillet's "A Clinical Lecture at the Salpêtrière," (Illustration 5), he captures the clinical gaze of Charcot and his followers. Interestingly, Freud spent a few months at Charcot's clinic in 1895 and had this print on the wall of his office; yet it remained for him to supplement Charcot's subjective modes—the "gaze" and the interpretation of bodily movement—with language, the "talking cure." Visual artists such as Henry Fuseli, Robert Fleury, and Max Ernst have also represented the typical body posture of the female "hysteric" (Illustrations 6–9).

The interpretation of hysteria historically alternates between an expression of liberation and one of pathology, accompanied by feelings of either pain or pleasure. As A. R. G. Owen states in his book on Charcot: "Hysteria is a socially malleable disorder and the form and intensity of its manifestation tend to alter as the milieu changes" (p. 66). We might also add that this "socially malleable disorder" and the form of its manifestation alter as perspectives on and interpretations of women alter. Woolf, with her filigree interest in describing dream states and illness in women as an aspect of some broader conception of mind, suggests the underlying psychological pain in the abandonment of the conscious self

5.   André Brouillet, "A Clinical Lecture at the Salpêtrière." Photograph courtesy of Basic Books, reprinted from Henri Ellenberger, *The Discovery of the Unconscious* (1970); painting at L'Hopital Pierre Wertheimer in Bron, France.

in hysteria. Such views are represented by Bernard in *The Waves*, who speaks of the fact that:

For pain words are lacking. There should be cries, cracks, fissures, whiteness passing over chintz covers, interference with the sense of time, of space; the sense also of extreme fixity in passing objects; and sounds very remote and then very close; flesh being gashed and blood spurting, a joint suddenly twisted—beneath all of which appears something very important, yet remote, to be just held in solitude. (p. 263)

The pain, delusions, and hysteria of Rhoda and Rachel are expressed then through dream and body states. Woolf's representation of their mental landscapes is generally specular, and such treatment is fitting given the nature of delusions and hysteria. In general, symptoms of this disorder involve loss of consciousness and disturbances of vision, hearing, and language, as well as tremors, somnambulism, headaches, and paralysis. There is no attempt here to correlate physical symptoms with refined categories of hysteria. In one form of hysteria described by Charcot, the hysteric's hands, arms, and legs contract and there is a certain paresis or jerkiness in body movement, illustrated perhaps in descriptions of Rhoda's "ill-fitting body" or her statement "My body seemed paralyzed." Rhoda is estranged from her body, overflowing with dreams, and "always seeking some pillar in the desert" (p. 281).

The visual drama in this pathology, first witnessed in Charcot's clinic for hysterical women at Salpêtrière in the 1880's, is captured in his three volumes of photographs, *Iconographie Photographique de la Salpêtrière*,

6.   Henry Fuseli, "The Nightmare." Reprinted by permission of Freies Deutsches Hochstift, Frankfurt am Main.

7.   Robert Fleury, "Pinel Delivering the Madwomen of the Salpêtrière." Reproduced courtesy of the New York Public Library.

which later interested surrealist painters like André Breton. Male surrealists in France in the 1930's, in adapting Charcot's photographs, also framed hysteria visually and ignored the suffering expressed in the margins of his photographs of female hysterics. They chose instead to focus on the erotic in their collages and paintings of female bodily abandon. Breton wrote in *La Révolution Surréaliste* in 1929 that "the problem of women is the most marvelous and disturbing problem in the world," and

he and Louis Aragon put out an issue of this magazine that commemo-
rated the fiftieth anniversary of Charcot's naming of hysteria. This issue
was published in 1928, ironically also the year *A Room of One's Own*
was published, and it contained a series of photographs of women in
attitudes passionnelles in what they (and Charcot) interpreted as erotic,

8.   Max Ernst, *Une Semaine de Bonté*. Reprinted by permission of the Print Collection,
Miriam and Ira D. Wallach Division of Art, Prints, and Photographs, the New York Public Library,
Astor, Lenox, and Tilden Foundations.

9.   Max Ernst, *Une Semaine de Bonté*. Reprinted by permission of the Print Collection, Miriam and Ira D. Wallach Division of Art, Prints, and Photographs, the New York Public Library, Astor, Lenox, and Tilden Foundations.

ecstatic states, and this surrealist document contained the statement: "Hysteria is not a pathological phenomenon and can in every way be considered as a supreme means of expression."

Similarly, Max Ernst was interested in the feminine disorder described by Charcot, and he constructed his erotic collages of suspended, floating women in the last seven plates of *Une Semaine de Bonté* from illustrations of Charcot's hysterical women taken from his *Iconographie*. These were the same women that fascinated Freud as he witnessed them in Charcot's clinic in 1885–86—women who exhibited the bodily and mental gestures that were diagnosed and treated with the now-famous "talking cure," first taught to Breuer and Freud by their patients, Dora and Anna O. As Dianne Hunter notes, "Psychoanalysis entered the history of consciousness in dialogue with the subjectivity of women. Freud's discussion of the unconscious was a response to the body language of nineteenth-century hysterics" ("Hysteria," p. 114). He supplemented Charcot's visual approach to hysteria with language. The explorations of hysteria and delirium in the characters of Rachel in *The Voyage Out* and Rhoda in *The Waves* are the literary cases that establish the general category of the unconscious in narration and that have more detailed imaging of the subjective than Freud and Breuer's case studies.

In juxtaposing Woolf's poetic descriptions of mind-body states represented by Rachel and Rhoda, Freud and Breuer's case studies, and Max Ernst's collage novel, I am suggesting that these artists are investigating the unknown dream states of women and their silences as an aspect of mind. They are all cultural "framers" of the hysterical unconscious. In such juxtapositions of the psychological, the visual, and the literary, we discover that each perspective operates with a different cultural construction, and it throws into relief Woolf's narrative technique of allowing women's bodies to speak. As Ruth Salvaggio explains in her theory of space and women: "Woman's body is at once marginalized and radically transformative. As the object of representation, it is not the ultimate message of the discourse. Yet when this body is allowed to speak, it breaks with the very symptoms of representation in which it has been imprisoned" (p. 275).

"DOUBLE FLOWERS": THE DIALECTICS OF OUTSIDE AND INSIDE

Woolf, Freud, and Ernst, in exploring these states in women, dramatize the much-remarked-upon splits in women's experience:

body	mind
unconscious	conscious
visible	invisible
public	private
primitive	civilized
surface	depths

semiotic   symbolic
irrational   rational
presence   absence

If we structure these divisions in terms of the dialectics of outside and inside, Gaston Bachelard's thinking in *The Poetics of Space* is useful: "Outside and inside form a dialectic of division, the obvious geometry of which blinds us as soon as we bring it into play in metaphorical domains. It has the sharpness of the dialectics of 'yes' and 'no,' which decides everything" (p. 211). This structural analysis, the dialectic of outside and inside, starts with mental disturbance and its bodily expressions of paralysis and somnambulism, and it operates in the writings of Woolf, Freud, and the representations of the surrealists. They illustrate how the dialectic sometimes leads to deformity, excess, and almost monstrous estrangement from the body as well as a fascinating kind of beauty. Breuer notes the doubleness in the state: "The overflowing productivity of their minds had led one of my friends to assert that hysterics are the flower of mankind, as sterile, no doubt, but as beautiful as double flowers" (Freud, *Standard Edition* 2, p. 240). The expression "double flowers" preserves the beauty, the deformity, and the split state of mind-body that characterizes what has traditionally been labeled "hysteria."

The "split" between the outside and the inside is exhibited first in body-mind states such as Rachel's immobile delirium at the end of *The Voyage Out* and Rhoda's "estrangement from her body" in *The Waves*: examples of women's bodies constrained by the workings of their minds. Similarly, in Breuer and Freud's study of Anna O., they observe and interpret the rigid paralysis of her arms and legs, the paresis of her neck muscles, and somnambulism as hysterical expressions of her disturbance of mind. Also, the surrealist artist Max Ernst in the last seven collages of *Une Semaine de Bonté* presents disturbing collages of women floating or falling in air, exploring "outside" in space, the "inner" terrors of a woman's mind. The mind-body split is a metaphor for a split in consciousness: the alternation of conscious and unconscious states of mind or the movement between rational and dream states. Under the stress of these splits of mind, linear, rational language breaks down, as is illustrated in the delirious language of Rachel and Rhoda and in the "bilingualism" of Anna O. and Dora as reported by Freud and Breuer, who "break the silence" like the male novelists described in Chapter 2.

All three artists—Woolf, Freud, and Ernst—were driven by a strong and marvelous poetic sense, and they never stopped searching for ways to express the nature of these dream thoughts. Given the enigmatic nature of these splits in mind, body, and language, we will engage in a new kind of analysis—what Freud called "dream work" in talking to his patients, and what we will term "deciphering" since we are interpreting bodily expression in women who have escaped the alphabet in operating outside the domain of words and speech.

Rhoda's bodily symptoms, which might be pathologically labeled hysteria or, under a different cultural construction, a means of expression, are represented by Woolf as a series of visual-mental-body gestures: mental "pictographs." Sleep, dreams, and illness in Woolf's life and work are often associated with an extreme state that brings a new awareness of other aspects of the mind, the unconscious. Through Rhoda, Woolf explores an aspect of the mind, the dream state. There is little in this state, as Freud has taught us, that corresponds to the linear in syntax or proposition in the realm of reason, as described in Chapter 1. Dream logic transgresses linguistic and social codes, and Woolf, like Barnard, did not wish "to describe what we have all seen so it becomes a sequence" (*The Waves*, p. 37).

Rhoda's mind-body state is a widening gyre of "white loops" in "white spaces"—vague, undefined, incomplete—a feminine space that we are challenged to "experience" as well as read. Such bodily descriptions are poetic correlatives for the silences, the periodic interruptions of her speech, which Breuer in his case study of Anna O. labels "absences." These alternations of consciousness, or splits, are recognizable in Rhoda as the literary embodiment of the "presences" and the "absences" of mind that Breuer clinically describes in Anna O.:

These "absences" had already been observed before she took to her bed; she used then to stop in the middle of a sentence, repeat her last words and after a short pause go on talking. These interruptions gradually increased till they reached the dimensions that have just been described. . . . At moments when her mind was quite clear she would complain of the profound darkness in her head, of not being able to think, of becoming blind and deaf, of having two selves. (p. 24)

And though Breuer at first was puzzled by the "pauses" and found the "absences" unintelligible, he learned to read her silences and bodily codes that led to therapeutic talk. Breuer also describes another alternation of mind in his case history of Anna O.:

Two entirely distinct states of consciousness were present [in Anna O.] which alternated very frequently and without warning and which became more and more differentiated in the course of the illness. In one of these states she recognized her surroundings; she was melancholy and anxious, but relatively normal.

In the other state she hallucinated and was "naughty"—that is to say, she was abusive. (p. 24)

This "having of two selves," one conscious and the other unconscious, is revealed by Woolf also in the alternation of the actual presence and the hallucinatory absences of Rhoda in *The Waves*, as well as in the narration of Rhoda's interiority with its rhythm of words and silence (pauses, interruptions). Anna O. herself named her absent states "clouds," reminding us of Rhoda's psychic space variously described by Woolf's narrator as "vagueness" or "emptiness." And it is in the tension between these states that Woolf's interest lies, the "différance." Rhoda's "mind lodges in those white circles; it steps through those white loops into emptiness alone" (p. 22).

Freud, in his interpretation of Dora, was stymied by her silence, her "loss of voice." But he did not always "hear" Dora's expression of her middle-class, Jewish, orthodox background: the social and cultural factors that contributed to her intellectual and social confinement. As Elaine Showalter suggests in *The Female Malady*: "Freud failed Dora because he was too quick to impose his own language on her mute communications. His insistence on the sexual origins of hysteria blinded him to the social factors contributing to it" (p. 160).

If we are to avoid Freud's blindness to the larger cultural and social dimension of women or of Rhoda's experience, we need to assert certain values: first, the value of women's experiences, which are often considered culturally "marginal"; and second, the value of new language, which Woolf as a writer uses to describe women's experience, including subjectivity. In her essay "On Being Ill," Woolf states: "Yet it is not only a new language that we need, more primitive, more sensual, more obscene, but a new hierarchy of the passions" (*The Moment*, p. 11). We must be aware that a deconstructionist or feminist reading as advanced by Mary Jacobus—the formulation of "reading" a woman's body as a "text"—constitutes as well as articulates what feminine space is. A word like "reading" represents a certain kind of mental operation: a text, after all, is linear and does not always suggest the looping rhythms, spaces, and sensations that we experience and decipher in Rhoda. Limiting ourselves to "reading a body as a text" is reductionist and, perhaps, enforces an oppressive hierarchy in that we reduce a new form—physical sensations in space as a basis for female thought and imagination, a new kind of mentality—to a better known critical formulation of "text."

With what words and letters then—if not the alphabet of the text—can women preserve themselves and their own versions of themselves and their bodies and minds? What assumptions, ask Sandra Gilbert and Susan Gubar in their newest critical work on twentieth-century women's literature, *No Man's Land*, can we make, as women, about the use of the alphabet, about conventional language? "How can" a woman "employ the alphabet to perpetuate the most elementary trace of her identity?" (p. 237). How can women like Rhoda and Rachel, and Janie in Zora Neale Hurston's *Their Eyes Were Watching God*, "name" themselves in a language that has historically been used by men to reinforce their own conceptions of women? Janie, in Hurston's novel, says she was nicknamed Alphabet " 'cause so many people had done named me different names" (p. 21), and, as is true of women historically, not names of her own choosing. Gilbert and Gubar perceptively suggest in their analysis of this novel that Janie, and perhaps, by extension, the Rhoda and Rachel "named" by men, "would seem to have become no more than a character (letter of alphabet) who signifies nothing for herself—while facilitating a 'circulation of signs' that reinforces communication among men" (p. 238).

In order to escape the alphabet, Woolf has used images relating to the "deciphering of pictographs" or the "decoding of hieroglyphs" in relation to the reading of women's dreams, delirium, hysteria: all states of "absence" of the conscious mind and the "presence" of the unconscious. Some of Rhoda's bodily gestures can be read as "hysterical," and Freud compared the symptoms of hysteria to a "pictographic script which has become intelligible after the discovery of a few bilingual inscriptions" (*Standard Edition* 2, p. 129). Lacan extends this view of woman in stating that "there is always something about and in her which escapes discourse" (*Écrits*). Freud and Breuer learned to read hysteria in women, and Breuer, in his case study of Anna O., describes the "deep-going functional disorganization" of her speech, which is not unlike Rachel's silence during her delirium or Rhoda's estranged and disembodied manner of communicating. Because of the "absences," "lapses," and "silences" as well as disorganization of conventional speech, we, like Breuer, must learn to read the unconscious through symbolic dreams, delusions, and body gestures. The unconscious, dreaming parts of Rachel, Rhoda, and even Lily and Mrs. Ramsay in *To the Lighthouse* are aspects of women not as thoroughly explored by other twentieth-century authors. In Woolf, women's mind states do not correspond to "the keyboard of a piano, divided into so many notes, or like the alphabet . . . ranged in twenty-six letters all in order" (*To the Lighthouse*, p. 53).

Reading Mrs. Ramsay in *To the Lighthouse* is compared to reading "a wedge-shaped core of darkness" or "tablets bearing sacred inscription" (p. 82), enigmatic shapes to be read in a different way than the linear alphabet of mind represented by Mr. Ramsay. Also, Rhoda in *The Waves* assumes enigmatic shapes as she "dreams" with a "suspended," "clumsy, ill-fitting body" (p. 50), "no weight," "no face," "always seeking some pillar in the desert" (p. 281), a pillar that recurs in surrealist paintings and, interestingly, in the poetry of Sappho.

In escaping the alphabet and comparing Mrs. Ramsay and Rhoda to foreign scripts, Woolf not only addresses the patriarchal "alphabet of mind"—the teleology of reaching Q—represented by Mr. Ramsay that feminist critics focus on, but she also decenters Western notions of mind, writing, and voice. Derrida, in *Of Grammatology*, speaks of Chinese characters as more philosophical than our Western alphabet, built upon intellectual and not phonetic considerations—detached strokes as if "invented by a deaf man" (p. 79). Woolf's decentering of Western values, script, and logocentrism is sometimes missed by feminists intent upon the patriarchal transgression. As described in this chapter, then, reading is closer to the process of decoding a foreign script than to "girl-watching," a gendered metaphor of reading alluded to by Geoffrey Hartman in *The Fate of Reading*. It is a way of reading that is less involved with "gazing at" and "distancing" the text than "participating in" its sensations, feelings, and thoughts. It is a way of creating the text in the spirit of Genette's moebius strip of the intertwining of reading and writing.

The issue of men's and women's uses of language or ways of reading has emerged in feminist discussion in works like Luce Irigaray's *The Sex Which Is Not One* and Judith Fetterly's *The Resisting Reader*. Are women still too absorbed in men's words and representations of "reality"? Are they trapped in categories and ways of knowing and reading that are not their own? Yes and no. We have only one English language, and women have always, in spite of their social position, as argued here, found ways to use words and silences and situations to their best effect. However, as Robert Frost says, "The important thing is to know a moment when you have one," and we cannot help but know that this is a historical moment for women. The full realization is upon us that women need to be in a position, educationally and socially, to have control and mastery over language in order to represent and "name" their own visions in their lives and their institutions. Whether we accept women's use of the alphabet, accept a gendered use of the alphabet, or take a more militant and, I believe, utopian stance on the creation of a new women's language written in "white ink," as Hélène Cixous of *l'écriture féminine* school advances, we can, in the meantime, begin to read differently and invest women's silences with a new psychic life. Woolf captures women's interiority through metaphors of the body in the poetics of space, as Gaston Bachelard might say. The landscape, or perhaps mindscape, of this chapter includes then a discussion of four kinds of "space": bodily, material space; mental space; narrative space; and critical space.

The body existing in its own physical space is mute and is inextricably intertwined with the mind. Three meanings of "body" will be explored in our discussion of Woolf: women's telling "the truth" about their physical bodies; women's bodies interpreted as the reflection of women's minds and cultural constructions; and the materiality of women's bodies as the origin of thought and metaphors of mind and narration in women's writing. First, "the truth about the body" and women's ways of being and knowing must be acknowledged; second, this "truth" can only be expressed in a receptive cultural and literary climate; third, the hierarchy of cultural and literary values must change so that the body—in sickness and in health—can become a legitimate subject for literature; fourth, creative representations of the body must be constructed in literature; and fifth, we need to learn to "read" these representations.

First, then, the truth about the physical body. Women have to know what they feel and what they are experiencing in their bodies—"différance"—and then must name the difference. The knowing and the naming are culturally and psychologically problematic, given what we know about traditional definitions of men and women and mechanisms of repression. This simple acknowledgment of difference does not come easily to women, as Virginia Woolf notes: "All I can tell you is that I discovered when I came to write that a women—and it sounds so simple, but I should be ashamed to tell you how long it took me to realize this for myself—is not a man. Her experience is not the same. Her traditions are different. Her values, both in art and life are [her own]" (Speech of January 1931, p. 33). In the same speech, Woolf notes that "she thought of something, something about the body, about the passions which it was unfitting for her as a woman to say. . . . She could write no more" (p. 33). A Victorian woman's own inhibitions about the discussion of sexual passion parallel the social conventions, and the extent to which others can bear to hear "the truth about the body" can become an issue. Woolf notes a common incident in the life of a woman novelist: "She has to say I will wait. I will wait until men have become so civilized that they are not shocked when a woman speaks the truth about her body.

The future of fiction depends very much upon what extent men can be educated to stand free speech in women" (pp. 39–40).

ILLNESS AND THE BODY

In 1930, just one year before the publication of her novel *The Waves*, Woolf published an essay, "On Being Ill," in which she observes how literature still was doing its best to ignore the body:

Literature does its best to maintain that its concern is with the mind; that the body is a sheet of plain glass through which the soul looks straight and clear, and, save for one or two passions such as desire and greed, is null, and negligible and non-existent. . . . It becomes strange indeed that illness has not taken its place with love and battle and jealousy among the prime themes of literature . . . to hinder the description of illness in literature, there is the poverty of the language. . . . Yet it is not only a new language that we need, more primitive, more sensual, more obscure, but a new hierarchy of the passions; love must be deposed in favor of a temperature of 104. (*The Moment*, pp. 9–11)

Clearly Woolf is interested in the contributions of the body to engendering thought and, more particularly, in what the body reveals about women's minds. What Woolf is questioning in the passage above is nothing less than the standards of the canon or "hierarchy of the passions": for if love is deposed in favor of a fever of 104, then an aspect of women—their illnesses—ignored during Victorian times will be attended to. When Woolf was writing, the aesthetic position that prevailed toward women could be compared to Henry Louis Gates's description of racial exclusion: "When men were men, and men were white, when scholar-critics were white men . . . none of the members of the black community, the minority community of color or the women's community, were ever able to discover the reflection or representation of their images or hear the resonances of their cultural voices" (*New York Times*, Feb. 26, 1989, p. 7).

Illness is often the mute expression of the Victorian woman's psychological and cultural dilemma, and if we acknowledge Carol Smith-Rosenberg's observation that "passion and desire caused political disorder in the eighteenth-century novel" (speech, Barnard College, Feb. 1988), then we must similarly observe that female "illness" caused disorder in the Victorian novel. As Dianne Hunter perceptively states: "Hysteria can be considered a self-repudiating form of feminine discourse in which the body signifies what social conditions make it impossible to state linguistically" (pp. 113–14). Illness, and particularly female mental illness with somatic expression, was ascribed in Victorian medical texts such as George Savage's *Insanity and Allied Neurosis* (1884) to women's sexuality; in fact, most female insanity, illness, and disorders are described in this text as "hysteria," the female malady. Jane Marcus's "Virginia Woolf and Her Violin: Mothering, Madness and Music" admirably explores interpretations of this malady in the Victorian age.

The name "hysteria" has a long history. A. R. G. Owen, in his book about the work of Charcot, gives a brief sketch of the label:

In ordinary parlance, we think of hysteria as either a state of overanxiety or an attack of "the hysterics": excitable laughing or crying. The ancients regarded the condition as characterized by these latter attacks, which have, of course, from time immemorial occurred also in more violent and convulsive forms. Hysteria was regarded as primarily a female disorder, and the famous theory ascribed to Hippocrates referred its origin to hystera (the uterus). Aretaeus, who lived in the first century A.D., was more specific in asserting that the uterus is liable to be suddenly carried upward within the abdominal cavity. Violently compressing the vital organs, it gives rise to "hysterical suffocation"—a choking sensation leading to a fainting fit. . . . Until 1900 or so one could still find learned savants who were convinced that hysteria was a kind of uterine fury and an exclusively feminine weakness. (pp. 58–59)

Such a view of feminine illness created difficulties in legitimizing it as a subject for literature. In the deciphering of feminine illness, doctors constructed a social reality and definition of women and, ultimately, a system of values that informed literature. Hysteria, the catchall description of female disorder, was connected with sexuality and symptoms of hysterical conversion.

It was not only in the medical profession, but also in the aesthetic realms of the surrealist painters in the 1930's in France that such notions of women's illness and sexuality existed. Just as actual women's senses of themselves and their own interpretations of their disorders did not inform medical views of hysteria, so too women's views of pain, love, and sex were absent from surrealist discussions and representations. Whitney Chadwick, in her book on female surrealist artists, states that women came late to the movement, although wives—Simone Breton, Gala Eluard, and other women—sometimes attended surrealist sessions as observers (see the paradigms in Chapter 2). "And when, in 1928, a group discussion on the subject of sexuality took place, only Louis Aragon suggested that in a discussion of women's sexuality, 'it would have been preferable to have had a woman present'" (Chadwick, p. 11). This comment perhaps epitomizes the surrealist stance on women's experience. The ideality of women or men's fantasies of women were preferable to the actuality of women.

However, Virginia Woolf, in her depiction of Rachel in the latter part of *The Voyage Out* and Rhoda in *The Waves*, and Charlotte Perkins Gilman, in *The Yellow Wallpaper*, explore the illness and silences of women, which are both diseased and creative. They acknowledge the pain so often denied by the eroticization and infantilization of women in the Victorian medical profession and, later, in the surrealist movement. In contrast, Woolf's ambition, as Makiko Minow-Pinkney states, "is to summon 'silence' into the order of speech, to reintroduce the repressed into an order made possible only by that exclusion of 'the other' " (p. 159). Traditional exploration and sometimes exploitation of women's eroticism, as in D. H. Lawrence's novels, would not yield the same aspects or exaggerations of mind and body. Undaunted by the disturbing aspects of women's minds and lives, Woolf describes in Rachel and Rhoda that which is psychologically and culturally repressed in women.

THE BODY AS THE ROOM OF THE MIND

In illuminating "the undiscovered countries that are then disclosed . . . when the lights of health go down" (*The Moment*, p. 9)—whether in common illness or in the delirium of Rachel's fever or Rhoda's dreams and hysteria—Woolf turns in her narration to the body. It remains to be seen in the next hundred years whether this is a distinctively "feminine" turn. It is in the "descriptions of the phantasmagoric riot of Rachel's sick brain," which Phyllis Rose evaluates as the best writing in the novel, that we become immersed in the fantasia of the unconscious:

She had come to the surface of the dark, sticky pool, and a wave seemed to bear her up and down with it; she had ceased to have any will of her own; she lay on the top of the wave conscious of some pain, but chiefly of weakness. The wave was replaced by the side of a mountain. Her body became a drift of melting snow, above which her knees rose in huge peaked mountains of bare bone. . . . But for long spaces of time she would merely lie conscious of her body floating on top of the bed and her mind driven to some remote corner of her body, or escaped and gone flitting round the room. (*The Voyage Out*, p. 347)

What makes this state so vivid is the expansion and contraction of the body, the odd angle of vision, and the discontinuity in the shifting symbols of water and mountain; in other dreams the space is a tunnel that turns into a vault. Clearly the enclosed space of the room opens out into dreams of enclosure.

Woolf's interest in the lived moment and the body is a moment that shows "not merely visual and audial scorings on consciousness . . . but felt impulses from the body as well. In other words, the multi-dimensional response to the moment included a body-ego whose presence had never before been taken into account by fiction writers" (Richter, p. xi). It is in this space of the body in the sick room with a fever of 104—a space the Victorian novelist had not claimed—that Woolf, the novelist, dwells. She makes the silent speak here by bringing into being the symbolic weight of female consciousness in the sick room. She infuses women's silence with a new psychic life.

It is in the sick room—a room that is marginal to a house, a room that is quarantined by Victorian society—that the body and the unconscious is unleashed: the female imagination flourishes in this delirium. It is a room of Rachel's own that holds creative possibilities so important to her throughout the novel because, in sickness and in health, it is a place where she establishes a reality, separate from social definitions, that no one else can enter. It is here where she plays the piano and "the body alone listens to the passing bee; the wave breaking; the dog barking" (*Mrs. Dalloway*, p. 59). It is a musical room; it is a narrative room; it is a room of musical narration that contains Woolf's exciting descriptions of women's subjective states, which have the scent of disease as well as of health. We, as readers, enter into rhythmic descriptions of strange chambers of women's minds repressed during the daylight hours of society (to be described in Chapter 5). And, as Woolf will suggest a few years later in *A Room of One's Own*, it is also a place where women like Rachel and Rhoda, unable to find a place in society, can explore the self and even write, temporarily.

Refuge is temporary because both Rhoda and Rachel lose speech in hysteria and delusion in their rooms, and though Woolf explores this domain outside speech, both women die young and symbolically present an ending of female voice. Rhoda is silenced through suicide; Rachel, through a mysterious illness that ends in death. They embody their womanly sense of loss and inability to cope with life through their bodily expressions, which Elaine Showalter demonstrates so effectively in *The Female Malady*. Their silence, then, is part of a double denial. It can be a defiance, a refusal to enact the social subordination or roles expected of women—Rachel in fearing and delaying marriage, Rhoda in resisting the maternal and the sexual roles of Susan and Jinny—and thus is silence as a ritual of truth as described in Chapter 2. However, silence can also be a capitulation, a refusal to make the effort to shore up one's self against the ruins: the choice of death.

Woolf's preoccupation with silence and female illness is not to be interpreted as a literary symptom of Woolf's own manic-depressive states or, as Lee Edwards argues, a manifestation of "schizophrenia as narrative." Positing that both Woolf and Rhoda's selves are "defined in dissolution," Edwards warns readers that their "madness" is "another country" (pp. 28–29), neglecting Woolf's broader explorations of mind and writing in her novels. What Derrida says of Dr. La Forgue's psycho-analytical study of Rousseau applies to this way of reading: "The reading of the literary 'symptom' is most banal, most academic, most naive. And once one has thus blinded oneself to the very tissue of the 'symptom,' to its proper texture, one cheerfully exceeds it toward a psychobiographical signified whose link to the literary signifier then becomes perfectly extrinsic and contingent" (*Of Grammatology*, p. 159). There is a need to de-pathologize readings of Woolf and to freely observe that the "disembodied mood" of Rhoda is a narrative exploration of the temporary loss of what we ordinarily refer to as the "self," or Woolf, "the egotistical self": this is an exploration of mind and dream space. Those critics who "institutionalize" Rhoda and Rachel, and even Woolf describing them as "defective," "disturbed" or "abnormal," create definitions that limit the reader's exploration and appreciation of the richness of these women's minds, and, in Woolf's case, of her work and productivity (Richter, pp. 56, 89; Edwards, pp. 28–29).

Illness in Rachel, whatever its origins—typhoid or hysteria about her imminent entrance into sexuality and marriage with Terence—becomes part of the "curious, silent unrepresented life" of women. A fever of 104 confines Rachel to the room of her body, described as "enchanted" and "isolated." Her body and consciousness are represented as occupying a chamber, a chamber within a chamber. She has her music as a creative outlet but her world, like her body, is a sheltered "room" as described by her aunt, Helen Ambrose: "A room in which she could play, read, think, defy the world, a fortress as well as a sanctuary. Rooms, she knew, became more like worlds than rooms at the age of twenty-four. Her judgment was correct, and when she shut the door Rachel entered an enchanted place, where the poets sang and things fell into their right proportions" (*The Voyage Out*, p. 123). Rachel's room is a place for daydreaming. Similarly, Freud's Anna O. "Embellished her life in a manner which probably influenced her decisively in the direction of her illness, by indulging in systematic day-dreaming, which she described as her 'private theater'" ("Studies on Hysteria," p. 22). In addition to daydreams, Rachel has nightmares. Her terrors and anxiety about sexuality

revealed in her dreams following her experiences with Richard Dalloway, and later Terence Hewet, are absent from Rhoda, whose "still . . .
disembodied mood" (*The Waves*, p. 228) is generally upon her. Rhoda
loathes her body and does not define herself in the conventional ways
that Rachel does.

It is like a Chinese box: the room is a metaphor for body, and within
that the body is a metaphor for mind. The spaces that contain Rachel's
mind in *The Voyage Out* are largely "rooms" that admittedly open out
through her music, her reading, her "enchanted" imaginings, and her
delusions, but that also remain a "fortress" for the inexperienced, sheltered Rachel. The metaphor of the "room" and confinement pervades the
body as "her mind is driven to some remote corner of her body" (p. 347)
during her delusions.

Woolf refines and develops her concepts of the mind and body evident in this first novel until, in *The Waves*, each character would represent its various aspects. *The Waves*, published sixteen years after *The
Voyage Out*, exists outside of time and logic in a space of narrative and
psychological "suspension"—"the spaces between hour and hour"—unlike *The Voyage Out*, which escapes conventional time and plot in part
only. Although Woolf begins to explore the margins of consciousness in
dreams in isolated sections of *The Voyage Out* and in the long section describing the fantasia of Rachel's state of delusion and illness, this remains
a conventional novel in its preoccupation with plot and character. While
Woolf invents or describes the character of Rachel, she "thinks" Rhoda.
Traditional notions of character and body are diminished in Rhoda, who
has "no face" and "no weight." Compare this conception of "character"
to the Rachel described by Helen Ambrose as: "This girl, though twenty-
four, had never heard that men desired women, and until I explained it
did not know how children were born" (p. 96).

Rhoda's body is post-Freudian and exists not as flesh and blood
in "rooms" such as Rachel inhabits, but as a poetic correlative for the
dreaming mind in the large spaces of nature and the cosmic interludes
and silences of the novel. Critics sometimes misread the "disembodied mood" in Rhoda, criticizing her lack of "at-homeness in the body"
(Hussey, p. 19), but Woolf is simply presenting another aspect of the
self here—the dreaming self in a bodily quiescent state—in Rhoda. Her
imaginative spaces are larger than Rachel's, reflecting Woolf's desire to
describe Anon., an anonymous She. Rhoda is an aspect of psychological
investigation of the unconscious, a metaphysical embodiment of woman
as an aspect of mind or life and does not necessarily add a new dimen-

sion to our sense of human relations or the unexpressed emotion that interests Woolf in her first novel. Rhoda, a brilliant character created in defiance of time and conventional social space, is a dreaming woman, an aspect of mind.

The origin of Rhoda's subjectivity, however, is present in Rachel's delusionary state. In illness, Rachel retreats and immerses herself in the phantasmagoric riot of her mind, a state that Woolf, like other women authors, such as Charlotte Perkins Gilman in *The Yellow Wallpaper*, links with creativity. Illness brings the solitude, the gulf between the outer and inner worlds, that is the prerequisite for creativity. Rachel's outward, spatial voyages are metaphors for her psychic voyaging in dreams and delirium. The narrator and character intertwine in this description of Rachel:

> For six days indeed she had been oblivious of the world outside, because it needed all her attention to follow the hot, red, quick sights which passed incessantly before her eyes. For this reason, the faces,—Helen's face, the nurse's, Terence's, the doctor's,— . . . were worrying because they distracted her attention and she might miss the clue. . . . The sights were all concerned in some plot, some adventure, some escape. . . . Now they were among trees and savages, now they were on the sea; now they were on the tops of high towers; now they jumped; now they flew . . . she fell into a deep pool of sticky water which eventually closed over her head. She saw nothing and heard nothing but a faint booming sound, which was the sound of the sea rolling over her head. While all her tormentors thought that she was dead, she was not dead, but curled up at the bottom of the sea. There she lay, sometimes seeing darkness, sometimes light, while every now and then some one turned her over at the bottom of the sea. (*The Voyage Out*, p. 341)

There is something in the sweep of this inner voyage that reminds one of Satan's inner and outer voyages in *Paradise Lost*, "the mind itself" being "its own place," and of Ernst's collages (see Illustrations 2, 3, and 4).

This represents a personal as well as a narrative voyage for Woolf, and in her letters she sometimes writes of the creative benefits of mental and bodily illness: "As an experience, madness is terrific I can assure you, and not to be sniffed at; and in its lava I still find most of the things I write about. It shoots out of one everything shaped, final, not in mere driblets, as sanity does. And the six months—not three—that I lay in bed taught me a good deal about what is called oneself" (*Letters* 4, p. 180). Also, given the amount of time that Julia Duckworth, Woolf's mother, spent in sickrooms tending the ill as described in her writings, one wonders whether the states of mind explored in Rachel's "sick room" are not also connected with Woolf's attempts to get closer to or deal with her obsession with her mother's death. It is fascinating that both mother and daughter are "in" sick rooms: Julia Duckworth in nursing, Virginia Woolf in her own illness and as a writer interested in states of mind during illness. We think back through our mother's rooms. (Perhaps women "cure" themselves of the pain of social positioning through "curing" others in the domains of action, talking, and writing. One senses that the motherless Rachel, like Woolf in her narrative "sick room" of *The Voyage Out*, calls out for a nurturing mother. In her *Diary* Woolf writes of her obsession with her mother's death until the "writing cure" of *To the Lighthouse*.)

The well-defined spatial domain of Rachel's room in *The Voyage Out*, however, gives out to a much larger, more encompassing subjective view of space in the character of Rhoda and nature in *The Waves*. The mental perspective of Rhoda is no longer confined to the themes of the Victorian house: confinement, chastity, illness, and marriage. Rhoda's psychic dream space is available to more subjective kinds of response and relationship, not only to people but also to nature and to life and to things that exist when we do not. Rachel may dream but Rhoda becomes the poetic correlative for the dream in Woolf's narrative experimentation.

DEFORMITY AND EXAGGERATION: THE BODY AS MONSTROUS

Charcot, in his studies of hysteria, stressed the principle that hysteria produces its symptoms in exaggerated form, and he, in the late nineteenth century, was unsympathetic to this quality in his hysterical patients. He comments: "They certainly take pleasure in distorting, by exaggerations, the principal circumstances of their disorder, in order to make them appear extraordinary and wonderful" (Owen, p. 73). Freud takes a more sympathetic and sophisticated view of the function of distortion in wish-fulfillment dreams and hysterical states. He states:

We may therefore suppose that dreams are given their shape in individual human beings by the operation of two psychical forces (or we may describe them as currents or systems); and that one of these forces constructs the wish which is expressed by the dream, while the other exercises a censorship upon this dream-wish, and by the use of that censorship, forcibly brings about a distortion in the expression of the wish. (*The Interpretation of Dreams*, p. 177)

If in "dream work," according to Freud, "the latent wish is translated into imagery of manifest content" (*Standard Edition* 4, p. 277), then the "body work" required in the interpretation of hysteria is the opposite. The bodily gestures that are outside and "manifest," often in an exaggerated form, parget, cover, the "latent" wishes of women that the interpreter must uncover.

When the invisible or the repressed is made visible, it takes on disturbing forms because it has been re-pressed or bottled up, psychically and culturally. If "desire" is the cosmological principle of our age, it is important to articulate two definitions: sexual desires and, by extension, the energy of this principle, which, when sublimated, becomes a vitalizing force in women's work and careers. Woolf's women are identified by their own sense of themselves in body and mind, their dreams, their relationships with men and women, their work, and their fulfillment in the culture. When this repression of the many aspects of women's self in the culture—not just the sexual repression, which informs so many interpretations of the Freudian paradigm—is unleashed, it sometimes assumes deformed, monstrous, or exaggerated shapes.

In Rachel's dreams after her infatuated encounter with Richard Dalloway, there is deformity and the exaggeration of animality. Sexuality surfaces in silent dream images. The "little deformed man who squatted on the floor gibbering with long nails. His face . . . pitted like the face of an animal" (*The Voyage Out*, p. 77) is a distortion, perhaps, of a repressed sexual wish in relation to Richard Dalloway, who has excited her. When expressed, it is all out of proportion and monstrous. "Awed by the discovery of a terrible possibility in life" (p. 176), Rachel now has trouble repressing her feelings, which escape into her dreams. They are "pre-conscious," for when she awakes the "horror" of the dream does not go away at once: "She felt herself pursued so that she got up and actually locked her door. A voice moaned for her; eyes desired her. All night long barbarian men harassed the ship" (p. 77). After the flowering of her relationship with Terence Hewet, she is drawn again into unknown sexual waters but is navigated by love. During their courtship, "Her own body was the source of all the life in the world, which tried to burst forth here—there—and was repressed now by Mr. Bax, now by Evelyn, now by the imposition of ponderous stupidity—the weight of the entire world" (p. 258). This is no less than Woolf's summary of civilization and its discontents and is the origin of her ellipses, which signal the sexual taboos of her time. Rachel escapes the "alphabet" of repression and drifts off into her own mind and body states:

Her body became a drift of melting snow, above which her knees rose in huge peaked mountains of bare bone. . . . And though she pushed her voice out as far as possible until sometimes it became a bird and flew away, she thought it doubtful whether it ever reached the person she was talking to. There were immense intervals or chasms, for things still had the power to appear visibly before her, between one moment and the next. . . . But for long spaces of time she would merely lie conscious of her body floating on the top of the bed and her mind driven to some remote corner of her body. All sights were something of an effort, but the sight of Terence was the greatest effort, because he forced her to join mind to body in the desire to remember something. (pp. 346–47)

Rachel suffers in her state of delirium from her lonely effort to join body to mind: she is psychically suspended.

Suspension—floating, sinking, falling, mounting, escaping, turning, and tumbling in space or water or sticky pools as described in the passage above—suggests, ever since Freud, a dream state that is sometimes connected with sexuality. Suspension in both theme and narration relates to silence because it is a state somewhere between actuality and sleep or dream, figured also in Ernst's collages of women (Illustrations 2, 3, and 4). Silence is a part of Woolf's suspension because, in exploring unconscious, dream states Woolf must "break the sensuous enchantment and enchainment, turn aside from the actual, establish between what he has felt and what he is going to think, an interior distance, a zone of calm, of reserve, and of silence" (Poulet, p. 77). This zone of calm and reserve and silence is a mental zone and the "zone of art" that Woolf writes of in her essay on Walter Sickert (*Collected Essays* 2).

In her delirious state, Rachel in *The Voyage Out* is "conscious of her body floating on top of the bed," an image that will reappear in Frida Kahlo's paintings of women's dream states. Woolf also describes Rhoda in *The Waves* in immobile states of suspension, which we connect with dreams: "Now I spread my body on this frail mattress and hang suspended" (p. 27). Suspension relates to both sleep and illness, silent states in which the body expresses aspects of mind, the unconscious, that "wideawake" language cannot. Rachel's dream state is induced by illness, and it is these body states that create certain states of mind and language. Freud states in *Dora*: "Although hysterical fever does undoubtedly occur, yet it seemed too arbitrary to put down the fever accompanying this questionable illness to hysteria instead of to some organic cause operative at the time" (p. 122). Rhoda's night dreaming is causally connected with the organic state of approaching sleep but in the daytime is induced by a mental state that eventually leads to Rhoda's suicide. Rhoda's hallucinatory states are triggered by looking at a blackboard, into a mirror, approaching sleep:

"There Rhoda sits staring at the blackboard," said Louis, "in the schoolroom, while we ramble off, picking here a bit of thyme, pinching here a leaf of southern-wood while Bernard tells a story. Her shoulderblades meet across her back like the wings of a small butterfly. As she stares at the chalk figures, her mind lodges in those white circles; it steps through those white loops into emptiness, alone." (p. 22)

As Rhoda's absent states become more frequent, her body like Milton's angels seems to become transparent and turn "all to spirit": "Month by month things are losing their hardness; even my body now lets the light through; my spine is soft like wax near the flame of the candle. I dream. I dream" (p. 45). She levitates, a modern "saint." Rhoda is almost disem-bodied but the sensory richness of her body surfaces before sleep. This state of heightened body consciousness ironically comes just before the "still and disembodied mood" descends and the body drops away. Just before going to bed, Rhoda meditates: "Now I spread my body on this frail mattress and hang suspended. I am above the earth now. I am no longer upright" (p. 27). This sense of the body is different from Jinny's sensations of bodily rapture when,

The gentleman pulls up the window. I see reflections on the shining glass which lines the tunnel. I see him lower his paper. He smiles at my reflection in the tun-nel. My body instantly of its own accord puts forth a frill under his gaze. My body lives a life of its own. . . . And I lie back; I give myself up to rapture; I think that at the end of the tunnel I enter a lamp-lit room with chairs into one of which I sink, much admired, my dress billowing round me. But behold, looking up, I meet the eyes of a sour woman, who suspects me of rapture. My body shuts in her face, impertinently, like a parasol. (*The Waves*, p. 63)

One almost feels that one is in a surrealist painting in this passage. Couldn't René Magritte capture the impertinence of Jinny's gesture?

In *The Voyage Out*, Rachel, in her delirium, is also suspended like Rhoda above her bed. She embodies a Cartesian split as her mind flits about the room: "But for long spaces of time she would merely lie con-scious of her body floating on the top of the bed and her mind driven to some remote corner of her body, or escaped and gone flitting round the room" (p. 347). This phenomenon of the mind leaving the body is described by Freud as a hysterical symptom, and when described as the "soul" leaving the body in the meditative tradition of the seventeenth century (discussed in Chapter 2), it is viewed as a state of rapture, ecstasy, dream, or contemplation. Andrew Marvell's description of ecstasy in "The Garden" comes to mind:

> Here at the Fountains sliding foot,
> Or at some Fruit-trees mossy root,
> Casting the Bodies Vest aside,
> My Soul into the boughs does glide:
> There like a Bird it sits, and sings,
> Then whets, and combs its silver Wings.

Religious exaltation can transform into the psychological flight of the mind in hysteria from the seventeenth to the twentieth century.

   Clearly this state of bodily and psychological suspension opens up for Marvell, as for Woolf, the portals of the unconscious and creative states of language. In illness, says Woolf, "with the police off duty, we creep beneath some obscure poem . . . and the words give out their scent and distil their flavour, and then, if at last we grasp the meaning, it is all the richer for having come to us sensually first" (*Collected Essays* 4, p. 200). Woolf evokes the sensuous power of words just before Rachel enters her delirious state. She is tellingly listening to Terence read aloud Milton's poem "Comus," on the theme of chastity:

The words, in spite of what Terence had said, seemed to be laden with meaning, and perhaps it was for this reason that it was painful to listen to them; they sounded strange; they meant different things from what they usually meant. Rachel at any rate could not keep her attention fixed upon them, but went off upon curious trains of thought suggested by words such as "curb" and "Locrine" and "Brute," which brought unpleasant sights before her eyes, independently of their meaning. (pp. 326–27)

Three mind-body themes, then, are connected with suspension: first, "the truth about the body," released in the suffering of illness or approaching sleep or death, a truth that Woolf, as a woman particularly, had an interest in articulating. Woolf explores "the truth about the body" through the suspended experiences or themes of dream, sleep, and death. Second, body states are viewed as an entrance into and a metaphor for mental states and sensations. This dream space, as Poulet says, "is not, like external space, the place of isolated points of view. It is, on the contrary, the place where thought can see simultaneously the different relations and the different aspects" (p. 44). Third, the female body state can be viewed as the entrance into aspects of the unconscious that then open up creative dimensions of language.

NARRATIVE SUSPENSION

Woolf's starting point for her descriptions of Rachel and Rhoda in her novels is a place of sensory and body awareness, which becomes, in time, a place of mental stillness. This "interior distance" traveled in Woolf is apprehended in a reflective distance of mind, not in what we call actuality. This space is doubly silent because of Woolf's technique of narrative suspension: she not only arrests the conversation of the novel to allow Rhoda, Rachel, and the reader to turn inward to contemplate, to meditate, to listen to dreams, but, in suspending the speech and narration of the novel, Woolf also absorbs it for a time in a contemplative silence. She suspends narrative movement in linear time through the creation of dream and sleeping themes and poetic representations of the process.

This initial space or arrest between the actuality and the "reflective distance" is marked by a separation, a shift of theme, tense, or register, a verbal repetition—"border" techniques described with convincing clarity in Mary Ann Caws's *Reading Frames in Modern Fiction* (pp. 3–26). A sense of spatial distance or temporal remoteness from events, as discussed in Chapter 3, is created. For example, in the passage below we note the shift of register and the separation of the actual and reflective realities of Rhoda. Lying in bed, she says:

I will stretch my toes so that they touch the rail at the end of the bed; I will assure myself, touching the rail, of something hard. Now I cannot sink; cannot altogether fall through the thin sheet now. Now I spread my body on this frail mattress and hang suspended. I am above the earth now. I am no longer upright, to be knocked against and damaged. All is soft, and bending. . . . Out of me now my mind can pour. . . . Oh, but I sink, I fall! (p. 27)

At other times, "distance" is marked not by a bed rail but by a lexical item like "gulf" or by the metaphor of "glass." In order to create her dream space, Rhoda must separate herself from contact with people who often threaten her, "people pursuing, pursuing" (p. 27). Similarly, Rachel in her delirious state experiences a gulf between her and the world:

The second day did not differ very much from the first day, except that her bed had become very important, and the world outside, when she tried to think of it, appeared distinctly further off. The glassy, cool, translucent wave was almost visible before her, curling up at the end of the bed, and as it was refreshingly cool she tried to keep her mind fixed upon it. (p. 329)

The qualities of glassiness and coolness, "the glassy, cool, translucent wave," are important, for as Poulet says:

The dream exists only by reason of the glass, that is to say, the distance. . . . It is necessary then, at all costs, not to break the glass, to maintain between the ideal and the self the intermediate distance. For this distance is not simply the obstacle which forbids us from approaching it. It is also the protective medium—make-up, veil, or windowpane—which shields us from mortal contact. (p. 244)

Rhoda shuns crowds, shuns people, and creates her "interior distance." Rachel too, during her illness, "was completely cut off, and unable to communicate with the rest of the world, isolated alone with her body" (p. 330). Both women by reason of the "glass" of sleep or illness withdraw into their own isolated creative states separate from people. This "glass" too is a kind of silence that acts as a buffer and protects the "dream"—like "The Window" in the first section of *To the Lighthouse* protects a childhood image or dream of the family.

Mirrors, another aspect of glass imagery, are used by Woolf for distancing, but mirrors create a reflective distance from other aspects of self, not from other people, as glass does. Mirrors contain repetition and present various aspects of the self: "Individuality raised to a new power" as Kierkegaard states in his philosophical novel, *Repetition*. Rhoda says at one point, "That is my face . . . in the looking-glass behind Susan's shoulder—that face is my face. But I will duck behind her to hide it, for I am not here. I have no face. . . . Therefore, I hate looking-glasses which show me my real face" (pp. 43–44). Rhoda's "looking-glass shame"—the distancing of unfamiliar, frightening aspects of the self—is similar to Woolf's autobiographical description of a looking-glass dream in "A Sketch of the Past." She states: "I dreamt that I was looking in a glass when a horrible face—the face of an animal—suddenly showed over my shoulder. I cannot be sure if this was a dream or if it happened" (*Moments of Being*, p. 69). Rhoda witnessing her own face, and Woolf witnessing the terrifying face of an animal in the mirror, retreat, fearing the "passionate impulses of which the dreamer is afraid, whether they are his own or those of other people. . . . It might be said that the wild beasts are used to represent the libido, a form dreaded by the ego and combatted by means of repression" (Freud, *Interpretation of Dreams*, p. 445). This may connect with Louise deSalvo's speculations about Woolf's childhood sexual experiences, and the aspects of self that are revealed may also connect with Woolf's own dread of mirrors, which led her to remark: "My natural love for beauty was checked by some ancestral dread. Yet this did not prevent me from feeling ecstasies and raptures spontaneously and intensely and without any shame or the least sense of guilt, so long as they were disconnected with my own body"

(*Moments of Being*, p. 68). The crucial phrase, "so long as they were disconnected with my own body," relates to the mind-body splits that Woolf captures in Rachel and Rhoda, and it is described by Freud in cases of hysteria and by the surrealists' representation of women whose minds are "absent."

Consequently, buffer zones like the images of the "bed rail," "glass," and "mirrors" and spatial lexical items such as "gulf," "interval," and "chasm" function as themes, images, markers, and symbols of an "interior distance." They signal a character's retreat from sensory experience and entrance into silent unconscious states. As Poulet said of mental-space feelings: "Space is precisely that: an hiatus, a cleft or gap that widens between reality and consciousness, the virtual place in which the mind discovers the powers to evolve, where, without risk of running afoul of matter and being trapped in the actual, it can 'travel open spaces.' Space is freedom of mind" (p. 72).

Rhoda, the dreamer, does have freedom of mind. Her origin or existence is not to be found in her body or in her past or present experience. She is somehow fallen from the skies, and Woolf's writing of her is a kind of skywriting. She exists in a realm of silent dreams, and the bare visual outlines of Rhoda represent Woolf's intention to portray only the abstract essence of character or aspect of mind in *The Waves*. As Bernard says of the fin of a porpoise on the horizon, "it is unattached to any line of reason." So is the shape of Rhoda in this novel. And she is suspended in a mental space that cannot be situated or positioned in the external world, though Woolf must strive for bodily metaphors to express it. Rhoda is reminiscent of Woolf herself in her description of a suspended moment in her childhood in "A Sketch of the Past": "There was the moment of the puddle in the path; when for no reason I could discover, everything was suddenly unreal. I was suspended; I could not step across the puddle; I tried to touch something . . . the whole world became unreal" (*Moments of Being*, p. 78). This state of bodily and mental suspension and paralysis relates also to hysterical symptoms described by Freud in his analysis of the case of Dora.

Rhoda thus represents a double movement for Woolf: the concentration and contraction of self necessary for stillness of mind, and yet, in Woolf's metaphoric descriptions and surrealist painters' representations, a movement of expansion of the body and mind as a woman voyages toward cosmic, not lived, time. As always with Woolf, common dichotomies of body and mind, contraction and expansion, collapse, and it is the overall pattern or the rhythm of seeming contraries that becomes important in her narrative style rather than either term of the opposition. Foregrounding the dynamism between inside and outside in her descriptions of the body, which are metaphors for mind, Woolf makes her experimental contribution to the modern novel. The body is her metaphor for the dreaming mind of a woman. Woolf liberates Rhoda from social and historical positioning in her imaginative narrative space.

Suspension involves both time and space and represents a state of mind where contraries like outside and inside, mind and body, self and cosmos, space and time collapse. Suspension suggests not only a double space (physical space and the mental space of dreams) but also a double-time. Extra-spatiality and extra-temporality are conferred upon thought, and the use of the present tense is an indication of the extra-temporal character of this state. And because there is no external time or space, the dream space is "the place where thought can see simultaneously . . . different relations and different aspects . . . [not] isolated points of view" (Poulet, p. 44).

This is the same interior distance that surrealists foreground in their paintings of women's dream and hysteria states. Rhoda must wait for the time of sleep to enter this dream state: "There are hours and hours . . . before I can put out the light and be suspended on my bed above the world, before I can let the day drop down" (p. 56). She desires to stretch this state and time of dreams: "I have longed to float suspended. . . . I desired always to stretch the night and fill it fuller and fuller with dreams" (p. 205). In suspending Rhoda in time and space, Woolf, from a psychological viewpoint, as Gaston Bachelard says of another writer, "demolished the lazy certainties of the geometrical intuitions of intimacy. Even figuratively, nothing that concerns intimacy can be shut in" (p. 220). Rhoda's intimate dream states are outside instead of inside, as are the dream states of women represented by surrealist artists. The study of this reversal, the turning of inside out, making the invisible or the marginal visible, brings women out of their exclusion. It also introduces a play of values, a deconstructive reading that is, as Barbara Johnson says,

An attempt to show how the conspicuously foregrounded statements in a text are systematically related to discordant signifying elements that the text has thrown into its shadow or margins. . . . Deconstruction thus confers a new kind of read-ability on those elements in a text that readers have traditionally been trained to disregard, overcome, explain away, or edit out—contradictions, obscurities, ambiguities, incoherences, discontinuities, ellipses, interruptions, repetitions and plays of the signifier. ("Rigorous Unreliability," p. 279)

Conventionally, when confronted with outside and inside, we think in terms of being and non-being. Woolf collapses this distinction as dream states, conventionally categorized as non-being, become for Rhoda and the reader "moments of being."

The physical states of suspension or levitation—jumping, flying, turning over, somersaulting in the air, lying on the bottom of the sea or in a sticky pool—reflect the dream state. It is a state in which the body loses its qualities of materiality, of "hardness." Rhoda's body becomes fluid, "soft and bending." "Out of me now," she says "my mind can pour" (p. 27); "Now my body thaws; I am unsealed" (p. 57) The sense of paralysis or frozen states mentioned in Freud's descriptions of hysteria in the case of Dora and Anna O. is suggested here, but Rhoda works her own cure in entering into the dream state. She is literally disembodied in this state of mind, and Louis comments that "She has no body as the others have" (p. 22). She is faceless: she says, "I have no face. Other people have faces; they are here" (p. 43). Indeed, she is eyeless: "Rhoda with her intense abstraction, with her unseeing eyes" (p. 200). What she sees is "behind the eyes," and all of this, of course, prepares her to be a seer of another kind since she is not positioned in rational psychic space.

She refers to herself as "incandescent," a word that in its Latin origins, "candere," contains the process of becoming white, hot, shining: "emission by a hot body of radiation that renders it visible." She is transparent: "I shift and change and am seen through in a second" (p. 43), and she is often in that disembodied mood "when the walls of the mind become transparent" (p. 228). Rhoda notes her bodily sensations with a filigree interest not unlike Woolf's as recorded in her diary. Rhoda observes, "Now my body thaws; I am unsealed, I am incandescent" (p. 57). Her "body is hot and burning" as she states, "I am thrust back to stand burning in this clumsy, this ill-fitting body to receive the shafts of his indifference, and his scorn" (p. 105). In the heat of life, of the lived moment, she longs for, and eventually achieves through suicide, the coolness of marble, of death: "I who long for marble columns on the other side of the world where the swallow dips her wings" (ibid.). These are peaceful images. Rachel's dreams in *The Voyage Out*, on the other hand, are more violent and remind us of allegories and surrealism in Latin American novels: an old woman slicing a man's head off with a knife (p. 339); the good woman with a face like a white horse at the end of the bed (p. 206).

SUSPENSION IN SURREALIST
ART: THE DREAM STATE

If Virginia Woolf develops the narrative technique of "suspension" to capture dream states, Max Ernst too is driven by a marvelous poetic sense to capture the nature of dream thoughts in visual terms in *Une Semaine de Bonté*. His disturbing creations of suspended women are visual correlatives—as Woolf's Rhoda is a poetic correlative—for dream states or hysteria. In ten of the collages in this "novel," women are the central element, and in the last seven women are falling or floating in space. One woman wildly gesticulates, suspended in air next to a bed; other women with loose flowing hair and gowns float with sensuous pleasure outside the windows of a building; other images of floating women are starker and more chaste, figures constructed from Charcot's illustrations of hysterical women in *Iconographie*. Ernst was interested in the dream symbolism and new psychoanalytic theories of Freud that were widely read and discussed at the University of Bonn where Ernst was a student in 1910. *The Interpretation of Dreams* and *Dora: An Analysis of a Case of Hysteria* were sources for Ernst's floating, falling women who, according to Freud, were symbols "of surrendering to erotic temptation." In *The Interpretation of Dreams*, Freud states: "In other women I have found that flying dreams express a desire 'to be like a bird'; while other dreamers became angels during the night because they had not been called angels during the day. The close connection of flying with the idea of birds explains how it is that . . . flying dreams usually have a grossly sensual meaning" (p. 429). Such states suggest the attraction and terrors of sexuality, as well as other kinds of disorientation, including the cultural. Split states of mind can be read in the bodily gestures of the women.

Ernst's floating women also suggest a "suspension" of meaning. A "sign" can both offer and suspend meaning, and a floating woman as a visual sign both offers meaning—the frustration of desire—and suspends the attainment, delays the fulfillment and definition of the woman. A floating woman in an Ernst collage is in a space that is free from pressure of social "signs" and context; she is unnamed and unfixed, positioned in a poetic space of possibility. This "deferral" of meaning is also an aspect of "différance" as described by Derrida.

Similarly, Virginia Woolf's poetic "signs" in *The Waves* are suspended. The language she uses to describe Rhoda is language dreaming:

"Rhoda's face mooning, vacant, is completed, like those white petals she used to swim in her bowl" (p. 41). Woolf's themes of unfinished women—the suicide of Rhoda and the death of Rachel, both young women—somehow leave them in narrative suspension on a Grecian urn of Woolf's own making. However, instead of the legend of a damsel being pursued by men, her urn is fringed by tales of women pursuing dreams, sometimes tragic. The metaphysical meaning of woman is suspended, though Woolf has "made" their meaning, created their "signs," and summoned them from the silence of illness and dream states in her novels. They are unfinished and to be deciphered and philosophically discussed in the next hundred years, Woolf's usual century of projection. And the language she uses to describe their delirium or hysterical states is separate from everyday language, and it is purposely distanced from the actual to create a poetic "gap." "Poetic language," according to Genette, "is defined in relation to prose, as a 'gap' (*écart*) in relation to a norm" (p. 78), and it is in this gap that new terms and definitions of women are created.

THE BODY AS THE BASIS FOR FEMININE DISCOURSE

Whitney Chadwick, in her study *Women Artists and the Surrealist Movement*, highlights differences between male and female visions of dream and hysteria states. For example, Remedios Varo, after marrying the poet Benjamin Peret, became active in surrealist circles and took the same hysterical postures seen in Charcot's illustrations, eroticized by Ernst, and made them into a Bayer Aspirin promotion in the mid-1940's. She titled it "Dolor" (pain) (Illustration 10). What distinguishes her treatment—commercial though it be—is her awareness of the body and her perception of pain in the hysterical stance that the male artists eroticized. Similarly, Frida Kahlo perceives the pain, not the ideality in women's body-dream states. Two of her paintings, "Henry Ford Hospital" (1933) and "The Dream" (1940), present women floating in beds in space: representations of dream and birth states that are reminiscent of Woolf's descriptions of the sleep states of Rachel and Rhoda: "Now I spread my body on this frail mattress and hang suspended. I am above the earth now" (p. 27); "so I dream falling off the edge of the earth at night when my bed floats suspended" (p. 223); "Now the bed gives under me. The sheet spotted with yellow holes lets me fall through" (p. 206). In "Henry Ford Hospital" (Illustration 11), a woman is naked and bleeding on a

10.   Remedios Varo, "Dolor" (Pain). Reprinted by permission of Walter Gruen.

hospital bed with symbolic objects connected to her stomach, one of which is a fetus. She blends her own history of miscarriage and hospital reminiscences into a message of pain. In "The Dream" (Illustration 12), a woman, perhaps the artist, sleeps beneath a mocking skeleton wired with explosives. Both of Kahlo's paintings introduce the actualities of decay, disease, and pain of the female body ignored by the male surrealist idealizations.

Other female surrealists reveal their alienation from the Surrealist cult of desire and the "male gaze" that eroticizes sleeping, dreaming

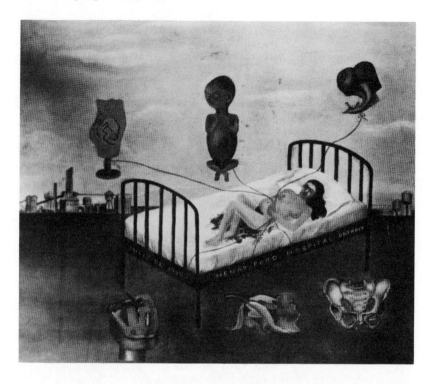

11.   Frida Kahlo, "Henry Ford Hospital." Reproduced courtesy of the New York Public Library.

women in physical states of bodily abandon through mockery. Leonor Fini, a friend of Ernst and Paul Eluard in the 1930's surrealist circles, parodies male obsessions in "Chthonian Divinity Watching Over the Sleep of a Young Man" (1947). In this painting, a young man sleeps under the gaze of a female deity—toppling male surrealist conventions (see Illustration 13).

These three female surrealists—Remedios Varo, Frida Kahlo, and Leonor Fini—are aware of the relationship between their own experience of their bodies and their painting. This exploration of women's illness and hysteria is different from the male surrealists who, though in love with the Idea of woman and intrigued by "the problem of woman," deal with her as muse, virgin, child, celestial creature, sorceress, erotic object, and femme fatale—and not as an actual woman. The treatment of female hysterics in the 1928 issue of *La Révolution Surréaliste* is an example of women as a necessary part of the male dynamic and of the artists'

aestheticization and eroticization of women's pain: women's own bodily
sensations are not perceived or perceived as important in the hierarchy
of the passions.

In Woolf's Introduction to *Life as We Have Known It*, she states
that "The imagination is largely the child of the flesh. One could not
be Mrs. Giles of Durham because one's body had never stood at the
wash-tub; one's hands had never wrung and scrubbed and chopped up
whatever the meat may be that makes a miner's supper" (p. xxi). Woolf
here is presenting a material, bodily basis for the imagination as well as
the sense of diverse women, experiences, and imaginations. She does not
come to a conclusion about "the true nature of women" (*A Room of
One's Own*, p. 6).

With this kind of writing about dream-body states, perhaps distinctively feminine writing, Woolf puts "into discursive circulation," as
Minow-Pinkney suggests, "that which normative writing represses, the
realm outside the Cartesian subject"—an exploration of the subjective.
Woolf more than other modern writers is concerned with representing

12.   Frida Kahlo, "The Dream." Reproduced courtesy of the New York Public Library.

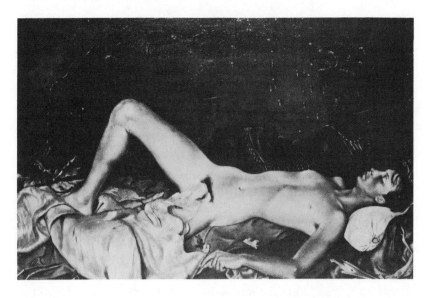

13. Leonor Fini, "Chthonian Divinity Watching Over the Sleep of a Young Man." Reprinted by permission of the artist; photograph courtesy of Whitney Chadwick.

the full range of sentient experience, objective and subjective, contrary to what critics say about her aloof, impersonal style. Her interest in and methods for capturing the subjective emanates from a different concept of mind than that of a writer like Charlotte Brontë, who, in the nineteenth century, still wrote of the mind as an entity, a thing, rather than the immaterial mentality that Freud conceptualized at the beginning of the twentieth century. Brontë represents the faculty of the mind as endowed with "will" and conscious control and awareness: Jane Eyre states "I ordered my brain to find a response." Woolf abandons the "I" and the "order" in finding language and metaphors for unconscious aspects of mind, as well as the conscious dimensions that Brontë favors in her language. She acknowledges and trusts the unconscious, irrational dimensions of mind, abandoning the conscious control of the Cartesian "I." She finds the figurative language to express the three dimensions of experience related in this chapter: body, mind, and language.

Rachel is silent about her sex: waking and sleeping. She chooses not to enter into public discourse with Terence, and Woolf suggests that she, as a woman, is historically slumbering, not yet ready to reveal the secrets of her sex, "reserved for a later generation to discuss them philosophically." In her time and place in a Victorian household in Victorian England, Rachel will find other means of expression: music and somatic expression, both wordless. In contrast, less domesticated, mad, visual impressions spring from Rhoda, dissolving the normative sense of self in *The Waves*. They expand like a gyre in the mind of the reader: the gyre of delirium and, possibly, hysteria.

CHALLENGING CULTURAL CONSTRUCTIONS OF THE FEMININE

In deciphering women's bodies and, consequently, aspects of mind such as unconscious dream and sleep states, Woolf challenges current interpretations of women's minds and bodies advanced by disciples of Freud, literary theorists like Kristeva, and visual artists like the male surrealists. Thomas Caramagno, in "Manic-Depressive Psychosis and Critical Approaches to Virginia Woolf's Life and Work," reports readers' and critics' confusion about Rachel's disturbing delirium, the narrative gap of her illness at the end of the novel, "leaving the reader to deal with a naturalistic close to an otherwise impressionistic, almost poetic novel" (p. 20). Some critics, notably Mitchell Leaska and Louise deSalvo, in her early criticism, subscribe to a Freudian paradigm and establish a cause-effect relationship between hidden events and Rachel's illness, positing that "everything is there not by chance, but by choice" (Caramagno, p. 35). Clearly, this something hidden, they imply, as revealed in Leaska's study of the earlier versions of *The Voyage Out*, is sexuality and bestiality.

The final draft of *The Voyage Out*, even with its omission of earlier references to sexuality and violence, offers a seemingly fertile field for such interpretations. Rachel is presented as a repressed, middle-class, Victorian girl brought up by her widowed father and unmarried aunts in a conservative household similar to those described by Freud in the cases of Dora and Anna O. Rachel is described by her Aunt Helen as a "girl [who] . . . though twenty-four, had never heard that men desired women" (p. 96). Rachel tells Terence Hewet, her fiancé, that she spends time "in interminable walks round sheltered gardens, and the household gossip of aunts" (p. 124), suggesting medieval images of a cloistered nunnery and a state of chastity. We are given other signs of Rachel's repressed sexuality. When Rachel at the age of twenty-four witnesses Helen and Ridley Ambrose embracing, she senses "the smooth green-sided monsters of the deep" (pp. 27–28); later, in a flirtatious encounter with Richard Dalloway, she herself is kissed, and Richard becomes "terrifying" as "a chill of mind and body crept over her" (p. 76). A dream follows this encounter that reveals her unconscious, the structure of which is knowable, according to Freud, only by "displacement" and "conversion." Rachel's dreams reflect a displacement of her own emergent desires and fears concerning sexuality onto the figure of a deformed man with the face of an animal, as quoted above.

However, despite the numerous references to repressed sexuality in this novel, it is important to note that no causal relation is established between Rachel's sexual feelings and the fever in the novel. In distinguishing, as Freud advises in his case of Dora, between a "motive" for and a "liability" to illness, we must discard a simple causality. As Freud states, "A single symptom corresponds quite regularly to several meanings simultaneously" (p. 70), and so with Rachel. It is a part of Woolf's philosophy of the obscurity and multiplicity of origins—of illness or anything else. A Freudian interpretation of Rachel's withdrawal into delirium is possible, but is probably an "overreading" or, perhaps, an "underreading," given that the reason for Rachel's illness and death is deliberately left unclear in the text. We cannot pinpoint whether it is typhoid fever or a psychological withdrawal from the erotic life opening before her—probably both, as with Milly Theale in Henry James's *Wings of the Dove*. However, given Woolf's declared interest in "a fever of 104," there is another possible view—that Rachel's fever is simply a physical illness that affects her mind. Given modern views that psychological conditions, for example manic-depressive conditions and even traits such as shyness, are biologically or genetically based, Rachel and Rhoda's illnesses may be seen anew. Also, given Woolf's own manic-depressive states, her lifelong interest in illness and the "material" aspects of body, she may have been more captivated by dramatizing scenes of illness in *The Voyage Out* and a kind of madness in *The Waves* than with the subject of love or sex, upon which she is often "silent."

Isn't there a particular energy in the descriptions of Rachel's fantasia—perhaps the best writing in this early, sometimes stilted novel? Hasn't Woolf herself written in her letters of the creative power of withdrawal into illness? Is she perhaps asserting, early in her novelistic career, the primacy of the body as the basis for female feeling and illness, and her interest in the working out of an expressive feminine discourse of illness: not through Freud's "talking cure" but her own "writing cure"? Rachel's illness is not an "absence" from life, as women's illnesses have often been seen (Freud and Breuer actually labeled Anna O.'s states "absences"), but a creative "presence" in the novel. Their silences are infused with a new psychic life.

Makiko Minow-Pinkney has written perceptively about Woolf's notions of the "subject" using the theories of Julia Kristeva, and she offers some provocative but debatable comments about reading Rhoda:

The extreme enactment of the negative aspects of rejecting the symbolic and the thetic are seen in Rhoda, who suffers a dispersal of the self of pathological proportions. Excluded from the domain of propositions and positionality, she exists (if this is indeed the right word for her tenuous mode of being!) only in the margins of the symbolic order, in "the white spaces that lie between hour and hour." Associated with whiteness and emptiness, outside time and logic, Rhoda marks out the locus of a feminine space, that non-symbolizable "other" that must be repressed but none the less exist for a normative discourse to be installed. . . . A feminine discourse of the white spaces remains strictly a contradiction, impossible except as silence. (p. 145)

Certainly, the "dispersal of the self" is evident in Rhoda. But what is the nature of the "self" that is dispersed? Does Rhoda simply reject the cultural definitions of female "self"? Is she unable to find a cultural or bodily space as a woman in which to be her "self"? Do the traditional maternal and erotic roles cast her as an "object" struggling to be "subject"? It is, perhaps, the cultural construction of the feminine "self" that Rhoda cannot bear that leads her to what Minow-Pinkney terms "the extreme enactment of the negative aspects of rejecting the symbolic and the thetic." Rhoda, like Bertha Pappenheim in Freud's case of Anna O., rejects the cultural identity being offered her as a nineteenth-century woman and uses her body—its suspension, its somnambulism, its mesmerization, its paralysis—to express her psychic state. Her "ill-fitting body" is a metaphor of mind. Her body is the visible expression of the "ill-fitting" mind and "self," a visual gesture that is represented in surrealist paintings and collages also.

Certainly such expressions in Rhoda are not, as Minow-Pinkney suggests, "a feminine discourse . . . impossible except as silence" expressed as they are on the pages of Woolf's novels. Learning how to "read" Rhoda precludes silence. What kind of a body does the contemplative woman, the dreaming Rhoda, have? The wonder is that Woolf creates a metaphor of mind through the body of a dreamer in space. Rhoda who longs always "to float suspended . . . [desiring] always to stretch the night and fill it fuller and fuller with dreams" (p. 205); Rhoda who "flies with her neck outstretched and blind fanatic eyes, past us" (p. 198) like a crazed female figure in Picasso's "Guernica"; Rhoda with her inward-turning eyes like Giorgio de Chirico's surrealist painting "The Child's Brain." This is a "woman caught in the thicket of definitions" who retreats from the body.

Authors before and since Woolf have captured the erotic raptures of a Jinny, the maternal tranquillity of a Susan: bodily poles that the culture presents as models of womanhood. Rhoda states, "As I fold up my frock and my chemise, . . . so I put off my hopeless desire to be Susan, to be Jinny" (p. 27). Unlike Susan and Jinny, Rhoda does not define herself in relation to a man. Both Jinny and Susan do. Who before Woolf created such a woman? Who before Woolf used the body of a dreaming woman as a metaphor of mind? Who captured the desire to put off the female body and represented those meditations, reveries, and dreams that are a mode favored by, but not confined to, the feminine imagination in Woolf? Rhoda is not the "thinking" woman or the "thinking" mind that Bernard represents, but the visionary, dreaming mind made flesh— floating like a figure in a Chagall landscape.

In the latter section of *The Voyage Out* and throughout *The Waves*, we are presented with strong visual impressions and bodily sensations, metaphors of mind that we may, in time, learn to "read." The discourse of body-mind states is "silent" only to those who have not learned to hear and read through the ears and eyes of women and their different cultural constructions of "reality." In learning to "listen" to texts, as de Man urges in *Blindness and Insight* and as Freud and Breuer demonstrate in their case studies of hysteria, we challenge the culture's and Kristeva's definitions and the relegation of women to the conventional margins of texts and life.

In capturing Rhoda's dream states through metaphors of the body, Woolf makes her mind "transparent" by making it visible. She thus externalizes the internal and creates a narrative mind space. Here as elsewhere in Woolf, "The imagination is largely the child of the flesh" (*Life as We Have Known It*, p. xxi). Woolf is suspending the rational, linear movement of mind by arresting the narrative movement in the novel to focus on interior dream states—the feminine subjective. This reading of the body, a "discordant signifying element" that Woolf throws into the text, is, as Barbara Johnson says of practices of deconstructive reading, "An attempt to show how the conspicuously foregrounded statements in a text are systematically related to discordant signifying elements that the text has thrown into its shadows or margins" ("Rigorous Unreliability," p. 279). Released from the body, the mind is free to explore these states yet dependent on body states for its description of mental voyaging. Woolf stakes out a feminine space here that is not in the realm of the conscious mind but is, nevertheless, "symbolic" in its marking of unconscious states of body and mind through writing. And the "marking," the "stroke" of the symbolic pen, is the marking of a metaphor of mind, not just a "spastic" feminine expression typical of women. A character like Rhoda in *The Waves* embodies for Woolf, the writer, and for us, as readers, a feminine way of knowing, imagining, and being, and she subverts through her silences, through her dreaming body, the claim-making "phrases" of Bernard, a talk-producer who dominates the end of the novel.

If we unfix literary and visual signs from their conventional literary and historical associations, as in Woolf's experimental novel, *The Waves*, in the female surrealists, and in the juxtapositions of Ernst's *Une Semaine de Bonté*, we create a new metaphysical space for women—in narration, in imagination, in our thinking practices. For Ernst this was an erotic space; for Woolf, a poetic correlative of mind, the dream state; for female surrealists, the actualities and pain of the body. All found freedom of mind in this space.

5

Listening to Silence

THE RHYTHMS OF 'THE WAVES'
AND 'BETWEEN THE ACTS'

ALTERNATING RHYTHM is a fact of Virginia Woolf's style. She "out-plays the codes on which she seems to rely" (Culler, p. 26) and elicits from her readers an emotional and visceral response to rippling sentences, oscillating themes, alternating structures, and flickering visions of reality. More than any other twentieth-century novelist, she reaches for a condition of poetry:

The power of music, the stimulus of sight, the effect on us of the shape of trees or the play of colour, the emotions bred in us by crowds, the obscure terrors and hatreds which come so irrationally in certain places or from certain people, the delight of movement, the intoxication of wine. Every moment is the centre and meeting-place of an extraordinary number of perceptions which have not yet been expressed. Life is always and inevitably much richer than we who try to express it. (*Granite and Rainbow*, p. 23)

There is a beat of silence that accompanies words in a sentence: words as notes, silence as pauses. Septimus in *Mrs. Dalloway* ruminates about these rhythms that preoccupy the madman and the poet: "Sounds made harmonies with premeditation; the spaces between them were as significant as the sounds" (p. 33). Her conscious use of rhythm is a kind of meta-syntax that relieves the oppressiveness of "words with short wings for their heavy body of meaning" (*Complete Shorter Fiction*, p. 88) and enables her to express the richness that is concealed within them. Music is also a channel for feeling that is unexpressed in words. Rachel observes in *The Voyage Out*: "It appeared that nobody ever said a thing they meant, or ever talked of a feeling they felt, but that was what music was for. Reality dwelling in what one saw and felt, but did not talk about" (p. 37).

In her essay "The Narrow Bridge of Art," Woolf describes how the modern novel will take on the attributes of poetry: its ambiguity and its intensity. Its rhythms, she says, will embody the incongruous content of the mind, and the unspoken will surface indirectly in dreams and symbols in the novel: "It will take the mould of that queer conglomeration of incongruous things—the modern mind" (*Granite and Rainbow*, p. 20). The modern mind for Woolf will be encased in an elastic sentence of her own making, and it will take on a different rhythm and mood that passes easily and naturally from poetry to prose, prose into poetry. Rhythm—composed of sound, silence, time, and movement in thematic and technical alternation—is a poetic aspect of her prose style.

She wistfully writes in her diary one morning, "Could I get my tomorrow morning's rhythm right—take the skip of my sentence at the right moment—I should reel it off; . . . it's not the style exactly—the right words—it's a way of levitating the thought out of one." Rhythm contributes to meaning and lends order to Woolf's other ideas about fiction. Realizing that it is "getting the rhythm" in writing that matters, she states that "writing is nothing but putting words on the backs of rhythm. If they fall off the rhythm, one's done." The pulse of her mind takes on rhythms that enter her narrator, her characters and sentences, and incorporates in the genre of the novel a new music. And this music levitates thought and feeling out of the reader in new ways, lightening his being.

The musical metaphor Woolf sometimes chooses to describe her composition of novels is congruent with her desire to write texts that are "impersonal," written "standing back from life, because in that way a larger view is to be obtained of some important features of it" (*Granite and Rainbow*, p. 22). This perspective is related to but distinguishable from today's fashionable designation of an "authorless" text described by Jacques Derrida in his discussion of Lévi-Strauss: "The absence of a center is here the absence of a subject and the absence of an author. The myth and the musical work thus appear as orchestra conductors whose listeners are the silent performers. If it be asked where the real focus of the work is to be found, it must be replied that its determination is impossible" ("Structure, Sign and Play," p. 25). Readers of Woolf's novels—like readers of myth and listeners of musical works—are silent performers; her works require of us a certain quality of attention. But her "orchestration," her conviction that "everything in a work of art should be mastered and ordered" (*Granite and Rainbow*, p. 22), and the reader, consequently, focused and concentrated, differs from Derrida's view in its sense of determinacy. This chapter will analyze her attention to rhythm as an organizing and emotional dimension of her writing, as a way of creating meaning for the reader that is beyond words.

Through rhythm or music, Woolf can represent things of the spirit that cannot be heard—Keats's "ditties of no tone." While at work on *To the Lighthouse* in 1926, she writes to Vita Sackville-West: "Style is a very simple matter; it is all rhythm. Once you get that, you can't use the wrong words. But on the other hand here am I sitting after half the morning, crammed with ideas, and visions, and so on, and can't dislodge them, for lack of the right rhythm. Now this is very profound, what rhythm is, and goes far deeper than words" (*Letters* 3, p. 247). Rhythm, an undertow in language, "goes far deeper than words," for as Woolf says of *To the Lighthouse* in her diary, "the sea is to be heard all through it" (3, p. 34). It is a kind of metalanguage of which linguists dream and upon which poets insist, important because it communicates emotional and intellectual as well as aesthetic meaning.

Rhythm in Woolf's style relates to her exploration of space of various kinds: emotional or bodily space or the space of a sentence, a page, an artistic canvas. The conjunction of space with silence and rhythm suggests that she approached this dimension of outward form in the same way as a painter or an architect or a composer. Blank spaces (emotional, bodily, textual, thematic, structural) are seminal to her work, as they are to modern painters like Kazimir Malevich, "White on White," and Ad Reinhardt, "Black on Black." In her essay "The Anatomy of Fiction," Woolf speaks of how "Between the sentences . . . a little shape of some kind builds itself up" (*Collected Essays* 2, p. 132), suggesting again a sense of space and silence blocked into narration. Space and rhythm are metaphors for silence.

In her diary and novels, Woolf often refers to the "white space" of the mind as a page or an artistic canvas waiting to be filled. This white space represents the writer's mind as well as the reader's—the reader who is provided with white space in the text (various kinds of silences) by the writer for the play of his emotion and thought. As Gérard Genette observes: "Every book, every page, is in its own way a poem of the space of language, which is played out and performed under the reader's eye" (p. 69). White space is sometimes a material space on a page. Laurence Sterne textualized this concept in his novel *Tristram Shandy* (as represented here on p. 175). Here Sterne's blank page allows the reader textual and psychological space to imagine Uncle Toby's love for the Widow Wadman. The reader is invited into the text and into a dialogue with the narrator. As with Woolf's punctuation, metaphors, and rhythms of silence, a reciprocal relation of reading the author's thoughts and then pausing to consult one's own mind and imagination is established: read-pause; words-silence; author-reader. Such an overt space leads the reader to ask why the white space is there in the text and what he is to do with it. In some of Woolf's earlier transcripts of, for example, *Between the Acts*, she marked sections such as "The Lamp" and "The Garden," and in the final typescript these markings were replaced by added space. In fact, Leonard Woolf directed the printers—this novel having been published posthumously—to "Leave two white lines" with a downward arrow to separate scenes of the text. These intentional white spaces or silences and breaks in narration are, surprisingly, left out of both the American and English editions. Similarly, Edward Mendelson notes in his clever article, "The Death of Mrs. Dalloway" (p. 280), that there are twelve divisions in the novel, each marked by white spaces in the text in the British editions of this novel, but in all American editions some of these spaces are absent: an editorial decision that ignored the structural intention, the narrative breaks and silence on the page.

However, in addition to literal space, Woolf and other authors play with covert psychological, social, and narrative space. Blankness is often a metaphor for hidden or secret aspects of self and culture rather than emptiness. For example, an old storyteller in Isak Dinesen's wonderful short story, "The Blank Page" says:

"Who then," she continues, "tells a finer tale than any of us? Silence does. And where does one read a deeper tale than upon the most perfectly printed page of the most precious book? Upon the blank page. When a royal and gallant pen, in the moment of its highest inspiration, has written down its tale with the rarest ink of all—where, then, may one read a still deeper, sweeter, merrier and more cruel tale than that? Upon the blank page." (*Last Tales*, p. 100)

This book is about this blank page, which has often represented women's lives in the fiction of men and, sometimes, of women also. The female storyteller, eager to tell the story upon the blank page, continues. She tells of a princess of noble family in the country of Portugal who, on the morning after her wedding night, fails to hand over to the town chamberlain her wedding sheet that would proclaim "Virginem eam tenemus—

we declare her to have been a virgin." Instead, in a long row of framed sheets of royal princesses, there is one plate on which "no name is inscribed, and the linen within the frame is snow-white from corner to corner, a blank page" (p. 104). Inscribed on this white sheet, this blank page, is a rich story, not emptiness: an apt metaphor for this book that looks at this blank page—women's silences.

Similarly, for Woolf, the blank page is transformed into "white spaces" of the mind. It is suggestive, it confronts all writers: it is "empty" and "white" yet it holds, for Woolf, the potential for creativity and story. In the *Pointz Hall* manuscript, the earlier typescript of *Between the Acts*, the narrator contrasts the "whiteness" of this underground space in the mind with the "greenness" of certainty: "A man after all must have a hidden underground bubbling spring; which never comes to the top. . . . Perhaps—under its shelter as many ideas grow as there are blades beneath a stone; but all white; denied the green that the fresh air of certainty gives" (p. 38). This white space of the mind is also present in Rhoda, whose "mind lodges in those white circles; it steps through those white loops into emptiness alone" (*The Waves*, p. 22). This "whiteness" has its affinity with feelings of isolation, loneliness, desolation, and silence.

White spaces are also discernible in the sentence, the blank page, the artistic canvas. Lily, facing the "white space" of her artistic canvas, feels a "rhythm" just as Woolf speaks in her diary of a "rhythm" she achieves in her sentences: "Some rhythm which was dictated to her (she kept looking at the hedge, at the canvas) by what she saw, so that while her hand quivered with life, this rhythm was strong enough to bear her along with its current . . . white hideously white difficult space" (*To the Lighthouse*, p. 247). The "hideously white difficult space" here is the empty canvas of the artist or the form of the sentence waiting to be filled. Despite the brilliance of her words, Woolf is seeking something as impersonal and abstract as modern art in representing her characters. Lyndall Gordon, in her biography of Woolf, notes that in her letters she touches on the idea of art "that could shape infinite strange shapes . . . she wanted her writing to be judged as a 'chiseled block' . . . so that it could be disconnected from its author" (p. 97). This perspective is revealed in the description of her characters, who are often spatially fixed in the novels as geometric shapes representing something about their personality or relations with others. Mrs. Ramsay and James are a "purple triangle" reading together; Mrs. Ramsay, when alone, is associated with mystery and silence as a "wedge-shaped core of darkness"; Mrs. Dallo-

way is somehow cold and sharp and "diamond-shaped"; Mr. Ramsay in his alphabetic progression in life is a "line"; Eleanor of *The Years* is the "I" at the center of a concentric form. Such epiphanic shapes and forms representing character mark the white space of her page.

The space is also structural in Woolf's plotting of the broad outlines of a novel. In her diary, when working on the mammoth manuscript of *The Years*, she writes: "I think I see how I can bring in interludes— I mean spaces of silence and poetry and contrast" (*Diary* 4, p. 332). Similarly, the interludes in *The Waves* and the presence of the absence of Mrs. Ramsay in the "Time Passes" section of *To the Lighthouse* are plotted structurally according to a narrative rhythm on a broad scale.

These various representations of silence and connections between silence and space are thus part of the rhythm, the combination and permutation of sounds and silence, language and space. As mentioned earlier, Woolf often compares the rhythms of writing to music and paint-ing, and gestures of one kind or another—up/down, in/out, stroke/pause—contribute to the alternating rhythm of her style. Like the phi-losopher Roman Ingarden and the music critic Leonard Meyer, she is struck by the similarity of some aspects of musical experience to other types of aesthetic experience. Through the abstraction of rhythm in these domains, she is able to capture something about the pulses of the mind and life that is beyond words—a kind of silence. Learning to hear Woolf's sounding of the elements of "stroke" and "pause," a rhythm of marking and pausing in different domains, is the beginning of an appreciation of her style. More than other modern writers, she reshapes sentences into varied, energetic, elastic, and rhythmic forms. For example, the alterna-tions of sweep and pause in the movement of Lily's paintbrush in *To the Lighthouse*:

With a curious physical sensation, as if she were urged forward and at the same time just held herself back, she made her first quick decisive *stroke*. The brush descended. It flickered brown over the white canvas; it left a running mark. A second time she did it—a third time. And so *pausing* and flickering, she attained a dancing rhythmical movement, as if the *pauses* were one part of the *rhythm* and the *strokes* another, and all were related; and so, lightly and swiftly *pausing, striking*, she scored her canvas . . . a space . . . fluidity of life for the concentration of painting . . . some rhythm dictated to her. (pp. 235–37; my italics)

The gesture of "stroke" and "pause" is incorporated in Lily's "dancing rhythm" and is a metaphor for Woolf's incorporation of the rhythms of sound and silence into her writing. It is similar to the rhythm of Bernard's writing "on the lilt of the stroke" in *The Waves*. In penning a letter to "the girl with whom he is passionately in love," he reflects,

Byron of course. I am, in some ways, like Byron. Perhaps a sip of Byron will help to put me in the vein. Let me read a page. No; this is dull; this is scrappy. This is rather too formal. Now I am getting the hang of it. Now I am getting his *beat* into my brain (the *rhythm* is the main thing in *writing*). Now, without *pausing* I will begin, on the very lilt of the *stroke*. (p. 79; my italics)

This same vocabulary and rhythm of "stroke" and "pause" applies to the domain of light (the "strokes" of the beam of the lighthouse), to time (the "strokes" of time), and to action (the "stroke" of the oars of the boat on its way to the lighthouse). And in *Between the Acts*, there are the "strokes" of nature in creating the seven-sided flower representing the seven friends (p. 229), the "strokes" of brooms of men sweeping near the writing lady (p. 240), the "strokes" of women writing, and the "strokes" of painters (p. 157). Although the lexicon of each is borrowed from the domains of writing, music, and painting (mark/stroke, score/note/beat, pause/rest), the flickering facts of her style remain as she attempts to capture the dancing rhythms of life—her medium of words and spaces on a page. What Alfred Steiglitz said of Georgia O'Keeffe's paintings could be applied to the texture of Woolf's writings: "At last, a woman on paper."

Ezra Pound states that "Rhythm must have meaning." In Woolf's case it is feelings and images that infuse her rhythms with meaning: "A sight, an emotion creates this wave in the mind long before it makes words to fit it; and in writing (such is my present belief) one has to recapture this, and set this working (which has nothing apparently to do with words) and then, as it breaks and tumbles in the mind, it makes words to fit it" (*Letters* 3, p. 247). The writer renders in a poetic way the quality and rhythm of sensation, feeling, thought, and action as "a sight or emotion [that] creates this wave in the mind." The rhythms in a sentence or a structuring of a novel embody emotional patternings, rhythms, moods, and intensities of feeling. An emotion or "wave of the mind," its rise and fall, is then captured in the rhythm of Woolf's sentences. This space in which rhythm operates is emotional, visual, musical, and kinetic. One is almost tempted, at times, to score Woolf's text with a scansion of accented strokes (words and syllables) and pauses (caesuras or rests) marked by punctuation. To temporally or spatially systematize rhythm—as with earlier explications of Woolf's formal uses of silence in Chapter 3—does not destroy the experience or vitality of her fluid style for the reader. Instead, it confirms again our understanding of Woolf's appreciation of feeling as form and enables us, as readers, to observe the order in her inventive sentences and novels.

Woolf's gestures of alternation—in treating life and death, words and silence, actual time and mind time, men and women—is the capturing of thematic, visual, and musical counterpoint of sensation and mind. It matters to her more than anything else as a writer. For example, in *To the Lighthouse*, Lily ruminates: "For how could one express in words these emotions of the body? express that emptiness there?" (p. 265). Woolf invests the sight of empty steps with the rhythm of a bodily sensation: a hardness, a hollowness, a strain. Lucio Ruotolo, in *The Interrupted Moment*, mentions the time and effort that Woolf invested in the idea of empty rooms and the problem of supplying emptiness with a voice in *Between the Acts*. In one version of an empty drawing room in Pointz Hall just after the butler has left it, the narrator notes: "But who observed the dining room? Who noted the silence, the emptiness? What name is to be given to that which notes that a room is empty? This presence certainly requires a name, for without a name what can exist? and how can silence or emptiness be noted by that which has no existence?" (Ruotolo, p. 222). J. Hillis Miller subtly assesses the rhythmical nature with which Woolf invests these bodily sensations, emotions, and sights: "It takes what is given, the orts and fragments of reality, and fills the spaces between them with the intrinsic rhythmical order of the mind" (p. 214).

Form in a Woolf novel is an aspect of feeling that, as Harvena Richter claims, "when converted into such modalities as rhythm and pattern comprise[s] a largely unexamined area of Virginia Woolf's work" (p. 203). On the structural level, beyond a sight or an emotion expressed in a sentence, there is the flux and flow of certain emotional patterns that are captured in the form of the novel. Woolf, as discussed in Chapter 3, is concerned with the idea of mental and emotional strata of differing depths, a characteristic of phenomenological inquiry, and in her novels every stratum makes its contribution to the rhythm and polyphony of the whole: words, sentences, paragraphs, chapters, divisions, and overall structure. Division, repetition, and variation help to create the rhythm at every level.

Emotional patterns are a principle of organization in her novels. The musical and emotional form of *Mrs. Dalloway*, for example, might be charted as "lark," spatially upward movement (high pitch), and "plunge," downward movement (low pitch), with Mrs. Dalloway and Septimus representing the lark and the plunge of theme. Pitch, voice, and space create the overall harmonic ordering of the novel. As Joseph Joubert states, "In music pleasure is born of the intermixture of sounds and silences; in the same way it is born of architecture of the well-ordered intermixture of voids and plenums, of intervals and masses" (p. 83).

To the Lighthouse reveals a pattern of counterpoint or alternation between absence and presence, men and women, father and mother, life and death, sound and silence. *Between the Acts* contains a pattern of simultaneity or chords in which minds meet and unspoken voices of the past and present fuse. Music theory states that a given chord once struck liberates other tones that otherwise might not be heard. The unspoken thoughts of Isa, Giles, and Mrs. Manresa—along with the sounds of war, history, and literature as represented by Miss LaTrobe's pageant and the lines of poetry running through Isa's mind—create new chords of meaning and a blending of voices and sounds that is more complex than, for example, *The Voyage Out*, where Woolf holds to a single voice and mind.

New chords are also present in *The Waves*, written "according to a rhythm not a plot," emanating from Woolf's vision in 1931 that humanity and Nature are not separate but are in this world together. She writes in her diary of *The Waves*, "Thus I hope to have kept the sound of the sea and the birds, dawn and gardens subconsciously present, doing their work underground" (4, p. 165). Just as the subtle rhythms of Walt Whitman's free-verse have been likened to sea waves, so can we, at times, sense the same in the rhythms of *The Waves* or parts of *To the Lighthouse* with Woolf's intentional blurring of the lines between prose and poetry. In comparing some lines on death from Whitman's "Out of the Cradle Endlessly Rocking" to those in *The Waves*, we find the same free-verse lines with liquid, billowing waves, rising and falling, iambic and anapestic meters.

There is in *The Waves* a simultaneity and harmony in the cyclical rhythms of the stages of life, in life and death, in the seven voices, in the rising and the setting of the sun, and in the movements of the waves. Nature frames the novel in narration and philosophy, the first and last sentences of the novel being "The sun had not yet risen. . . . The waves broke on the shore." This reading contests Avron Fleischman's notion that "The thrust of all sequences in this work is linear" (p. 154). Nature in the nine interludes is as present as the seven voices of the novel. These interludes function in the novel like expanded parentheses in a sentence, and they enable Woolf to do two things: to capture two orders of time and reality, and to give us, as she says in her diary, "the sense of reading

the two things at the same time" (3, p. 106): life and nature. In the interludes we have a sense of the eternal renewal of time. Life and nature,
even though there is death (Percival's and Rhoda's), are in harmony. And
though words and narrative events proceed in time, Woolf arrests the linear sequence of writing by using the techniques of simultaneity through
the use of spaces of silence like the interludes of nature or parentheses in
a sentence. As a novelist working out experimental techniques, she defies
Ferdinand de Saussure's Principle II of language: "The Linear Nature of
the Signifier: The signifier, being auditory, is unfolded solely in time from
which it gets the following characteristics: a) it represents a span, and b)
the span is measurable in a single dimension; it is a line" (p. 70). Woolf
attempts to strike two notes, two orders of reality, two events at once in
the space of a sentence.

However, in *Between the Acts*, published posthumously in 1941, one
"hears" a different kind of music. The harmony of Nature and human
voices is shattered in war and the disjunctions of interruption are heard.
While writing this novel in 1939, Woolf writes in her diary of the air-raid
warnings early in the morning and the "endless interruptions" (5, p. 234).
In the novel, the Reverend Streatfield is also subjected to interruptions
as he speaks to the crowd assembled at Miss LaTrobe's pageant: "He
continued: 'But there is still a deficit' (he consulted his paper) 'of one
hundred and seventy-five pounds odd. So that each of us who has enjoyed this pageant has still an opp. . . .' The word was cut in two. A zoom
severed it" (p. 193). Virginia Woolf despairs of the daily "zoom" of war
that cuts her words in two: the death of friends; the daily bombings over
England that cause the destruction of her home, Tavistock, and London,
the city she loves; the lack of public for her work; the fears about the
Jews; and her death pact with Leonard in the event of a German invasion.
Bereft, she loses faith in "reason" and, like many people, experiences
the "transcendental homelessness" described by György Lukács in *The
Theory of the Novel* after World War I. The meaning of life and words,
lost in the war, is reflected in her vision and the way she patterns the relationships between words, sounds, silences, meaning, and people as well
as the characters and the narrator in *Between the Acts*. Whereas Woolf
intertwines human life and nature into a harmony in *The Waves*, she
sounds the obscurity and discordancy of human relationships through
Isa and Giles with the background disharmony of the war in *Between
the Acts*. Lacking the calm and sweeping rhythms of *The Waves*, this
novel contains the anxious counterpoint of a modern musical composition. Each rhythm—the calm sweep of *The Waves* and the halting beats

of *Between the Acts*—is determined by Woolf's planning the novels to a rhythm or a musical form that emerges from her vision of life.

Subscribing to Rousseau's philosophy that "One does not begin by reasoning but by feeling" (p. 11), Woolf's emphasis is on the curve of feeling as embodied in the shape of each book. She confirms this in her essay "On Rereading Novels." In her discussion of Percy Lubbock's use of the word "form," she insists that "Among all this talk of methods, that both in writing and in reading, it is the emotion that must come first. . . . Therefore, the 'book itself' is not form which you see, but the emotion which you feel" ("On Rereading Novels," in *The Moment and Other Essays*, pp. 161, 160). Although each of Woolf's novels is different in experimental intention, her commitment to feeling rhythms remains throughout. In 1931, "stumbling," as she says, "after my own voice, or almost, after some sort of speaker (as when I was mad)" (*Diary* 4, p. 10), she writes to Dame Ethel Smyth: "Though the rhythmical is more natural to me than the narrative, it is completely opposed to the tradition of fiction, and I am casting about all the time for some rope to throw the reader" (*Letters* 4, p. 204).

She needs "some rope to throw the reader" because, in her experimentation with "that cannibal, the novel, which has devoured so many forms of art," Woolf will seek to write in prose "but in prose which has many of the characteristics of poetry" (*Granite and Rainbow*, p. 18). The rhythm of Woolf's sentences is created by a certain lexicon and syntax (including punctuation) and by notational sounds and silences, and it is reflective of her attempt to capture different orders of mind and reality. As Miller states in his discussion of repetition in fiction: "The two rhythms interfere. They splash against each other like two waves intersecting. 'Thus' as Woolf says, 'a novel starts in us all sorts of antagonistic and opposed emotions. Life conflicts with something that is not life'" (p. 209). Her novels, then, contain the recognition that it is "getting the rhythm" in writing that matters. Silence, as much a dimension of rhythm as sound, is a part of her thematic and narrative intentions and contributes to her style. The pleasure of her writing is born of the presence of words and silence, scored in fluid sentences (often unpunctuated in her drafts) that move up and down and in and out in a style of rhythmic alternation unlike any other modern writer.

But what do we mean by the rhythm of narration in a novel? Woolf, like James Joyce, is interested in capturing "the wave of the mind." In *Ulysses*, Joyce not only constructed elaborate echoes between the eighteen episodes of his novel and Homer's text, but he gave each episode a series of correspondences: physical, temporal, symbolic, and rhythmic. So, for example, the rhythm of the Nighttown section is labeled "locomotor ataxia," and the jerky rhythms of the sentences embody this. Woolf shares Joyce's sensitivity to the rhythms and textures of language, but whereas in *Ulysses* he never tires, it seems, of repeating, transforming, and rearranging words, she does. Unlike Joyce, Woolf is drawn to issues of narrative and thematic silence, distrusting language in a way that Joyce did not.

It is important, therefore, to discuss different expressions of rhythm in narration, distinguishing those who write for the eye, like Laurence Sterne and sometimes James Joyce, from those who write for the ear— Jane Austen for the conversational ear; Woolf, for the poetic. Woolf is aware of these distinctions, and in her essay "The Strange Elizabethans" she notes that Gabriel Harvey's style "is interminable":

As we go round and round like a horse in a mill, we perceive that we are clogged with sound because we are reading what we should be hearing. The amplifications and the repetitions, the emphasis like that of a fist pounding the edge of a pulpit, are for the benefit of the slow and sensual ear which loves to dally over sense and luxuriate in sound—the ear which brings in, along with the spoken word, the look of the speaker and his gestures. (*Second Common Reader*, p. 16)

In developing this distinction between the sensual ear receptive to the spoken word and the words read on a page, Sterne, an eighteenth-century novelist whom Woolf admired, is helpful. In *Tristram Shandy*, when Uncle Toby and Tristram's father discuss why the midwife rather than the doctor has been sent for at Tristram's birth, the rhythms of discourse are punctuated by dashes (—) and asterisks (*) and CAPITAL LETTERS for the EYE, an incorporation of pauses and silences in the text:

Then it can be out of nothing in the whole world, quoth my uncle Toby, in the simplicity of his heart—but MODESTY:

—My sister, I dare say, added he, does not care to let a man come so near her ****. I will not say whether my uncle Toby had completed the sentence or not;— 'tis for his advantage to suppose he had,—as I think, he could have added not ONE WORD which would have improved it. (p. 100)

Woolf considered Sterne "the forerunner of the moderns": "In this preference for the windings of his own mind to the guide-book and its hammered high road, Sterne is singularly of our own age. In this interest in silence rather than speech Sterne is the forerunner of the moderns" (*Second Common Reader*, p. 81). Here Woolf consciously acknowledges the modernist and, of course, her own interest in the silence that "will give the relation of the mind to general ideas and its soliloquy in solitude" (*Granite and Rainbow*, pp. 18–19).

This same interest in the mind and the appeal to the eye is evident in Joyce's visual fragmenting of words in the ORTHOGRAPHICAL passage in chapter 6 of *Ulysses*:

Want to be sure of his spelling. Proof fever. Martin Cunningham forgot to give us his spelling bee conundrum this morning. It is amusing to view the unpar one ar alleled embarra two ars is it? double ess ment of a harassed pedlar while gauging at the symmetry of a peeled pear under a cemetery wall. Silly, isn't it? (p. 121)

Jane Austen, on the other hand, appeals in general to the conversational ear, as is evident in a passage of dialogue from *Emma*:

"I do not know what your opinion may be, Mrs. Weston," said Mr. Knightley, "of this great intimacy between Emma and Harriet Smith, but I think it a bad thing."

"A bad thing! Do you really think it a bad thing?—why so?" (p. 25)

Woolf, however, maximizes the poetic not the spoken word, and the silence in her writing is that which is sensed "behind the eyes" (*Between the Acts*) and behind the ears. After the death of Percival in *The Waves*, Rhoda's feelings are described: "But what can one make of loneliness? Alone I should stand on the empty grass and say, Rooks fly" (p. 161). The metrical emphasis in this prose sentence is a spondee, "Rooks fly," a poetic foot of two stressed syllables. This underlying rhythm reinforces the qualities of slowness and emptiness that are at the heart of the feeling of loneliness. Somehow Rhoda's rhythmic variation and bleak image— "Rooks fly"—captures this flatness of feeling, illustrating Woolf's involvement not mainly with the speaking voice but with the metrics of poetry in the writing of prose.

Woolf writes in her diary in 1908 that she is seeking some kind of whole or harmony through means of what she, in her early career, terms "discord." She begins in 1917 to write in a profusion of unshaped sensation and color and feeling, such as in the short story "Kew Gardens":

From the oval-shaped flower-bed there rose perhaps a hundred stalks spreading into heart-shaped or tongue-shaped leaves half way up and unfurling at the tip red or blue or yellow petals marked with spots of colour raised upon the surface; and from the red, blue, or yellow gloom of the throat emerged a straight bar, rough with gold dust and slightly clubbed at the end. (*Complete Shorter Fiction*, p. 84)

Reminding us of the lushness of D. H. Lawrence, this passage still lacks the mature sense of rhythm that contains not only the color and movement of description but also the steely backbone of meaning and pattern. In her later works, Woolf takes the same richness of sensation, feeling, and thought and creates aesthetic patterns and rhythms that are meaningful: "I attain . . . a symmetry by means of infinite discords, showing all the traces of the mind's passage through the world; achieve in the end, some kind of whole made of shivering fragments; to me this seems the natural process; the flight of the mind" (*Diary*).

Woolf's structuring of the "flight" or "wave" of the mind has much to do with rhythm and voices (inner and outer) and, it has been suggested, with musical forms as well. Leonard Meyer, the music critic, has noted that "when highly structured formal relationships are present in literature, they are often derived from or clearly associated with musical processes. . . . Repetitive or periodic structures in recent prose literature are often avowedly derived from music" (*Music, the Arts, and Ideas*, p. 114). Woolf's style, though fluid, is also highly structured, as revealed in this examination of her novels. She exclaims in her diary, "I cannot curve my mind to the line of a book. It's not the writing but the architecting that strains. If I write one paragraph, then there is the next and then the next . . . and the arches and the domes will spring into the air as firm as steel and light as cloud" (4, p. 306). Woolf here seeks support in her writing from the very lightest of things, "clouds," as well as from the strongest, "steel," capturing the modern notion of the lightness of gravity that preoccupies writers like Milan Kundera and the late Italo Calvino. This architecting—the patterning of sound, silence, and motion—can be found in sentences, chapters, and novels. For example, in *To the Lighthouse*, James, Cam, and Mr. Ramsay finally voyage out to the lighthouse together after Mrs. Ramsay's death. A rhythmic passage moves us from the outward to the inward. What is syntactically interesting is that the use of parentheses enables Woolf to capture both the outward motions of nature and the boat and the inward motions of the mind in a gesture of simultaneity, but, as illustrated in Chapter 3, the parentheses enclose the outward facts:

The sails flapped over their heads. The water chuckled and slapped the side of the boat, which drowsed motionless in the sun. Now and then the sails rippled with a little breeze in them, but the ripple ran over them and ceased. The boat made no motion at all. Mr. Ramsay sat in the middle of the boat. He would be impatient in a moment, James thought, and Cam thought, looking at her father who sat in the middle of the boat between them (James steered; Cam sat alone in the bow) with his legs tightly curled. (p. 242)

The body and the mind—the images and the sentences—move inward to the "still point" of Mr. Ramsay, who is syntactically encased in the middle of the passage: centered, guru-fashion ("legs tightly curled") in the middle of the boat and in the middle of his children's parallel trance-like thoughts ("James thought" and "Cam thought"). With slow rhythms and carefully balanced sentences, Woolf achieves the "interior distance" of art that separates the boat and the mind from the zone of actuality or "reality."

Larger musical structures beyond the sentence that support Woolf's works are apparent in the metaphors of critics. For example, E. K. Browne observes in his discussion of *To the Lighthouse* that the "three parts of the novel are related somewhat as the three big blocks of sound in a sonata" (pp. 69–70); *The Waves* has been described as an opera, and *Between the Acts* as a musical drama or, perhaps more accurately, a melodrama; *Jacob's Room* was described by Woolf herself as a "disconnected rhapsody" (*Diary* 2, p. 179), and *The Voyage Out* as a "harlequinade" (ibid., p. 17).

Such broad comparisons of music and the visual arts to writing are familiar, and they are welcome in an age that has come to value interdisciplinary thinking. However, all arts that represent human thought and feeling, though submitting to shared terms and borrowed aesthetics, can become strained if identifications among them become too rigid or thoroughgoing. The differences between, for example, the media of words and music must be acknowledged in the same glance that brings the gestures of similarity into view. As Brian Vickers, in his study of rhetoric, observes:

The prime difference between language and music is that language has a constant semantic dimension, uses words with definite meanings—subject, of course, to personal and regional differences: but these too can be registered—while music has no such fixed system of denotation. Certain modes, or in modern terms keys and tonalities, have traditionally been associated with certain feeling-states, but the association is not only arbitrary (in a much profounder sense than the "arbitrary" association, in language, of signified with signifier, which is at least widely shared within a country, dialect, or social group), but has suffered some drastic changes—before disappearing altogether in recent music. (pp. 363–64)

Understanding the limitations of comparing a language-based novel with a musical form, and Vickers's slighting of vocal music, we are still left with our experience of Woolf's language, which denotes rhythm or music.

How is this rhythmic trace or music experienced by the reader of her novels? What is that "rope" that she is casting about for "to throw the reader" in his or her experience of this "rhythm," which is more natural than the "narrative" to Woolf? What is the relationship between the rhythmic and the narrative? Does the musical form of authorial intention control the rhythm of reading? Do we read *The Waves* differently— perhaps *with* the long sweeping rhythm of the waves—and more slowly than the halting, interrupted rhythms of *Between the Acts*? And if so, how are these alternations of theme, structure, and vision transformed into the experience of rhythm, a new kind of musical element, in her novels? Finally, is there a unique rhythm in Woolf's style, that which, she claims, is expressive of a woman's mind or a "woman's sentence"?

Rhythm helps to create the "texture" of Woolf's style. But what is texture, that much-used and rarely defined literary term? It is composed of thematic as well as temporal and spatial counterpoint. One of the arguments of this chapter is that Woolf's alternations of theme and rhythm weave the fabric of language into new textures and patterns. Frequently, in a Woolf novel, a woman keeps the rhythm of conversation and life going so that women and their flowing and merging qualities become part of the texture of a novel. For example, Mrs. Ramsay in *To the Lighthouse* looks around her dinner party and notes that all of her guests sat separate, "and the whole of the effort of merging and flowing and creating rested on her" (p. 126). Men are represented as "sterile" and static. In *Between the Acts*, Lucy and Isa are driven to inward monologues, feeling stifled by the arrogance of the men who surround them: they expand their sense of themselves by thinking of famous women from the past— another of the silences of women that Woolf infuses with psychic energy. Sometimes a scene is structured by the rhythm of a woman's talking and silence while performing a craft: a woman doing two things at once. For example, Helen Ambrose talks to St. John while working on her embroidery in *The Voyage Out*, and the conversation is punctuated by rhythmic "lapses" and "pauses":

The embroidery, which was a matter for thought, the design being difficult and the colours wanting consideration, brought lapses into the dialogue when she seemed to be engrossed in her skeins of silk, or, with head a little drawn back and eyes narrowed, considered the effect of the whole. Thus she merely said, "um-m-m," to St. John's next remark, "I shall ask her to go for a walk with me." Perhaps he resented this division of attention. . . . There was a considerable pause. (p. 207)

Women's attention is divided, interrupted, and they are often doing two things at once—sewing, embroidering, knitting, painting. What they do creates a rhythm for the conversation and a metaphor for the alternating rhythm of the novel. Mrs. Ramsay in *To the Lighthouse* talks and pauses and sometimes knits and pauses; Mrs. Dalloway sews and talks and pauses while sitting with Peter; Lily in *To the Lighthouse* paints and talks and pauses. A counterpoint of talking and silence reflects relationships between men and women and the rhythm of women's lives.

A structuralist analysis of *The Waves* and *Between the Acts*, an attempt to isolate the general intellectual structures of Woolf's writing, is useful in extending what might be termed the poles of her oppositions. It enables the reader to observe her rhythms of alternation, the intellectual music of her style, from a higher plane of generality. For example, if we examine the "iron bolts," the underlying structures or patterns, that hold together the surfaces of plot, character, and theme in the novel *Between the Acts*, we find that it is based on the following oppositions: actors and audience; acts and intermissions; talk and silence; art and life; fiction and reality; war and the homefront; actual time and mind time; historical time and eternity; beginning and endings; and men and women. Since Saussure, our understanding of language in general, and Woolf's writing in particular, as a play of formal difference, enables us to subject the novel to such formal measure. The concepts below appear throughout Woolf's novels and contain the principle of meaning established by Saussure that there are no positive values in language, only difference. Each term is defined by the existence of the other: vision (light/dark); action (action/rest, spurt/stop, sink/rise, plunge/surface); mind (conscious/unconscious); time (actual/mind time, in time/out of time); writing (mark/pause); music (beat/rest, meter/rhythm); and visual art (stroke/space).

However, after making such structures "visible," we are not, after all, left with the rhythm or the music of Woolf's verbal texture but with the terms that combine to make the rhythm: we cannot rest with binary oppositions based on formal investigation as structuralists advise. It is important to note here as a point of methodology that, though certain textual claims are made on the basis of linguistic or semiotic principles, Woolf is, after all, a writer who writes rhythmically, and, consequently, she takes the above conceptual strands and weaves them, creating a "texture" unique among modern writers.

Throughout her works, Woolf's style turns on the above-mentioned differences, but "turn" is the crucial term just as "différance" is the structure that deconstructs structuralism. This second structure, deconstruction, then "turns" the structural oppositions like sound and silence into one another. Its perspective, which informs the spirit of this book with its philosophical concern with language and its hypothesis of heterogeneity, provides a rhythmic quality, one of "lightness" and "play" that becomes the working principle for reading Woolf. In the reading experience, the "scaffolding" of the novel turns into a Moebius strip. Lily's concept of her painting in *To the Lighthouse* expresses this doubleness: "The whole mass of the picture was poised upon that weight. Beautiful and bright it should be on the surface, feathery and evanescent, one colour melting into another like the colours on a butterfly's wing; but beneath the fabric must be clamped together with bolts of iron" (p. 255). In its steely concern with cognitive poles, the structuralist methodology resists the lightening of gravity, the rising of "a butterfly's wing" from "bolts of iron." Woolf achieves a lightening of being, like the writers Italo Calvino and Milan Kundera, through "narrativity," the act of writing, and this is communicated to the reader through the verbal, intellectual, spatial, and temporal counterpoint. Through her "quivering," "rippling," "oscillating," "flickering," "fluttering," and "dancing" words and sentences, she achieves a rhythm that fills the white spaces of the mind and the page. And as Calvino states in *Six Memos for the Next Millennium*, "The lightness is . . . something arising from the writing itself, . . . quite independent of whatever philosophic doctrine the poet claims to be following" (p. 10).

SOUND, SILENCE, AND TIME:
THE ELEMENTS OF RHYTHM

Sound and time are the elements that are generally acknowledged as contributing to the rhythm of a work: "The musical work is a multiphased structure in which the basic and elementary phenomena are sounding or rustling (percussive) qualities" (Ingarden, *Problems of Literary Evaluation*, p. 83). The fixed elements in this view are sounding qualities, those physically marked on a page, while the open, nonsounding elements, pauses or rests, are ignored in this definition of music. In this view, sound in an aesthetic work is privileged, silence being defined negatively as the absence of sound. If, on the other hand, the definition of sound and silence is established not on valuation of sound but on the basis of "différance," then silence is given a new status. Saussure observes that "in language, there are only differences without positive terms" (p. 121). If meaning exists in a network of differences, then sound and silence, when defined notationally and relationally, are not opposites or hierarchical or valued as positive or negative, but are counterparts in a general rhythm. Virginia Woolf knows this; her textual treatment of silence in her novels reveals it.

What is sound and what is silence becomes less predictable, but both are a "presence." As John Cage states of modern music: "In this new music nothing takes place but sounds: those that are notated and those that are not. Those that are not notated appear in the written music as silence, opening the doors of the music to the sounds that happen to be in the environment. . . . It is realized that sounds occur whether intended or not" (p. 7). If we accept this view of sound and silence, which blurs the conventional meaning of the words—indeed a view that "sounds" silence—then how does the mind's perception of silence change? If silence is not "an absence of sound" or simply a separation of two sounds or two groups of sounds or two sections of a musical work or punctuation, as Roman Ingarden would claim, then it becomes something else: silence is expressive and notationally equivalent to sound. "Sounds," according to John Cage, are "called silence only because they do not form part of a musical intention . . . [and] may be depended upon to exist" (pp. 22–23). If we abandon "intentionality" as the chief validation of "presence," as the variable that is more important than any other in the creation of a work (the New Critics' intentional fallacy), what are we left with? We, as readers, can only learn to listen—particularly to modern authors like Woolf who pipe new tunes that contain the innovation of textual silence as well as sound.

When we apply this musical aesthetic to our thinking about silence in narration, the breaks in the rhythm of a novel are not as discordant as J. Hillis Miller contends in his analysis of repetition: "*Between the Acts* is full of breaks in that rhythm, interruptions, silences, gaps, cacophonies, incompletions, as though the author were unwilling for some reason to trust her own verve and go all the way in the direction her creative energy leads her" (p. 220). It may be a matter of trust but not a failure of creative verve. It is more likely Woolf's trust in language, what George Steiner asserts as "the poetic challenge to the 'sayability' of the world" (*Real Presences*, p. 92), a crisis of meaning that began in earnest at the end of the nineteenth century. Miller fails to sound this modernist tone, the new music of sounds and silences in *Between the Acts* that functions positively toward the ordering of the whole, thematically and musically. As John Cage explains,

This music is not concerned with harmoniousness as generally understood where the quality of harmony results from a blending of sound elements. Here we are concerned with the coexistence of dissimilars, and the central points where fusion occurs are many: the ears of the listeners wherever they are. This disharmony, to paraphrase Bergson's statement about disorder, is simply a harmony to which many are unaccustomed. (p. 12)

Woolf's basic rhythmic elements in the novel are time (capturing present-ness, linear-historical time, cyclical-eternal time); thoughts (inaudible but marked in the text); words (spoken and unspoken and marked); voices (narrator's, character's, poetic, social, historical, journalistic, anonymous); the ambient sounds of nature and machines; the sounds of the city; and pauses, silences, fissures, cracks, crevices, gaps, gulfs, and abysses—to name a few "sounds," conscious and unconscious, to be further developed in this chapter. It is important to note at this point that the lacunae of pauses and gaps and silences are as schematized as the sounds in Woolf's writing. For Woolf, as for Ingarden, "the world of represented objects must contain undetermined spots because the work cannot afford an infinity of descriptions. . . . It is a schematized picture with inherent lacunae" (*The Literary Work of Art*, p. 166).

STYLE REFLECTS VISION

Woolf's alternating rhythm, however, is not just a fact of style: it is an embodiment of her vision of mind and life and reality. In assessing "how the novelist goes from one thing to another" (Hartman, "Virginia's Web," p. 71), we find that she is as concerned with "interpolation," the connection between two known points in the mind, as Geoffrey Hartman contends in "Virginia's Web," as "extrapolation," the movement from the known point to the unknown that Miller describes in *Fiction and Repetition*. Woolf is concerned with both the alternation and "différance" of interpolation and extrapolation in the mind, not exclusively with either, illustrating again the deconstruction of opposites. Contrary to what Hartman asserts, *Between the Acts* does not reveal "the same voracious desire for continuity as *Mrs. Dalloway* and *To the Lighthouse*" (p. 79), because each of Woolf's novels has a different experimental intention, and her works do not necessarily reflect the narrative progression from "realism" to "expressionism" that he posits (p. 48). In addition, Hartman misperceives Woolf's vision of life in underlining "her wish for the affirmative": "Mrs. Woolf sought to catch the power of affirmation in its full extent" (p. 81). Miller recognizes the affirmative but at the same time acknowledges that *Between the Acts* "is full of breaks in that rhythm, interruptions, silences, gaps, cacophonies, incompletions" (p. 220), and he offers a more persuasive reading. He, more than Hartman, reads the discontinuites in style that reflect the dark spaces of Woolf's vision, noting that "there may be a hidden presence behind the apparent gap" (p. 222).

Woolf incorporates the "negative" shocks of life in her novels in her lexicon of silence, and it is her philosophy and practice as a novelist to capture the moment whole, "whatever it includes." She seeks to preserve the interrupted "Un . . . dis . . ." of the gramophone, the unity and dispersal of the times and of the mind and to embody this in the form of the novel. Hartman suggests that Woolf is not in touch with the "unconscious" and, therefore, with the "negative" in her drive toward the "affirmative" vision:

Considered as notes toward a supreme fiction the novels of Virginia Woolf say "It must be affirmative." They suppose a mind with an immense, even unlimited, power to see or build continuities. It is almost as if the special attribute of the unconscious, that it does not know the negative, belonged also to mind in its freest state. The artist is either not conscious of the negative (i.e. his unconscious speaks through him), or fiction is generally the embodiment of the negative . . . in purely affirmative terms. The reader, of course, may reconstitute the negative; this task is one of the principal aims of interpretation. (p. 81)

The somewhat confusing equations of the unconscious and the negative in this passage lead us to the kind of bipolar thinking about Woolf's style that ignores her alternations of rhythm and theme and that collapses the contraries Hartman posits. One could also quarrel with Hartman's statement that the "unconscious" or the artist's mind in the creative state does not know the "negative." As illustrated later in this chapter, Woolf, particularly in *Between the Acts*, is aware of the "dark places of psychology," the decay of life, the cut of death, and the horrors of war, and she reveals this conception of life in her themes and style. Such expressions are not, as Hartman posits, "power failures" in Woolf's writing (p. 79). As Ruotolo claims in *The Interrupted Moment*, "To be open to life in Woolf's fictional world is to remain open to an aesthetic of disjunctions at the heart of human interplay" (p. 2). The wish for the "affirmative," the desire to ignore the anomalies and gaps of Woolf's text, is clearly Geoffrey Hartman's and not Virginia Woolf's. He is most attuned to Woolf when he shifts his Romantic stance slightly toward the end of his article, touching her darkness as well as her light, noting our interest in "her continuous doubting of the continuity she is forced to posit" (p. 74).

Although the interpretations of Hartman and Miller are certainly incisive, there is something amiss in their narrative expectations and models. The narrative model for Woolf should be one based on her practices of alternation in theme and style—the creativity and the emptiness at the heart of life—without "fitting" the critic's desire for unity, continuity, and harmony in traditional terms. Woolf's style is one of rhythmic alternation, "différance," interpolation and extrapolation, and of keeping the silences and gaps of life narratively marked in her text as part of the female rhythm discussed in Chapter 2 and this chapter. She develops a sentence that is suited to express a woman's mind, and it incorporates silence in its various guises and spaces. The themes of nothingness and flatness of feeling as well as the theme of effort and creativity mounted against despair are both present in *The Waves* and *Between the Acts*, revealing counterpoint of style and vision. Woolf makes no false "affirmations."

This discussion of techniques of interpolation and extrapolation reflects the bipolar categories of thinking of many critics of Woolf mentioned earlier. Hartman's and Miller's "interpolation" and "extrapolation" of narration, as well as Alex Zwerdling's and James Naremore's "real" and "poetic" worlds, are useful articulations of aspects of Woolf. However, now is the moment in Woolf criticism for the collapse of contrary categories into a third vision of alternation as a principle of her style.

MUSICAL FORMS OF 'THE WAVES' AND 'BETWEEN THE ACTS'

Woolf describes *The Waves* as a "playpoem" in her diary (3, p. 107), combining the drama and poetry of soliloquy: " 'Drop upon drop,' said Bernard, 'silence falls. It forms on the roof of the mind and falls into pools beneath. For ever alone, alone, alone,—hear silence fall and sweep its rings to the farthest edges. Gorged and replete, solid with middle-aged content, I, whom loneliness destroys, let silence fall, drop by drop' " (p. 17). The feeling of loneliness and silence is captured in the rhythmic iambs "For ever alone, alone, alone."

Every element (animate and inanimate) in *The Waves* somehow has its voice and is part of a gigantic cosmic conversation. The seven disembodied voices, dramatic soliloquies, reflect the majesty of an opera, a drama that is primarily sung, and this distinguishes it from the drama in *Between the Acts*, in which human voices are fragmented and not as central to the music of the novel. Since music is central in *The Waves*, the poetic inner songs or soliloquies of the seven characters dominate the work. However, the voices represent not ordinary talk but songs for the poetic ear, comparable in subjective experience to the sound of voices reverberating in a seashell.

Between the Acts, in contrast, is a novel more concerned with art than nature, and it increases the variables in the field of sound of the novel. It voices silent thoughts (unspoken thoughts and unfinished lines of poetry) and the sounds of nature (cows coughing) and of machines (the "zoom" of planes, the gramophones' "tick-tick") as part of its musical composition. Woolf's fearlessness in constructing the "music" of *Between the Acts* contains the recognition that John Cage articulates:

> Where it is realized that sounds occur whether intended or not, one turns in the direction of those he does not intend. This turning is psychological and seems at first to be a giving up of everything that belongs to humanity—for a musician, the giving up of music. The psychological turning leads to the world of nature, where, gradually, or suddenly, one sees that humanity and nature, not separate, are in this world together; that nothing was lost when everything was given away. In fact everything is gained. In musical terms, any sounds may occur in any combination and in any continuity. (p. 8)

Cage's own musical experiments involving natural sounds would challenge a critic like Ingarden, who briskly dismisses such sounds as irrelevant to musical experience. Woolf, however, is preoccupied with a "song" inspired by the natural world as revealed in her last essays, "Anon" and "The Reader," written about the same time as *Between the Acts*.

Although not technically equipped, as we are today, Woolf was linguistically equipped to transform her awareness of nature and the environment's manner of operation into art. Her incorporation of sounding and nonsounding elements of voices (narrative, human, poetic, historical, journalistic), nature, machines, and silence (the unvoiced, the unsaid) all contribute to the totality of the rhythm in *The Waves* and to the even more musically inclusive *Between the Acts*. She approaches in these novels "the world seen without a self," a narrative concept about which Italo Calvino speculates just before his death in 1985:

Think what it would be to have a work conceived from outside the self, a work that would let us escape the limited perspective of the individual ego, not only to enter into selves like our own but to give speech to that which has no language, to the bird perching on the edge of the gutter, to the tree in the spring and the tree in the fall, to stones, to cement, to plastic. (p. 124)

In her diary, Woolf speaks of a play she would like to write with "voices speaking from the flowers" (4, p. 275). Had Calvino read Woolf closely, he would have found the beginnings of this work "conceived from outside the self" with all its strange sounds and multiple rhythms and perspectives.

And each rhythm has its meaning. Note the halting rhythm of sentences in *Between the Acts* in the talk of the Reverend Streatfield:

"Dare we, I asked myself, limit life to ourselves? May we not hold that there is a spirit that inspires, pervades . . ." (The swallows were sweeping round him. They seemed cognizant of his meaning. Then they swept out of sight.) "I leave that to you. I am not here to explain. That role has not been assigned me. I speak only as one of the audience, one of ourselves. I caught myself too reflected, as it happened in my own mirror" . . . (Laughter) "Scraps, orts and fragments! Surely, we should unite?"

   "But" ("but" marked a new paragraph) "I speak also in another capacity. As Treasurer of the Fund. In which capacity" (he consulted a sheet of paper) "I am glad to be able to tell you . . . ." (pp. 192–93)

This rhythm of seeming interruptions is developed in response to loss. Reason is no longer a handle on the world for Woolf in the late 1930's in war-torn England, and language bereft of stable referents and a stable public does not resonate in the same way: it lurches on. Casting about for another force to organize her world, she finds rhythm, and she traces the anxious counterpoint of the conscious and unconscious mind in her narration. Like Dr. P., the title character in Oliver Sacks' "neurological opera," *The Man Who Mistook His Wife for a Hat*, an aging singer and teacher who has developed visual agnosia, Woolf holds onto the world with music. In this modern opera, Dr. P. loses the ability to interpret visual information, to recognize faces, to distinguish between his shoe and his foot, indeed, between his wife's head and his hat on a rack. But in losing his body image he develops his body rhythm, and "when the music stopped, he stopped." So too Woolf's *Between the Acts* is organized according to a rhythm, a modern music to compensate for other kinds of loss that relate to the meanings of words. This is revealed in the interrupted rhythms:

"But you don't remember . . ." Mrs. Haines began. No, not that. Still he did remember—and he was about to tell them what, when there was a sound outside, and Isa, his son's wife, came in with her hair in pigtails; she was wearing a dressing gown with faded peacocks on it. She came in like a swan swimming its way; then was checked and stopped; was surprised to find people there; and lights burning. She had been sitting with her little boy who wasn't well, she apologized. What had they been saying?

"Discussing the cesspool," said Mr. Oliver. (p. 4)

More than other modern authors—even Joyce, with his density and precision of words in *Ulysses*—Woolf tries to incorporate her sense of the rupture in words and reason in her style, admitting the unconscious and the irrational into the halting rhythms of *Between the Acts*.

The rhythm of the novel has an organizing and lightening effect not only on the writer, Woolf, but also on the reader and the audience, demonstrating the role of art during times of cultural disorder like World War I. Collective "music," otherwise known as art, draws together and preserves individuals, as the "death" of Percival in *The Waves* draws together his friends, and as the people on the street are drawn together in *Mrs. Dalloway* to look up at the skywriting. In *Between the Acts*, Miss LaTrobe realizes the importance of music to her audience as Virginia Woolf does to hers—particularly when other organizing forces like culture, language, and reason have become disordered. For example, when the actors delay during Miss LaTrobe's play, she fears that "Every moment, the audience slipped the noose; split up into scraps and fragments. Music! she signalled" (p. 122). And as the audience assembles, they too realize the importance of the rhythms of music and life: "For I hear music, they were saying. Music wakes us. Music makes us see the hidden, join the broken" (p. 120). Woolf, like the phenomenologists, believes that art is not an independent entity. The readers of a Virginia Woolf novel are rescued from distraction and fragmentation in collectively constructing art. They join "the broken" as they listen to the art and music of her writing: "The tune began; the first note meant a second; the second a third. Then down beneath a force was born in opposition; then another. On different levels they diverged. On different levels ourselves went forward; flower gathering some on the surface; others descending to wrestle with the meaning; but all comprehending; all enlisted" (p. 189). "All enlisted" in the participation in art, and listeners or readers become silent performers in the work. This effort against despair is apparent in Woolf's diary where she records at times that she fears losing her readers—distracted as they are from the aesthetic by the daily specter of war—for her, "part of one's death."

This collective fragmentation and participation is one of the major themes of *Between the Acts*: unity and dispersal. The theme appears in language in the unified words and broken syllables; in human relationships in the harmony and discordancy of Giles and Isa; and in culture in the unity of the homefront and the dispersal of the war. The gramophone picks up the theme, "Dispersed are we. . . . The gramophone gurgled Unity-Dispersity. It gurgled Un . . . dis . . . and ceased" (pp. 196, 201). This sense of fragmentation and dispersal of self and society is captured also in the actual and metaphorical mirrors that the actors hold up to the audience at the end of the play. We, as readers, mirror Miss LaTrobe's audience in this musical reading activity, for in reading we, in some sense, mirror the text: "The whole world is a work of art. . . . There is no Shakespeare, there is no Beethoven; certainly and emphatically there is no God; we are the words; we are the music; we are the thing itself" (*Collected Essays* 1, p. 72).

When viewing the major paintings of John Constable, one senses that the sky is the place where the emotions of the artist are chiefly to be felt; when reading *The Waves*, the drama of Woolf's emotions is in the rhythm and sweep of the waves in nature, in the mind, and in the sentences and structure of the novel. She writes of *The Waves* during its composition in 1929 that it is constructed "according to a rhythm not a plot" (*Diary* 3, p. 316), and after completing this work, she states "I want to write another four novels: Waves, I mean" (*Diary* 4, p. 63). Such statements attest to Woolf's visceral sense of the structuring rhythm of this novel, and waves figure throughout as theme, motif, rhythm, and emotion, pulsing always in the voices of the seven characters.

In terms of theme, the wave of nature breaks on every one of the figures or aspects of consciousness, reminding them that the rhythms of nature prevail over human life in the end. The rhythm of characters' voices and the rhythms of nature, the waves, blend. Louis, the self-conscious son of an Australian banker, who loves the office and money-making, hears "always the sullen thud of the waves; and the chained beast stamps on the beach" (p. 58). Reminiscent of the rhythms and character of T. S. Eliot's Prufrock, Louis tries to reduce the world to consciousness and order: "And the grinding and the steam that runs in unequal drops down the window pane; and the stopping and the starting with a jerk of motor omnibuses; and the hesitations at counters; and the words that trail drearily with human meaning: I will reduce you to order. . . . I see the men in round coats perched on stools at the counter; and also behind them, eternity" (pp. 95–96). Fearing eternity and the "beast" of nature, death, he wishes "to feel close over me the protective waves of the ordinary, catch with the tail of my eyes some far horizon" (p. 94).

Similarly, Susan, representing maternity, seeks comfort in domestic rhythms and in her children, who are "the waves" of her life: "My children will carry me on; their teething, their crying, their going to school and coming back will be like the waves of the sea under me. . . . I shall be debased and hide-bound by the bestial and beautiful passion of maternity" (p. 132). And Bernard, the storyteller, always seeking to integrate his disparate selves and to find the perfect phrase, speaks of "the shock of the falling wave which has sounded all my life. . . . Once more, I who had thought myself immune, who had said, 'Now I am rid of all that,' find that the wave has tumbled me over, head over heels, scattering my possessions, leaving me to collect to assemble, to heap together, summon my forces, rise and confront the enemy" (pp. 291, 293). And as Bernard says, it is impossible to order these friends, these faces, to deal with them separately: "What a symphony with its concord and its discord, and its tunes on top and its complicated bass beneath, then grew up! Each played his own tune. . . . With Neville, 'Let's discuss Hamlet.' With Louis, science. With Jinny, love" (p. 182).

Nature is also a silent backdrop created in the interludes between the chapters and in the vision of characters like Bernard, the storyteller, who views life intermittently from the cosmic perspective of nature. Consciousness in these passages is presented as an enveloping psyche emanating from the harmonious rhythms of nature—the rising and setting of the sun, the repetitions of the waves, the "blank melody" of the birds' songs. Nature has a voice, a view. But how does the silence of nature speak? As Rousseau says of the representation of nature: "Whatever one does, noise alone does not speak to the spirit at all. The objects of which one speaks must be understood. In all imitation, some form of discourse must substitute for the voice of nature. The musician who would represent noise by noise deceives himself" (p. 58). One of the ways to represent nature is to provide a bird's-eye view of the world:

And then tiring of pursuit and flight, lovely they came descending, delicately declining, dropped down and sat silent on the tree, on the wall, with their bright eyes glancing, and their heads turned this way, that way; aware, awake; intensely conscious of one thing, one object in particular. Perhaps it was a snail shell, rising in the grass like a grey cathedral, a swelling building burnt with dark rings and shadowed green by the grass. Or perhaps they saw the splendour of the flowers. (*The Waves*, p. 74)

The enveloping psyche here, the narrator, views nature as Bernard does when he reflects on human life from the perspective "that the earth is only a pebble flicked off accidentally from the face of the sun" (p. 225)—of which the 1989 pictures of Neptune taken in space by Voyager II remind us.

Just as the reader thinks he is about to disappear into a modern Noh play written by Yeats, lulled by the trance-like repetitions that create a stillness, Bernard states: "But now listen, tick, tick; hoot, hoot; the world has hailed us back to it" (p. 225). Against this backdrop of enveloping silence and consciousness, then, the "tick, tick" of time enters, and Woolf's textures of space and time, the warp and woof of her style, emerge again.

In addition to the "tick" of time, we experience gaps in *The Waves* that represent the pulses of the unconscious. By introducing the unconscious into the text through the structure of a gap—to use Woolf's refined vocabulary, the crevices, gashes, fissures, rents, cracks, abysses, and gulfs (all spatial terms and suggestively "feminine")—Woolf introduces the pain of the mind into *The Waves*. These "gaps" allow unknown aspects of mind into the text: the repressed fears, shocks, and disasters of life seep in through the psychological and lexical spaces that punctuate her text. Jacques Lacan, writing of Freud, states: "Impediment, failure, split. In a spoken or written sentence something stumbles. . . . It is there that he seeks the unconscious. . . . It is the function of the unconscious to be in relation with the concept of the 'cut'" (*The Language of the Self*, pp. 25, 43). Woolf, in touch with the concept of the unconscious and death, structures its "cuts" into her novels lexically, syntactically, metaphorically, and thematically. Profoundly affected by the death of her mother when Woolf was just thirteen, she writes in *Moments of Being*: "But at 13 to have that protection removed, to be tumbled out of the family shelter, to see *cracks* and *gashes* in that fabric, to be cut by them, to see beyond them—was that good?" (p. 118; my italics). Sometimes she relates the "cuts" or "wounds" to the feminine. However, it is incorporated into her texts structurally, much like Georgia O'Keeffe cuts small square spaces in the canvas of her sky in "Starlight Night" to represent stars, silence, death, the unconscious.

Rhoda in *The Waves* is finely attuned to shocks "sudden as the springs of a tiger," and she speaks of the devices invented "for filling up the crevices and disguising these fissures" (p. 64) that open up the unexpected in life. She describes an experience of coming to a "grey, cadaverous space" of a puddle, a physical and psychological "gap," and being unable to cross it. The psychological impediment is mirrored in Woolf's similar experience described in both "A Sketch of the Past" and her diary: "Life is, soberly and accurately the oddest affair; has in it the essence of reality. I used to feel this as a child—couldn't step across a puddle once, I remember, for thinking how strange—what am I? etc. But by writing I don't reach anything. All I mean to make is a note of a curious state of mind" (*Diary* 3, p. 113). This impulse to record strange states of mind, inchoate, swelling into image and sound, leads Woolf to sometimes find a rhythm—a gap—rather than a word for an emotion.

This physical and psychological inability to cross puddles interests Woolf and Freud. He, through psychoanalysis, and Woolf, through her writing, set out to admit the presence of and then to explain such gaps and suspensions. After Percival's death, Rhoda has to cross an "enormous gulf" (p. 151); her world is "rent" by lightning, and oaks are "cracked asunder" (p. 159) upon the death of her friend—part of the "seven-sided flower" of the group. Unexpected death, an abyss, "cuts" through the harmony of life creating the "rents" and "cracks" in Rhoda's vision.

Lacan, writing about Freud, also stresses the rhythms of the unconscious: "the pulsative function, as it were of the unconscious, the need to disappear that seems to be in some sense inherent in it" (*The Four Fundamental Concepts*, p. 43). The alternating rhythm of Woolf's style discussed earlier—the movement from the conscious to the unconscious, the external to the internal—aesthetically captures this same pulsative function described by Freud. Woolf's vocabulary of "gaps" admits the unconscious pulses into narration only to disappear quickly into the rhythms of life in the novel. Louis in *The Waves*, "conscious of flux, of disorder; of annihilation and despair," expresses this intertwining of the conscious and the unconscious in a waltzing rhythm:

The rhythm of the eating-house. It is like a waltz tune, eddying in and out, round and round. The waitresses, balancing trays, swing in and out, round and round, dealing plates of greens, of apricot and custard, dealing them at the right time, to the right customers. The average men, include her rhythm in their rhythm ('I would take a tenner; for it blocks up the hall') take their greens, take their apricots and custard. Where then is the break in this continuity? What the fissure through which one sees disaster? The circle is unbroken; the harmony complete. Here is the central rhythm; here the common mainspring. I watch it expand, contract; and then expand again. (p. 94)

And so the fact of alternation, the movement in Woolf's style from the rhythms of life to the gaps and silences—the presence of the unconscious in fissures, breaks, cracks, and a broader sense of life and death—takes yet another form: the pulsing movement from the conscious to the unconscious. It is in the splits and gaps that the unconscious is admitted. This lexicon introduces unknown aspects of mind into the text and represents the psychological spaces for the repressed—fears, shocks, and disasters of life.

In addition to marking the unconscious in spatial "gaps," Woolf is equally concerned with giving "pauses" their effect in nature. "Pauses" mark time in nature and music in the interludes; "gaps" represent Woolf's spatialization of ruptures in the mind. "Pauses" are a temporal marker in the surface melody of nature and sometimes in the mind in *The Waves*, while "gaps" are a spatialization of mind. In Chapter 3, "pauses" were associated with the suspension of the "ordinary cotton-wool of experience," marking the moment before the mind sank to meditative, perhaps unconscious depths. In *The Waves*, pauses are still part of the alternating pattern, not of mind, but of nature. They function more like "rests" in a harmonious patterning of sounds and silences in nature.

"Pauses" occur more frequently in the interludes, where nine separate episodes interspersed throughout the novel are controlled by nature. The rising and setting of the sun, the movements of the waves, and the birds' songs demonstrate that nature is not silent. As the sun rises higher and higher and then sets over the space of the interludes, the "sounds" of nature are made audible. At the beginning of the first interlude, for example, "the sun had not yet risen," and Woolf's lexicon of silence signals a sunken order of reality until the light of the sun "struck" and creates a visceral, visual, auditory, and linguistic pattern that includes "pauses" and "rests":

The light *struck* upon the trees in the garden, making one leaf *transparent* and *then another*. One bird chirped high *up*; there was a *pause*; another chirped *lower down*. The sun sharpened the walls of the house and *rested* like the tip of a fan upon a white blind and made a blue *fingerprint of shadow under* the leaf by the bedroom window. The blind stirred slightly, but all *within* was dim and unsubstantial. The birds sang their *blank* melody *outside*. (p. 8; my italics)

The sounds and "pauses" at different distances, the motions and "rests" "within" and "outside" intermix in this passage as in music. The pauses; the rests; the repetitions; the sounds that are lower, higher; the shadows that are under, within, inside, and outside are a part of the confluence of nature and do not "rend" like the gaps discussed earlier. Viewing sound and silence relationally, we discover, like John Cage, that though nature (breezes, birds, waves, sun) is generally not considered part of the sound of a novel, Woolf expands or, as J. Hillis Miller asserts, "extrapolates" the field of sound in *The Waves*, and she continues to do so in *Between the Acts*.

The rhythmical is natural to Woolf, a re-creation of "the wave of her mind" as she casts about for rhythms for different emotions, sights, individuals, classes, professions, generations, and genres, particularly in a novel like *Between the Acts*. Though only acknowledged in the past decade, her novels contain an awareness of "the social life of discourse outside the artist's study, discourse in the open spaces of the public square, streets, cities and villages, of social groups, generations and epochs": the social and philosophical dimension of style that Bakhtin, the Russian formalist, so rightly reminds us of in "The Discourse of the Novel" (*The Dialogic Imagination*, p. 259). Such awareness of voice and the social rhythms of war in *Between the Acts* places Virginia Woolf squarely, if intermittently, in the "real world." However, Bakhtin's theories will carry us only so far in an appreciation of silence and Woolf's style, since he devalues the "subjective" and "individual," as demonstrated in his discussions of Proust and Joyce (*Problems of Dostoevsky's Poetics*, pp. 63–64), in favor of the collective social "reality" and psychology he discerns in the writings of Dostoevsky. Bakhtin's devaluation in theory and practice of interiority and subjectivity in the novel extrapolates to the devaluation of the silent subjective states that preoccupy Woolf, and thus to the neglect of the experience of women. Women, having been sociologically and historically positioned—not in the public-collective but often in the individual-subjective—have traditionally lacked the opportunity to develop a public voice and thus join Bakhtin's chorus of social dialects. Women are sometimes silent, not speaking subjects in Woolf's novels, as described in Chapter 2, but they are definitely "present" and their silence is expressed.

There are also the voices of society and different philosophical discourses. Brenda Silver has noted in her introduction to *Virginia Woolf: Reading Notebooks* that Woolf mentions a projected critical work: "Four Voices: A Discourse for 4 Voices Realism Romance Psychology Poetry" (XLV, A.1, A.2, p. 17) in 1934. And if these discourses were to be sought in the women's voices in *The Waves*, then Realism, Romance, Psychology, and Poetry—different aspects of mind and voice—might well apply to Susan, Jinny, and Rhoda. The gestures of Susan's maternal body, the textures of Jinny's desire, the mystery of Rhoda's dreams, indeed, the "social life of discourse outside the artist's study," as Bakhtin reminds us (*The Dialogic Imagination*, p. 259), enter into the soliloquies of the women in *The Waves*. We can hear the difference between Susan's calm Maternal voice, Jinny's rippling Desire, and Rhoda's vague Dreaminess, aspects of women's private and social selves. Susan's voice is like a lullaby:

Sleep, sleep, I croon, whether it is summer or winter, May or November. Sleep I sing—I, who am unmelodious and hear no music save rustic music when a dog barks, a bell tinkles, or wheels crunch upon the gravel. I sing my song by the fire like an old shell murmuring on the beach. . . . I am no longer January, May or any other season, but am all spun to a fine thread round the cradle, wrapping in a cocoon made of my own blood the delicate limbs of my baby. Sleep, I say. (p. 171)

Jinny's voice, inviting, contains staccato notes of action combined with sentences flowing with desire:

I am rooted, but I flow. All gold, flowing that way, I say to this one, "Come." Rippling black, I say to that one, "No." One breaks off from his station under the glass cabinet. He approaches. He makes towards me. This is the most exciting moment I have ever known. I flutter. I ripple. I stream like a plant in the river, flowing this way, flowing that way, but rooted. (p. 102)

Rhoda's voice is dream-like:

Month by month things are losing their hardness; even my body now lets the light through; my spine is soft like wax near the flame of the candle. I dream. I dream. (p. 45)

These different voices leave the reader not only with the perception of individual minds but also with a sense of the opera of this novel—the centrality of voice. But these are not spoken voices as many critics claim; they are voices of different tones sounded from different aspects of being: sensation, perception, intellect, memory, imagination. Our attention is directed toward the music and collectivity of seven voices, seven aspects of being, a construct of a higher order. Bernard notes that,

Faces recur, faces and faces—they press their beauty to the walls of my bubble— Neville, Susan, Louis, Jinny, Rhoda. How impossible to order them rightly; to detach one separately, or to give the effect of the whole—again like music. What a symphony with its concord and its discord, and its tunes on top and its complicated bass beneath, then grew up! Each played his own tune, fiddle, flute, trumpet, drum or whatever the instrument might be. (p. 256)

Like the characters at the farewell lunch for Percival, we see "a seven-sided flower, many-petalled, red, puce, purple-shaded, stiff with silver-tinted leaves—a whole flower to which every eye brings its own contributions" (p. 127). But the beauty of the seven-sided flower, the seven aspects of mind and discourse represented by the characters, must be "broken" to remain beautiful, to remain fluid. Into this harmony, Woolf introduces the death of Percival and Rhoda, the shocking "gaps" of death in life that, nevertheless, are part of nature's plan and triumph over life.

In *Between the Acts*, on the other hand, Woolf is less concerned with the harmony of voice and nature that preoccupies her in *The Waves*. It is the contrapuntal music generated by all the ambient sounds of the world that focuses her attention: voices speak but so do thoughts, nature, society, and even the unconscious spaces between people. Silence is literally blocked into the text as the unexpressed feelings that occur between the acts of spoken thought are marked on the page. Silence tells the reader to pause and to feel what Woolf suggests. One is impressed with the quality of her attentiveness in this novel: no sound or thought is irrelevant, and all—even interruptions—becomes part of her music. Her ability to listen to voices of all kinds—conscious and unconscious, animate and inanimate, intended and unintended—involves her in extending the borders of the field of sound and thought and narration. This also extends the novel in giving voice to those who cannot always speak for themselves, the voices of the obscure, and it includes the collective voices from society—the journalists, the gramophone, and the war planes as well as the voice of memory and lines of poetry from past voices. In the following passage, Woolf captures the triple melody of the gramophone, the view, and the cows:

The gramophone, while the scene was removed, gently stated certain facts which everybody knew to be perfectly true.

The view repeated in its own way what the tune was saying. The sun was sinking; the colours were merging; and the view was saying how after men toil men rest from their labours; how coolness comes; reason prevails; and having unharnessed the team from the plough, neighbours dig in cottage gardens and lean over cottage gates.

The cows, making a step forward, then stood still, were saying the same thing to perfection.

Folded in this triple melody, the audience sat gazing. (*Between the Acts*, pp. 158–59)

The gramophone, the view, and the cows were all saying the same thing as in a fugue of voices.

FRAMES OF SILENCE

Given this relationship of sound and silence, sound is always present within silence as a possibility, just as silence is always present within sound. Each contains the other and can turn into the other. In the last scene of *Between the Acts*, Isa—whose discordant relationship with her husband, Giles, has been suggested throughout the novel—finally sits down with him to talk. The narrator notes that she "let her sewing drop," reminding us of Penelope upon Odysseus' return home. This Odysseus, Giles, returns to Pointz Hall from work and infidelity. But Woolf enlarges this moment of domestic talk into a cosmic scene in a primitive time of beginnings—the time of cave men with undeveloped language, or the beginning of talk in a marriage relationship:

The great hooded chairs had become enormous. And Giles too. And Isa too against the window. The window was all sky without colour. The house had lost its shelter. It was night before roads were made, or houses. It was the night that dwellers in caves had watched from some high place among the rocks.
    Then the curtain rose. They spoke. (p. 219)

These last words of the novel suggest the growth of talk, human talk, from the silent prelude of the novel. In fact, this novel, like Eric Roehmer's film "Reinette and Mirabelle," is framed by silence. The novel about silence is a prelude to talk. Most of the communication among characters in this novel is inaudible, unspoken but verbally recorded: the silences, the split words, the words of one syllable, the thought without words, the unvoiced poetry, the interrupted conversations, and the unvoiced communication among people. Finally, "they spoke." Silence as in a musical work frames Woolf's novel. She not only suggests that the ending of *Between the Acts* is a beginning, but in doing so questions the borders and frames of words, plays, a play within a play, the novel, and fiction, in general. All open up, deconstruct, re-form. She refuses the usual frames of novelistic discourse.

To schematize what Woolf so gracefully incorporates as part of her style and philosophy, the sound/silence continuum below has been constructed. It illustrates the way sounds grow from so-called silences, with each step reflecting differing degrees and kinds of sound. All this creates a new attention to narrative voice as an organizing force of a broader range of sound, voice, and rhythm in the novel. Proceeding from sounds in nature to letters to syllables to words to voices of various kinds, here is a schema of Woolf's broad sound spectrum in *Between the Acts*:

Sounds of nature (rain, breezes)
Sounds of animals (cows coughing)
Sounds of machines (planes "zoom," gramophones "tick")
Words: letters (separate letters of a word)
Words: syllables (words that are split in two, interrupted)
Words rubbed out: voices of the obscure in history
Words: one syllable (focus on sound)
Words: one syllable (focus on meaning)
Repetition: words of one syllable; nursery rhymes
Human voices:
   Voiced sounds
   Voiced conversation
   Conversation interrupted by self; other people's thoughts;
      other people's voices or conversation; nature; machines
   Inner monologue (includes memory)
   Inner dialogue with others (unspoken, telepathy)
   Poetic voices: lines of poetry voiced and unvoiced
   Historical voices: obscure and great voices performed in the
      play
   Clerical voices
   Journalism: present time
   Megaphone voice: anonymous
   Narrator's voice

In presenting multiple voices and exploring the obscurity of human relationships and the fragmenting effect of the war on institutions and society at home, Virginia Woolf shows the force of cultural disruption in linguistic and aesthetic interruptions. The musical patterns of sound and silence are presented as a counterbalancing and unifying psychological and cultural force during a time of war. However, the ways in which words and language and meaning are deconstructed during a time of war are clearly marked in her text.

The deconstruction of words—their fragmentation, repetition, one-syllabled—throws into relief the "silences" surrounding them. She draws our attention to the fact that language is always saying less about the war than the sum of her experiences: the silence of the incommunicable surrounds them. Miss LaTrobe in *Between the Acts*, for example, asserts the value of one-syllable words in her play. As her historical pageant moves into present time, the actors hold up mirrors to the audience and a voice, "megaphonic, anonymous, loud-speaking," says:

Before we part, ladies and gentlemen, before we go . . . (Those who had risen sat down) . . . let's talk in words of one syllable, without larding, stuffing or cant.

Let's break the rhythm and forget the rhyme. And calmly consider ourselves. Ourselves. Some bony. Some fat. (The glasses confirmed this.) Liars most of us. Thieves too. (The glasses made no comment on that.) The poor are as bad as the rich are. Perhaps worse. Don't hide among rags. Or let our cloth protect us. (p. 187)

The words of one syllable in this context are honest words, without the cant of the multi-syllabled dissemblings of human nature that seeks to mask with language. It reminds us of the "little language" described in *The Waves* as the language "lovers use, words of one syllable such as children speak when they come into a room and find their mother sewing and pick up some scrap of bright wool, a feather, or a shred of chintz" (p. 295).

After the play is over, Miss LaTrobe visits the Inn and has a drink, and again words of one syllable arise, but this time not as sincere words, as in the above passage, but as wonderful sounds: "She raised her glass to her lips. And drank. And listened. Words of one syllable sank down into the mud. She drowsed; she nodded. The mud became fertile. Words rise above the intolerably laden dumb oxen plodding through the mud. Words without meaning—wonderful words" (p. 212). Here Woolf captures a sound-swell as the words of one syllable arise out of Miss LaTrobe's well-earned drunken stupor. Woolf's narration is unique in capturing sensations of sounds before swelling into thoughts and words. But then as she ruminates, as "The cheap clock ticked. . . . Suddenly the tree was pelted with starlings. She set down her glass. She heard the first words" (p. 212). This is a creative moment and suddenly she "hears," one suspects, words that begin another play. Sounds and words of meaning, the art of her play, organically grow out of the silent stir-rings of her mind. Woolf uses the image of the "intolerably laden dumb oxen plodding through the mind" to represent a "dumbness," a much-used Victorian variation on the word "silent," without our pejorative connotations. Dumbness is a drunken, heavy, yet fertile state of mind, referred to in other contexts that precede creativity. This state of mental sluggishness, a stupor of mind that compares to the movement of heavy oxen, prepares, in this context, the ground for fertile thoughts. Sound and meaning and creativity grow out of silence—a particular kind of "dumbness." Similarly, the word "stupid" is related to "dumbness," and in the *Pointz Hall* manuscript, Isa's mind after ruminating about books is compared to "a sea anemone when the feelers are curled up; like a dab of jelly on a plate, reflecting a window pane; placid; stupid" (p. 54). Such "stupid" or "dumb" states of mind are quiescent and fertile.

Somehow language in this novel is "sous-rature," as Derrida might claim: words split, syllables divide, sounds disappear, words are rubbed out and again re-form as soon as they are spoken. This philosophical stance on language—words do not seem to work anymore—leads Woolf to an appreciation of silence.

For example, Woolf targets the profession of the clergy and deconstructs its ineffectual rhetoric in a time of war in the person of the Reverend Streatfield. Woolf sketches him as "a piece of traditional church furniture . . . a butt, a clod, laughed at by looking-glasses; ignored by the cows, condemned by the clouds which continued their majestic rearrangement of the celestial landscape" (p. 190). In this time of war, the words of the clergy are ineffectual cant, Woolf seems to say, and while he is speaking, nature (the breeze and the rustling leaves) and the war machine (planes) play their part in fragmenting and interrupting his words:

His first words (the breeze had risen; the leaves were rustling) were lost. Then he was heard saying: "What." To that word he added another: "Message"; and at last a whole sentence emerged; not comprehensible; say rather audible. . . . Each is part of the whole. Yes, that occurred to me, sitting among you in the audience. . . .
He continued: "But there is still a deficit." . . . "So that each of us who has enjoyed this pageant has still an opp . . . ." The word was cut in two. A zoom severed it. Twelve aeroplanes in perfect formation like a flight of wild duck came overhead. *That* was the music. The audience gaped; the audience gazed. Then zoom became drone. The planes had passed. (pp. 191–93)

The words of the clergy are split in two by the "zoom" of war planes. "That was the music," the reality, brought to the homefront. There is a "gap" between Reverend Streatfield's words and referents; they do not correspond to life as Woolf knows it during the war, and the interruptions in this passage reflect the narrator's control of the contributions of nature and war to his meaning. "Scraps, orts and fragments" of sound and words in the environment become part of the totality—"complete with missing parts" (Beckett, *Tel Quel*).

The ambient sounds of nature that might traditionally be dismissed from the genre of the novel as "irrelevant" also play their part in the music of conversation in *Between the Acts*. The sounds of nature and the voices of people form a pattern. The novel opens:

It was a summer's night and they were talking. . . .
Mrs. Haines, the wife of the gentleman farmer, a goosefaced woman with

eyes protruding as if they saw something to gobble in the gutter, said affectedly: "What a subject to talk about on a night like this!"

Then there was silence; and a cow coughed; and that led her to say how odd it was, as a child, she had never feared cows, only horses. . . .

A bird chuckled outside. "A nightingale?" asked Mrs. Haines. (p. 3)

However, art as well as the institution of religion is deconstructed by nature. Art performed outdoors, Woolf suggests through Miss LaTrobe's play, must incorporate, not oppose, nature (in the Renaissance tradition). Nature too then becomes part author, as in John Cage's theory of music. For example, a chorus of cows fills an empty space in Miss LaTrobe's pageant. The stage was empty for a moment,

Then suddenly, as the illusion petered out, the cows took up the burden. One had lost her calf. In the very nick of time she lifted her great moon-eyed head and bellowed. All the great moon-eyed heads laid themselves back. From cow after cow came the same yearning bellow. The whole world was filled with dumb yearning. It was the primeval voice sounding loud in the ear of the present moment. Then the whole herd caught the infection. . . . The cows annihilated the gap; bridged the distance; filled the emptiness and continued the emotion. (pp. 140–41)

Here the gap, the distance, the emptiness in the play, in art, is "bridged" by nature, the cows. Note that the gap here is an interval of time, a space in the play to be filled, and not the "cut" of the unconscious mind as described in the discussion of *The Waves*. Nature and art are placed on a continuum as the sound of the bellowing cows "continues the emotion" of the play. We sense the presence of the narrator here connecting "scraps, orts and fragments" from nature and art, creating a rhythm from what we traditionally consider salient, the play, as well as the interpolations, nature and its ambient sounds, unacknowledged on the margins.

The humorous bass bellowing of the cows, however, creates a different tonal coloring from the conversational voices of the audience, which fill another "space" between the acts: "They're not ready . . . I hear 'em laughing" (they were saying); ". . . Dressing up. That's the great thing, dressing up. And it's pleasant now, the sun's not so hot. . . . That's one good the war brought us—longer days. . . . Where did we leave off? D'you remember?" (p. 120). Such internal and external chattering touches, nevertheless, on the theme of change in people; it is in a different key and tone from the fugue of human voices at Pointz Hall:

Across the hall a door opened. One voice, another voice, a third voice came wimpling and warbling: gruff—Bart's voice; quavering—Lucy's voice; middle-toned—Isa's voice. Their voices impetuously, impatiently, protestingly came across the hall, saying: "The train's late"; saying: "Keep it hot"; saying: "We won't, no, Candish, we won't wait." (p. 37)

This chorus of human voices, each one another instrument, is yet different from the impersonal, anonymous voice of the artist that comes through the megaphone during the play and the voice of Mr. Page:

It was the other voice speaking, the voice that was no one's voice. And the voice that wept for human pain unending said: The King is in his counting house / Counting out his money / The Queen is in her parlour . . . . Mr. Page, the reporter, licking his pencil noted: "With the very limited means at her disposal, Miss LaTrobe conveyed to the audience Civilization (the wall) in ruins; rebuilt (witness man with hod) by human effort." (p. 181)

Woolf's silences flow out of not only an individual but also a collective memory. Her feeling for words and silence or for solid and void reflect her interest, also, in those not only in the center but also on the margins of society: women, the obscure, the mad. In her introduction to *Life as We Have Known It*, about the Cooperative Working Women's organizations, Woolf notes of the writings of these women:

These pages are only fragments. These voices are beginning only now to emerge from silence into half articulate speech. These lives are still half hidden in profound obscurity. To express even what is expressed here has been a work of labour and difficulty. The writing has been done in kitchens, at odds and ends of leisure, in the midst of distractions and obstacles. (p. xxxix)

Because of this sympathy for obscure lives, Woolf inserts another kind of silence into Miss LaTrobe's play besides the wordless choreography of communication among people in the audience (oratio obliqua) and the sounds of nature. She inserts the village idiot into the play, representing madness or the surfacing of the socially unconscious as well as the historical silence of obscure people in English history. During the historical procession of scenes from English history, she marks the presence of the working class by marching villagers across the stage, representing Chaucer's pilgrims: "All the time the villagers were passing in and out between the trees. They were singing; but only a word or two was audible '. . . *wore ruts in the grass . . . built the house in the lane . . . .*' The wind blew away the connecting words of their chant" (p. 80). However, though the words of the villagers lose their connections, historically "sous-rature" (Derrida), the words being blown away as soon as spoken, Woolf later subjects the words of the great and powerful to the ravaging effects of nature and time also. The great, like the obscure, are leveled and endure historical silence sometimes: "The words died away. Only a few great names—Babylon, Nineveh, Clytemnestra, Agamemnon, Troy—floated across the open space. Then the wind rose, and in the rustle of the leaves even the great words became inaudible; and the audience sat staring at the villagers, whose mouths opened, but no sound came" (p. 140).

By encompassing all these voices in *Between the Acts*, Woolf represents a tonal sense of reality. Since she blends outer and inner voices, the inner ear of the reader is important in interpreting the blend. Different times in the past are voices that submerge the present, and all the variety of society is recognized. Sentences are unfinished, ellipses are frequent, public voices interrupt: all attesting to multiple views and voices that fragment language and life. Whether the plane ("zoom") or the train ("chuff chuff") or the gramophone ("tick tick") or nature (cows, rain, breezes) or the journalist's voice or that of other people, or the self interrupting the self, Woolf is deconstructing language, digressing from the matter at hand, and introducing silence: all to slow down time.

Repetition is another way of putting off the ending and of slowing down the course of time. Bernard, in his summary at the end of *The Waves*, finds repetition in nature, and he states, "Yes, this is the eternal renewal, the incessant rise and fall and fall and rise again" (p. 297), and in considering a certain Miss Jones for marriage, he observes, "And the little fierce beat—tick-tack, tick-tack—of the pulse of one's mind took on a more majestic rhythm" (p. 258). Woolf's new music is grounded in the repetition of verbal elements—as J. Hillis Miller suggests, "words, figures of speech, shapes or gestures, or, more subtly, covert repetitions that act like metaphors" (p. 1). Miller makes a useful distinction between Platonic and Nietzchean repetition: " 'Platonic' repetition is grounded in a solid archetypal model which is untouched by the effects of repetition. . . . The validity of the mimetic copy is established by its truth of correspondence to what it copies. This is, so it seems, the reigning presupposition of realistic fiction and of its critics in the nineteenth and even in twentieth-century England" (p. 6). The other mode of repetition is Nietzchean, which, like Woolf, "posits a world based on difference. Each thing, this other theory would assume, is unique, intrinsically different from every other thing. Similarity arises against the background of this 'disparité du fond.' It is not a world of copies but . . . 'simulacra' or 'phantasms' " (ibid.). Woolf's rhythmic alternating style emerges from this second Nietzchean reading of the world in which identity and difference are established in relation to one another, not in correspondence with a "true" reality. Miller's perspective here, though brilliant in its analysis of the elements of repetition, posits an expectation of harmony, a female rhythm of "filling spaces" (p. 229) that does not go far enough in expanding the field of sound to include the silence that operates in all of Woolf's writing. Woolf's narrative practices and notions of rhythm in the novel exceed Miller's theory.

THE CONTRIBUTION OF SILENCE TO TALK

The deconstruction of words and the patterning of sound and silence in conversation in this novel, as illustrated above, reflect Woolf's theme that silence contributes to talk. In *Between the Acts*, silence is part of a pattern, a space for personal interaction. In breaking from the demand for "realism" in the novel, the demand for so-called objectivity, Woolf makes the novel available for more subjective kinds of experience and response. Silence, for example, marks the "unheard rhythms of . . . [the characters'] own wild hearts" as well as the unconscious rhythms of communication as the narrator moves in and out of various minds, revealing inner lives. Feelings pass between people without any words, and people hear when no words are spoken, representing a kind of telepathy. The telepathy is somehow metaphorically mixed with Woolf's observations of the wireless radio of modern days. She writes of men and women:

Living on a long avenue of brick . . . cut up into boxes, each of which is inhabited by a different human being who has put locks on his doors and bolts on his windows to ensure some privacy, yet is linked to his fellows by wires which pass overhead, by waves of sound which pour through the roof and speak aloud to him of battles and murders and strikes and revolutions all over the world. (*Granite and Rainbow*, p. 15)

The waves that pass overhead in certain of Woolf's rooms are psychic. The communication is often a kind of omnicommunication, in which the unconscious and the discourse of the other are equivalent. It is a kind of communication of which Lacan writes: "The omnipresence of human discourse will perhaps one day be embraced under the open sky of an omnicommunication" (*The Language of the Self*, p. 27).

In a passage of psycho-narration in *Between the Acts* where narrator and character are intertwined, Isa listens and, through this act, contributes silence to the conversation. As Isa listens to the welcoming of Mrs. Manresa and William Dodge to Pointz Hall, the narrator notes her silent participation in the dialogue: "In all this sound of welcome, protestation, apology and again welcome, there was an element of silence, supplied by Isabella, observing the unknown young man" (p. 38). Being a silent observer is an activity for women, a presence, not an absence, as demonstrated in Chapter 2.

Often men and women in intimate relationships communicate word-lessly, as do Mr. and Mrs. Ramsay or Peter and Mrs. Dalloway. In *Between the Acts*, Isa often guesses the words that her husband, Giles, has not spoken. Isa is also attracted to William Dodge, and she communicates on an unconscious level with him. At one point in the novel,

> He [Giles] said (without words), "I'm damnably unhappy."
> "So am I," Dodge echoed.
> "And I too," Isa thought.
> They were all caught and caged; prisoners; watching a spectacle. Nothing happened. (p. 176)

Later Giles, who works in the city, comes to Pointz Hall for the weekend to find Mrs. Manresa and William Dodge, strangers, among the family. He too, the narrator notes, contributes silence to talk, like Isa: "What for did a good sort like the woman Manresa bring these half-breeds in her trail? [William] Giles asked himself. And his silence made its con-tribution to talk—Dodge that is, shook his head. 'I like that picture.' That was all he could bring himself to say" (p. 49). Such communication, "thought without words," is not unusual in this novel. Even though there is more focus on human relationships here than in *The Waves*, people often interact in concord or discord unconsciously, not through direct discourse. The pattern of relationship, abstract, has a kind of ping-pong effect on the reader as he watches a small white dot of thought play about the room, moving from one person or one level of reality or con-versation to another. It is a certain kind of unconscious "talk," heard though unspoken—somehow between the acts of consciousness in the recesses of the unconscious. Isa, preoccupied with her inner voices, lines of poetry continually running through her mind, mutters to herself at one point and is overheard by William Dodge. That he responds to her unvoiced yearnings shocks her and "She flushed, as if she had spoken in an empty room and someone had stepped out from behind a cur-tain" (p. 51). Woolf allows these sub-rosa dialogues to surface as if they were actual conversations, but they have the still rhythms of thought that appeal to the poetic, not the conversational, ear. Woolf admits these silent dialogues—"the things people don't say"—about taboo subjects (madness, unhappiness, marginality, sexuality) and multiplies the forces in the field of the novel.

Perhaps if Woolf had not been a woman, if she had not—despite her privileged upbringing—worked with women's organizations, lectured to working-class women at Morley College in 1906, and joined the Sussex Village Labour Party, she might not have had this concern with women, the obscure, the mad—those on the margins of society. In *Between the Acts* her thematic silences are more often associated with art and women than with nature, as in *The Waves*, and she is particularly preoccupied with silent women framed in portraits at Pointz Hall. The "silence" of these women frozen in art (a permanent looking-glass) is collective and expands outward in history. In describing two pictures of ancestors at Pointz Hall, a man and a lady, the narrator of *Between the Acts* comments:

He was a talk producer, that ancestor. But the lady was a picture. In her yellow robe, leaning, with a pillar to support her . . . she led the eye up, down, from the curve to the straight, through glades of greenery and shades of silver, dun and rose into silence. The room was empty.
Empty, empty, empty; silent, silent, silent. The room was a shell. (p. 36)

Not only does the lady lead the viewer "through glades of greenery . . . into silence," but the repetition of the words "empty" and "silent" also creates a kind of stillness and "slow time," as in Keats's "Ode on a Grecian Urn." The woman is a suggestive presence, not a "talk producer," whose actual and metaphysical function in the text is to present perhaps another way of being, a question, an alternative view, an insight, a possibility, a darkness, a mystery, another kind of consciousness. The silence not only comments on Woolf's historical sense of the evolving concept of woman, but also represents the indeterminacies in life. The inclusion of the silent presence of the woman in the portrait is mesmerizing, and William Dodge withdraws from conversation to look at the picture again: "They all looked at him. 'I was looking at the pictures.' The picture looked at nobody. The picture drew them down paths of silence" (p. 45). The silence of woman incites wonder, and they are drawn into the silence of the "zone of art."

The study of these rhythms in Woolf's writing draws us, as readers, down new narrative paths of silence—for the use of musical experience in the analysis of literature brings into sharper relief Virginia Woolf's expression of silence through a variety of narrative techniques.

Conclusion

THIS EXPLORATION of the theme, philosophy, and narration of "silence" in the novels of Virginia Woolf brings under scrutiny nothing less than the nature of gender, mind, being, knowledge, and language. In re-defining silence as a "presence," and not just an "absence" in life and narration, Woolf displaces the privileged place of the "speaking subject" and speech or dialogue as the only markers of presence in the novel. Like Derrida and Rousseau, she "is suspicious . . . of the illusion of full and present speech. . . . It is toward the praise of silence that the myth of a full presence wrenched from différance and from the violence of the word is then deviated" (*Of Grammatology*, p. 140). Woolf's "writing" of silence or perhaps arche-writing—"to think the unique within the system" (ibid., p. 112)—was explored in Chapters 1 and 3. There we found that Woolf is searching for a language of mind in the midst of concepts of mind in the twentieth century, and so she creates a lexicon of silence, a punctuation of suspension, metaphors, and scenes of silence that signal mind, particularly the unconscious, in fiction.

This marking of the presence of mind in narration is not just a formalist preoccupation of Woolf, however; it is intertwined with her perceptions of the social roles of men and women and a worldview. Talk, more often associated with men in Woolf's novels, has traditionally been valued as "presence mastered" (*Of Grammatology*, p. 159); women's silence, on the other hand, is marked as absence. However, as illustrated in Chapter 2, female authors are suspicious of the myth of "full presence" in speech and find methodologies to "sound" women's minds and silences. They represent women in a tradition of developing inwardness: Jane Austen creates observing women in her late novels, the women she knew so well from common sitting rooms; Charlotte Brontë develops soliloquies in female characters, adapting the seventeenth-century meditative tradition for women's use; and Woolf traces the inner fluency of thought and dreams in women, structuring silences into the text so that the reader can consult his mind. Silence in women is not viewed as a sign of personal or social oppression by these authors; it is a space in which to observe, to think, and to dream, and it is infused with a new psychic and narrative life. It is an enlightened "absence."

This perspective contrasts with the representation of women's silences in selected novels of eighteenth- and nineteenth-century male authors in Chapter 2. Here the gaps, blanks, "dumbness," and silence of women in the text are mimetic, and are marked to reflect women's absence from the social, public, and historical spheres of life. Women, in this tradition, are viewed from the "outside," like the legendary Mrs. Brown. However, women writing in the tradition of Virginia Woolf free female characters from dependency on social facts and subjective imprisonment, creating a space limned from the "inside."

If woman is no longer an "object" who is watched, gazed upon, restricted, and marginalized, then we can posit, along with Woolf, a new way of being and knowing for a woman dreamer, thinker, listener, observer, and reader of life. In valuing and preserving the "différance"— the silence of women as well as their language in her texts—Woolf is describing women in her time and place: undefined and evolving. Similarly, in the post-modern view of Woolf presented in this work, a static valorization of the silent woman is not advanced; rather, a process of reading her and her silences anew as enlightened and creative absence is presented. Within this position of flux, it is also acknowledged that women move in and out of silence, even today, as they evolve and become actors and participants in public and professional spheres in ways unknown to Woolf.

Woolf, in valuing and preserving the psychological, social, historical, and philosophical silences along with the silences of women in her texts, is also questioning the nature of knowledge and the logocentrism of those positioned like Mr. Ramsay, whose mind is "like the keyboard of a piano . . . [or] like the alphabet is ranged in twenty-six letters all in order" (*To the Lighthouse*, p. 53). In doing so, she practices a deconstructive form of writing. She, like Nietzsche and Derrida, is criticizing the logocentrism of Western thought, and she unmasks, through certain kinds of silence, including women's silence and presence, men's claims to systematic knowledge, the expressiveness of the Western alphabet and language, in general. She perceives women in the "phallic shadow" and suggests through the image of the "arid scimitar" the sterility of the need to dominate, or what Christopher Norris, the deconstructionist critic, labels "the intellectual will-to-power." She embodies women's ways of being and knowing in her novels, and "being" for the major female characters discussed in this work—Rachel of *The Voyage Out*; Mrs. Dalloway; Lily and Mrs. Ramsay of *To the Lighthouse*; Rhoda of *The Waves*; and Isa of *Between the Acts*—includes silence as well as language in narration: twin houses of being.

Finally, the reader of silence is implicated in the text in a new way in Woolf's novels, for she or he must join with the writer to understand and decipher the silences in the novel: a mode of subjectivity. As Foucault states, "the novelty lies no longer in what is said, but in its repetition. . . . Commentary's only role is to say finally, what has silently been articulated deep down" (*The Discourse on Language*, p. 221). Chapter 5 articulated the depths of the underside of the mind—the unspoken, the unsaid, the unsayable—as revealed in the varied and alternating rhythm of Woolf's style, an important and uncharted dimension of her style.

In questioning the nature of being and knowing through the concepts of presence and absence and men's "speech" and women's "silence," Woolf is also questioning the nature of language. She seeks ways of escaping language through spatializing thought and expressing mind through gestures of the body, as discussed in Chapters 4 and 5. For in exploring that which is unsaid, she is exploring what happens in the hiatus between word and thing. If, as Gérard Genette states, silence is one of the "signs by which literature draws attention to itself and points out its mask" (p. 28), then Woolf, in using silence more often than other modern authors, disturbs notions of language and narration. In rupturing the belief in the link between the word and the thing or "actuality," in acknowledging the silence, the ineffable, the limitations of language and interpretation, she questions language. As Derrida states in "The Violence of the Letter": "By one and the same gesture (alphabetic writing), servile instrument of a speech dreaming of its plenitude and its self-presence, is scorned and the dignity of writing is refused to non-alphabetic signs" (*Of Grammatology*, p. 109). If the alphabet is viewed as a metaphor of mind (Mr. Ramsay's getting to "R") and is a "servile instrument of speech," then we must restore the "dignity" that Derrida speaks of to the "nonalphabetic" signs of silence. And in learning to read Woolf's many silences—psychological, social, historical, philo-sophical, rhythmic, and structural—expressed in theme and method-ology, we become readers of a new rhetoric of silence.

Many critics have developed opposing theories of Woolf: a "real-ist" because of her faithful description of women's lives; a "modernist" because she breaks with literary conventions and normative structures; a realist manqué because of her Bloomsbury aestheticism; a modernist manqué because of her search for harmony in fragmentation. However, it is now the moment in Woolf criticism for viewing her seeming oppo-sitions as part of a pattern. As Poulet says, "On the one hand, every-thing becomes suspense, fragmentary arrangement, with alternation and opposite terms; on the other hand, everything contributes to the total rhythm." Together these movements, "complete with missing parts," con-stitute the experience of the lived moment that Woolf seeks to capture.

What can we say, then, that Woolf makes of silence in narration? In changing the metaphor of silence to one of value and presence rather than absence and negation, she changes the meaning of silence and in-fuses it with a new psychic life. Silence becomes a part of the whole, a constituent part of narration as she "traces the patterns of the mind" and its relation to women's ways of knowing and being. This relates not only to the methods used to place the many kinds of silence in a text, but also to a larger ensemble of relationships and "différance" in life—men and women, presence and absence, stasis and flux, language and silence—"to give the moment whole; whatever it includes."

WORKS CITED

Works Cited

Abel, Elizabeth. "Cam the Wicked: Woolf's Portrait of the Artist as her Father's Daughter." In Jane Marcus, ed., *Virginia Woolf and Bloomsbury: A Centenary Celebration*. Bloomington: Indiana Univ. Press, 1985.

———. "Narrative Structures and Female Development: The Case of Mrs. Dalloway." In Elizabeth Abel, Marianne Hirsch, and Elizabeth Langland, eds., *The Voyage In: Fictions of Female Development*. Hanover: Univ. Press of New Hampshire, 1983.

Abrams, M. H. *The Mirror and the Lamp: Romantic Theory and the Critical Tradition*. New York: Oxford Univ. Press, 1953.

———. *Natural Supernaturalism*. New York: Norton, 1971.

Anderson, Laurie. "Laurie Anderson Sings the Body Electric." *New York Times*, Oct. 1, 1989, pp. 1 and 41.

Ardener, Shirley, ed. *Perceiving Women*. London: Malaby Press, 1975.

Austen, Jane. *Emma*. 1816. Reprint. Ed. Lionel Trilling. Boston: Houghton Mifflin, 1957.

———. *Mansfield Park*. 1814. Reprint. Boston: Houghton Mifflin, 1965.

———. *Persuasion*. 1818. Reprint. Ed. R. W. Chapman. London and New York: Oxford Univ. Press, 1932.

Bachelard, Gaston. *The Poetics of Space*. Trans. Maria Jolas. New York: Orion Press, 1964.

Bakhtin, M. M. *The Dialogic Imagination*. Trans. Michael Holquist. Austin: Univ. of Texas Press, 1981.

———. *Problems of Dostoevsky's Poetics*. Trans. and ed. Caryl Emerson. Minneapolis: Univ. of Minnesota Press, 1984.

Beckett, Samuel. *Proust and Three Dialogues with Georges Duthuit*. London: Calder and Boyars, 1965.

————. "Tel Quel." In *Proust and 3 Dialogues with Georges Duthuit*. London: Calder and Boyars, 1965.

Beer, Gillian. "Beyond Determinism: George Eliot and Virginia Woolf." In *Arguing with the Past: Essays in Narration from Woolf to Sidney*. London: Routledge, 1989.

Belenky, Mary, Blythe Clinchy, Nancy Goldberger, and Jill Tarule. *Women's Ways of Knowing*. New York: Basic Books, 1986.

Bell, Quentin. *Virginia Woolf: A Biography*. New York: Harcourt Brace Jovanovich, 1972.

Bowlby, Rachel. *Virginia Woolf: Feminist Destinations*. Oxford: Basil Blackwell, 1988.

Breuer, Josef. *Studies in Hysteria*. Boston: Beacon Press, 1950.

Brontë, Charlotte. *Jane Eyre*. 1847. Reprint. New York: New American Library, 1960.

————. *Villette*. 1853. Reprint. London: Oxford Univ. Press, 1963.

Browne, E. K. *Rhythm in the Novel*. Toronto: Toronto Univ. Press, 1950.

Browning, Robert. *Robert Browning: The Poems*. Ed. John Pettigrew. New Haven and London: Yale Univ. Press, 1981.

Burrows, J. F. "Lively Measures." In *Computation Into Criticism*. Oxford: Clarendon Press, 1987.

Cage, John. *Silence*. Middleton: Wesleyan Univ. Press, 1961.

Calvino, Italo. *Six Memos for the Next Millennium*. Trans. Patrick Creagh. Cambridge, Mass.: Harvard Univ. Press, 1988.

Caramagno, Thomas. "Manic-Depressive Psychosis and Critical Approaches to Virginia Woolf's Life and Work." *PMLA* 103, no. 1 (1988): 10–23.

Caws, Mary Ann. *Reading Frames in Modern Fiction*. Princeton: Princeton Univ. Press, 1985.

————. ed. *Textual Analysis*. New York: Modern Language Association, 1986.

————. *Women of Bloomsbury: Virginia, Vanessa, Carrington*. London: Routledge, 1990.

Chadwick, Whitney. *Women Artists and the Surrealist Movement*. Boston: Little Brown, 1985.

Charcot, Jean Martin. *Iconographie Photographique de la Salpêtrière*. 3 vols. Paris: Lecrosnier et Babe, 1888.

Cixous, Hélène. "The Laugh of the Medusa." In Elaine Marks and Isabelle de Courtivron, eds., *New French Feminisms*. Amherst: Univ. of Massachusetts Press, 1980.

Cohn, Dorrit. *Transparent Minds*. Princeton: Princeton Univ. Press, 1978.

Cone, Edward T. *Musical Form and Musical Performance*. New York: Norton, 1968.

Cornuaille, Heldris de. *Le Roman de Silence: A 13th-Century Arthurian Verse-Romance*. Reprint. Cambridge, Engl.: Heffer, 1972.

Culler, Jonathan. *On Deconstruction: Theory and Criticism After Structuralism*. Ithaca: Cornell Univ. Press, 1982.

Defoe, Daniel. *Moll Flanders*. 1722. Reprint. Ed. Harold Bloom. New York: Chelsea House, 1987.

de la Cruz, Sor Juana Inés. *A Woman of Genius: The Intellectual Autobiography of Sor Juana Inés de la Cruz.* Trans. and Intro. Margaret Sayers Peden. Salisbury, Conn.: Lime Rock Press, 1987.

de Man, Paul. *Blindness and Insight: Essay in the Rhetoric of Contemporary Criticism.* 2d rev. ed. Minneapolis: Univ. of Minnesota Press, 1983.

Derrida, Jacques. *Speech and Phenomena, and Other Essays on Husserl's Theory of Signs.* Trans. David B. Allison. Evanston: Northwestern Univ. Press, 1967.

———. *Of Grammatology.* Baltimore and London: Johns Hopkins Univ. Press, 1974.

———. "Structure, Sign and Play." In Richard Macksay and Eugenio Donato, eds., *The Structuralist Controversy.* Baltimore: Johns Hopkins Univ. Press, 1972.

———. "The Voice That Keeps Silence." In *Speech and Phenomena, and Other Essays on Husserl's Theory of Signs.* Trans. David B. Allison. Evanston: Northwestern Univ. Press, 1967.

deSalvo, Louise. *Virginia Woolf: The Impact of Childhood Sexual Abuse on Her Life and Work.* Boston: Beacon Press, 1989.

DiBattista, Maria. "The Clandestine Fictions of Marguerite Duras." In Ellen G. Friedman and Miriam Fuchs, eds., *Breaking the Sequence: Women's Experimental Fiction.* Princeton: Princeton Univ. Press, 1989.

Dickens, Charles. *Hard Times.* 1854. Reprint. New York and Toronto: New American Library, 1961.

Dinesen, Isak. *Last Tales.* New York: Random House, 1957.

Donoghue, Denis. "A Criticism of One's Own." *The New Republic* (March 10, 1986): 30–34.

Eagleton, Terry. *The Rape of Clarissa: Writing, Sexuality and Class Struggle in Samuel Richardson.* Minneapolis: Univ. of Minnesota Press, 1982.

Edel, Leon. *The Psychological Novel: 1900–1950.* Philadelphia: Lippincott, 1955.

Edwards, Lee. "Schizophrenic Nature." *The Journal of Narrative Technique* 19, no. 1 (1989): 25–30.

Emerson, Ralph Waldo. *Essays.* New York: Grosset and Dunlap, 1948.

Empson, William. "Virginia Woolf." In Edgell Rickword, comp., *Scrutinies by Various Writers.* Vol. 2. London: Wishart, 1931.

Ernst, Max. *Une Semaine de Bonté.* Paris: J. Bucher, 1934.

Felman, Shoshana. *Writing and Madness.* Trans. Martha Noel Evans. Ithaca: Cornell Univ. Press, 1985.

Fetterly, Judith. *The Resisting Reader.* Bloomington: Indiana Univ. Press, 1978.

Fielding, Henry. *Tom Jones.* 1749. Reprint. New York: Modern Library, 1950.

Fleischman, Avrom. *Virginia Woolf: A Critical Reading.* Baltimore: Johns Hopkins Univ. Press, 1975.

Forster, E. M. *Virginia Woolf.* New York: Harcourt Brace, 1942.

Foucault, Michel. *Discipline and Punish: The Birth of a Prison.* Trans. Alan Sheridan. New York: Pantheon, 1977.

———. "The Discourse on Language." *Orders of Discourse* 10 (Apr. 1971): 7–30.

————. *The Foucault Reader*. Ed. Paul Rabinow. New York: Pantheon, 1984.

————. *The Order of Things: An Archaeology of the Human Sciences*. New York: Vintage Books, 1973.

Freud, Sigmund. *Dora: An Analysis of a Case of Hysteria*. New York: Macmillan, 1963.

————. *A General Introduction to Psychoanalysis*. New York: Liveright, 1920.

————. *The Interpretation of Dreams*. Trans. and Ed. James Strachey. New York: Basic Books, 1965.

————. *The Standard Edition of the Complete Psychological Works of Sigmund Freud*. Trans. James Strachey. 24 vols. London: Hogarth Press, 1953–1974.

Gallop, Jane. *The Daughter's Seduction: Feminism and Psychoanalysis*. Ithaca, N.Y.: Cornell Univ. Press, 1982.

Gauthier, Xavière. "Is There Such a Thing as Women's Writing?" In Elaine Marks and Isabelle de Courtivron, eds., *New French Feminisms*. Amherst: Univ. of Massachusetts Press, 1980.

Geertz, Clifford. *Works and Lives: The Anthropologist as Author*. Stanford: Stanford Univ. Press, 1988.

Genette, Gérard. *Figures of Literary Discourse*. Trans. Alan Sheridan. New York: Columbia Univ. Press, 1982.

Gilbert, Sandra. "Woman's Sentence, Man's Sentencing." In Gilbert and Gubar, *No Man's Land*.

Gilbert, Sandra, and Susan Gubar. *The Madwoman in the Attic*. New Haven: Yale Univ. Press, 1979.

————. *No Man's Land*. New Haven: Yale Univ. Press, 1988.

————, eds. *Shakespeare's Sisters: Feminist Essays on Women Poets*. Bloomington: Indiana Univ. Press, 1979.

Gilligan, Carol. *In a Different Voice: Women's Conceptions of Self and Morality*. Cambridge, Mass.: Harvard Univ. Press, 1982.

Gordon, Lyndall. *Virginia Woolf: A Writer's Life*. New York: Norton, 1984.

Hardy, Thomas. *The Mayor of Casterbridge*. New York: Modern Library, 1950.

Hartman, Geoffrey H. *The Fate of Reading*. Chicago: Univ. of Chicago Press, 1975.

————. "Virginia's Web." In *Beyond Formalism: Literary Essays, 1958–1970*. New Haven: Yale Univ. Press, 1970.

Haule, James M., and Philip Smith, comp. and eds. *A Concordance to 'To the Lighthouse,' 'The Years,' 'The Waves,' 'Between the Acts.'* London: Oxford Microform Publishers, 1981–84.

Heidegger, Martin. *On the Way to Language*. Trans. Peter Hertz. San Francisco: Harper and Row, 1959.

Hunter, Dianne. "Hysteria, Psychoanalysis, and Feminism: The Case of Anna O." In Shirley Nelson Garner, Claire Kahane, and Medelon Sprengnether, eds., *The Mother Tongue*. Ithaca and London: Cornell Univ. Press, 1985.

Hunter, Dianne, Lenora Champagne, and Judy Dworin. "Dr. Charcot's Hysteria Show." Theater and dance piece. New York, June 1989.

Hurston, Zora Neale. *Their Eyes Were Watching God*. Urbana: Univ. of Illinois Press, 1978.

Hussey, Mark. *The Singing of the Real World*. Columbus: Ohio State Univ. Press, 1986.

Ingarden, Roman. *Problems of Literary Evaluation*. University Park: Pennsylvania State Univ. Press, 1969.

——. *The Literary Work of Art*. Trans. George G. Grabowicz. Evanston: Northwestern Univ. Press, 1973.

Irigaray, Luce. *This Sex Which Is Not One*. Trans. Catherine Porter. Ithaca: Cornell Univ. Press, 1985.

Jacobus, Mary, ed. "Beyond Determinism: George Eliot and Virginia Woolf." In *Women Writing and Writing About Women*. London: Croom Helm; Totowa, N.J.: Barnes and Noble, 1979.

Jay, Martin. "In the Empire of the Gaze: Foucault and the Denigration of Vision in Twentieth-Century French Thought." In David Couzens Hoy, ed., *Foucault: A Critical Reader*. Oxford: Basil Blackwell, 1986.

Johnson, Barbara. *The Critical Difference: Essays in the Contemporary Rhetoric of Reading*. Baltimore: Johns Hopkins Univ. Press, 1981.

——. "Nothing Fails Like Success." In *Deconstructive Criticism: Directions*. SCE Reports 8 (1980): 9–10.

——. "Rigorous Unreliability." *Critical Inquiry* 2 (1984): 278–85.

Jones, Ernest. *The Life and Work of Sigmund Freud*. Vol. 1. New York: Basic Books, 1953.

Joubert, Joseph. *The Notebooks of Joseph Joubert: A Selection*. 1867. Reprint. Ed. and trans. Paul Auster. San Francisco: North Point Press, 1983.

Joyce, James. *Letters of James Joyce*. Ed. Richard Ellmann. Vol. 3. New York: Viking Press, 1966.

——. *Ulysses*. New York: Modern Library, 1961.

Kammer, Jeanne. "The Art of Silence and the Forms of Women's Poetry." In Sandra Gilbert and Susan Gubar, eds., *Shakespeare's Sisters: Feminist Essays on Women Poets*. Bloomington: Indiana Univ. Press, 1979.

Kearns, Michael. *Metaphors of Mind in Fiction and Psychology*. Lexington: Univ. Press of Kentucky, 1987.

Kenner, Hugh. "Bloomsbury." In *A Sinking Island: The Modern English Writers*. London: Barrie and Jenkins, 1988.

Kermode, Frank. *The Romantic Image*. London: Routledge and Kegan Paul, 1961.

Kierkegaard, Soren. *Fear and Trembling, Repetition*. Trans. and ed. Howard U. Hong and Edna H. Hong. Princeton: Princeton Univ. Press, 1983.

Kolodny, Annette. "Dancing Through the Minefields." In Elaine Showalter, ed., *New Feminist Criticism: Essays on Women, Literature and Theory*. New York: Pantheon, 1985.

Kristeva, Julia. *Desire in Language: A Semiotic Approach to Literature and Art*. Trans. Thomas Gora, Alice Jardine, and Leon Roudiez. New York: Columbia Univ. Press, 1980.

———. *Kristeva Reader*. Ed. Toril Moi. New York: Columbia Univ. Press, 1986.

———. "Oscillation Between Power and Denial." In Claire Marks and Isabelle de Courtivron, eds., *New French Feminisms*. Amherst: Univ. of Massachusetts Press, 1980.

———. *Revolution in Poetic Language*. Trans. Margaret Waller. New York: Columbia Univ. Press, 1984.

———. "Women Can Never Be Defined." In Claire Marks and Isabelle de Courtivron, eds., *New French Feminisms*. Amherst: Univ. of Massachusetts Press, 1980.

Kuhn, Thomas S. *The Structure of a Scientific Revolution*. Chicago: Univ. of Chicago Press, 1970.

Kundera, Milan. *The Unbearable Lightness of Being*. Trans. Michael Henry Heins. New York: Harper and Row, 1984.

Lacan, Jacques. *Écrits: A Selection*. Trans. Alan Sheridan. New York: Norton, 1977.

———. *The Four Fundamental Concepts of Psychoanalysis*. Ed. Jacques Alain Miller. Trans. Alan Sheridan. New York: Norton, 1978.

———. *The Language of the Self*. Trans. Anthony Wilden. Baltimore: Johns Hopkins Univ. Press, 1968.

Leaska, Mitchell. *Virginia Woolf's Lighthouse: A Study in Critical Method*. New York: Columbia Univ. Press, 1970.

Leavis, F. R. *The Great Tradition*. New York: George W. Stewart, 1952.

Marcus, Jane. *Virginia Woolf and the Languages of Patriarchy*. Bloomington: Indiana Univ. Press, 1987.

Mazzeo, Joseph A. "St. Augustine's Rhetoric of Silence." *Journal of the History of Ideas* 23 (1962): 175–96.

Meisel, Perry. *The Absent Father: Virginia Woolf and Walter Pater*. New Haven: Yale Univ. Press, 1980.

Mendelson, Edward. "The Death of Mrs. Dalloway: Two Readings." In M. A. Caws, ed., *Textual Analysis*. New York: Modern Language Association, 1986.

Meredith, George. *The Egoist*. London: Constable, 1909.

Meyer, Leonard. "The End of the Renaissance." *Hudson Review* 16 (1963):169–86.

———. *Music, the Arts, and Ideas: Patterns and Predictions in Twentieth-Century Culture*. Chicago and London: Univ. of Chicago Press, 1967.

Meyersohn, Marylea. "What Fanny Knew: A Quiet Auditor of the Whole." In Janet Todd, ed., *Jane Austen: New Perspectives*. New York: Holmes and Meier, 1983.

Miller, J. Hillis. *Fiction and Repetition: Seven English Novels*. Cambridge, Mass.: Harvard Univ. Press, 1982.

Minow-Pinkney, Makiko. *Virginia Woolf and the Problem of the Subject*. New Brunswick: Rutgers Univ. Press, 1987.

Moi, Toril. *Sexual/Textual Politics*. London and New York: Methuen, 1985.

Moore, G. E. *Proof of an External World*. London: H. Milford, 1939.

Naremore, James. *The World Without a Self*. New Haven: Yale Univ. Press, 1972.

Nicholson, Nigel. *Portrait of a Marriage.* New York: Atheneum, 1973.

Olsen, Tillie. *Silences.* New York: Delacorte Press, 1978.

Owen, A. R. G. *Hysteria, Hypnosis and Healing: The Work of J. M. Charcot.* New York: Garrett, 1971.

Pinter, Harold. *Plays.* London: Methuen, 1981.

Poulet, George. *The Interior Distance.* Trans. E. Coleman. Baltimore: Johns Hopkins Univ. Press, 1959.

Richardson, Dorothy M. *Pilgrimage I. Pointed Roofs.* New York: Knopf, 1967.

Richardson, Samuel. *Clarissa.* 1748–49. Reprint. Ed. Angus Ross. New York: Viking, 1985.

Richter, Harvena. *Virginia Woolf: The Inward Voyage.* Princeton: Princeton Univ. Press, 1970.

Rose, Phyllis. *Woman of Letters: A Life of Virginia Woolf.* New York: Oxford Univ. Press, 1978.

Rousseau, Jean Jacques. *On the Origin of Language.* Trans. John H. Moran and Alexander Gode. New York: F. Ungar, 1967.

Rubin, Lillian Breslow. *Worlds of Pain.* New York: Basic Books, 1976.

Ruotolo, Lucio. *The Interrupted Moment.* Stanford: Stanford Univ. Press, 1986.

Said, Edward W. *The World, the Text and the Critic.* Cambridge, Mass.: Harvard Univ. Press, 1983.

Salvaggio, Ruth. "Theory and Space, Space and Woman." *Tulsa Studies in Women's Literature* 7, no. 2 (1988): 261–82.

Saussure, Ferdinand de. *Course in General Linguistics.* Trans. Wade Baskin. New York: McGraw-Hill, 1966.

Saville-Troike, Muriel. "The Place of Silence in an Integrated Theory of Communication." In Tannen and Saville-Troike, eds., *Perspectives on Silence.*

Scollon, Ron. "The Machine Stops: Silence in the Metaphor of Malfunction." In Tannen and Saville-Troike, eds., *Perspectives on Silence.*

Showalter, Elaine. *The Female Malady.* New York: Pantheon, 1986.

———, ed. *New Feminist Criticism: Essays on Women, Literature and Theory.* New York: Pantheon, 1985.

Silver, Brenda. " 'Anon' and 'The Reader': Virginia Woolf's Last Essays." *Twentieth Century Literature* 25, no. 3/4 (1979): 356–441.

———. *Virginia Woolf: Reading Notebooks.* Princeton: Princeton Univ. Press, 1983.

Squier, Susan M. *Virginia Woolf and London: Sexual Politics of the City.* Chapel Hill: Univ. of North Carolina Press, 1985.

Steiner, George. *Language and Silence: Essays on Language, Literature, and the Inhuman.* New York: Atheneum, 1967.

———. *On Difficulty and Other Essays.* Oxford: Oxford Univ. Press, 1978.

———. *Real Presences.* Chicago: Univ. of Chicago Press, 1989.

Sterne, Laurence. *Tristram Shandy.* 1759. Reprint. Ed. James A. Work. New York: Odysseus Press, 1940.

Tannen, Deborah, and Muriel Saville-Troike, eds. *Perspectives on Silence.* Norwood, N.J.: Ablex, 1985.

Thackeray, William M. *Vanity Fair.* New York: New American Library, 1962.

Trilling, Lionel. *Sincerity and Authenticity*. Cambridge, Mass., and London: Harvard Univ. Press, 1971.

Vickers, Brian. *In Defense of Rhetoric*. Oxford: Clarendon Press, 1988.

Wong, Sau Ling. "A Study of Roger Fry and Virginia Woolf from a Chinese Perspective." Ph.D. diss., Stanford Univ., 1978.

Woolf, Virginia. *Between the Acts*. New York: Harcourt Brace Jovanovich, 1941.

——. *Collected Essays*. 4 vols. New York: Harcourt Brace Jovanovich, 1967.

——. *The Common Reader*. First Series. New York: Harcourt Brace Jovanovich, 1925.

——. *The Complete Shorter Fiction of Virginia Woolf*. Ed. Susan Dick. New York: Harcourt Brace Jovanovich, 1985.

——. *Contemporary Writers*. New York: Harcourt Brace Jovanovich, 1965.

——. *The Death of the Moth*. New York: Harcourt Brace Jovanovich, 1942.

——. *The Diary of Virginia Woolf*. Ed. Anne Olivier Bell. Intro. Quentin Bell. 5 vols. New York: Harcourt Brace Jovanovich, 1977–84.

——. *Granite and Rainbow*. New York: Harcourt Brace Jovanovich, 1958.

——. Introductory letter to *Life as We Have Known It*. By Cooperative Working Women. Ed. Margaret Llewelyn Davies. London: Hogarth Press, 1931.

——. *Jacob's Room*. New York: Harcourt Brace Jovanovich, 1922.

——. *The Letters of Virginia Woolf*. Ed. Nigel Nicholson and Joanne Trautmann. 5 vols. New York: Harcourt Brace Jovanovich, 1975.

——. *The Moment and Other Essays*. New York: Harcourt Brace Jovanovich, 1948.

——. *Moments of Being*. Ed. Jeanne Schulkind. New York: Harcourt Brace Jovanovich, 1978.

——. *Mrs. Dalloway*. New York: Harcourt Brace Jovanovich, 1925.

——. *Night and Day*. New York: Harcourt Brace Jovanovich, 1948.

——. *Orlando*. New York: Harcourt Brace Jovanovich, 1928.

——. *Pointz Hall: The Earlier and Later Typescripts of 'Between the Acts.'* Ed. Mitchell Leaska. New York: University Publishers, 1983.

——. *A Room of One's Own*. New York: Harcourt Brace Jovanovich, 1929.

——. *The Second Common Reader*. New York: Harcourt Brace Jovanovich, 1932.

——. "Speech Before the London/National Society for Women's Service, January 21, 1931." In Mitchell A. Leaska, ed., *'The Pargiters': The Novel-Essay Portion of 'The Years.'* New York: New York Public Library, 1977.

——. *Three Guineas*. New York: Harcourt Brace Jovanovich, 1938.

——. *To the Lighthouse*. New York: Harcourt Brace Jovanovich, 1927.

——. *To the Lighthouse: The Original Holograph Draft*. Transcribed and ed. Susan Dick. Toronto: Univ. of Toronto Press, 1928.

——. *The Voyage Out*. New York: Harcourt Brace Jovanovich, 1915.

——. *The Waves*. New York: Harcourt Brace Jovanovich, 1931.

——. *The Years*. New York: Harcourt Brace Jovanovich, 1937.

Zwerdling, Alex. *Virginia Woolf and the Real World*. Berkeley: Univ. of California Press, 1986.

Index

In this index an "f" after a number indicates a separate reference on the next page, and an "ff" indicates separate references on the next two pages. A continuous discussion over two or more pages is indicated by a span of page numbers, e.g., "57–59." *Passim* is used for a cluster of references in close but not continuous sequence.

238   *Index*

Semaine de Bonté (Ernst), 125–28 *passim*,
133–36 *passim*, 159, 169
Semantics, structural, 111, 113
Semi-colon, 92
Semiotics, 86; Kristeva and, 42, 57, 69–
70, 88, 125; Woolf and, 42, 69–70,
187; male novelists and, 79, 82; and
structural semantics, 111, 113; rheto-
ric of silence and, 125; and rhythm,
187. *See also* Language
"Sentience," 113–14, 116, 164
Separation: and moment, 53–54; of self
and society, 72; of realities, 105–10
passim
Sexuality: male novelists and, 78f; punctuation and, 108; and illness, 141–50
passim, 159, 165–66; Woolf's, 155
Shakespeare, Judith, 65
Shakespeare, William, 27, 49, 65
Showalter, Elaine, 9f, 36, 39f, 65, 75f, 95;
and body, 138, 145
Sickert, Walter, 105, 151
Sick room, 144–49. *See also* Illness
"Sign," 82, 114, 159–60; silence as, 5, 14,
97, 217
Silence, 1–12; and alphabet, 4, 123–69,
217–18; and interiority, 8, 12–55
passim; as "ritual of truth," 8, 36,
58–79 *passim*, 84, 145; women's, 8,
11–12, 35–47 *passim*, 55–88 *passim*,
108–9, 123–69, 201, 213–18 *passim*;
discourse of, 9, 15, 36–37, 41, 44,
59–60; rhythms of, 9–16 *passim*,
30–43 *passim*, 54–55, 119–20, 170–
213; metaphors of, 11f, 30, 38, 42,
60, 91, 97–101 *passim*, 113–19, 172,
215, 218; as "presence," 11, 33–42,
47, 69, 189, 215; zone of, 15, 101–7
passim, 151, 213; rhetoric of, 20, 87,
93, 125; male vs. female view of, 35–
36, 75, 84–86, 216; "snare of," 38;
ambiguity in, 42; configurations of,
42–55; structural, 42–43, 104, 107–
22, 120–22; "continuous" and "discontinuous," 43–44, 48; "unnatural,"
46, 76; negative and positive, 48–49;
keeping, 65–77; breaking, 77–88;
cosmic, 83–84; reading of, 89–96,
217; writing of, 96–122, 215; marked
and unmarked, 99–100; filled and
unfilled, 100; listening to, 170–213;
frames of, 204–11; contributing to
talk, 211–13. *See also* "Scenes of
silence"
Silences (Olsen), 46, 76

Silentius, 57, 61
Silver, Brenda, 23f, 33, 83, 89, 91, 118, 201
Sincerity, 28, 64, 72
Sinking, 35, 100–101
"Sketch of the Past" (Woolf), 51, 103,
155f, 199
Skywriting, 15
"Slater's Pins Have No Points" (Woolf),
104
Smith, Philip, 93, 102, 112
Smith-Rosenberg, Carol, 142
Smollett, T. G., 29
Smyth, Ethel, 7, 181
Social configuration of silence, 42–43,
47–49, 111ff
Social conversation of Austen, 71f
Social knowledge, and listener/ob-
server, 64f
Social realism, 40, 95
Sociology, 97
Soliloquies, 27–28, 72–73, 192, 202, 216
Solitary scenes, 44–45
Sor Juana Inés de la Cruz, 56–57
Soul: in *Jane Eyre*, 72–74, 116; leaving
body, 152
Sound, 12, 42, 188–90, 200–211 *pas-
sim. See also* Music; "Speaking"/
Speech; Talk
"Sous-rature," 15, 24, 207, 209
Space, 9, 12, 15, 53, 55, 59, 105, 156;
blank, 9, 12, 30, 108–9, 172–74;
"gaps," 9, 81, 160, 198–203 *passim*,
207f; in lexicon of silence, 112–
13; metaphors and, 117f; rhythm
and, 120, 172–76, 208; and body/
mind expressions, 125, 135, 138, 141;
feminine, 138, 168–69; bodily/ma-
terial, 141; critical, 141; mental, 141,
156; narrative, 141, 173; covert, 173;
psychological, 173; social, 173. *See
also* Distance; "Split"
"Speaking"/Speech, 20–23 *passim*, 71,
102, 215; inward, 17–21 *passim*, 36,
71. *See also* "Talk"; "Unspoken"
"Speaking subject," 69
"Split," 41–42, 67, 135–42, 156
Squier, Susan, 10
Steiglitz, Alfred, 177
Stein, Gertrude, 6
Steiner, George, 2–3, 17–27 *passim*, 52,
92f, 97, 189
Sterne, Laurence, 30, 108, 121f, 173, 182
Stevens, Wallace, 6
Stimpson, Catherine, 40
Strachey, Lytton, 52, 105

Library of Congress Cataloging-in-Publication Data

Laurence, Patricia Ondek, 1945–
     The reading of silence : Virginia Woolf in the English tradition /
  Patricia Ondek Laurence.
          p.   cm.
     Includes bibliographical references and index.
     ISBN 0-8047-1831-8 (cloth):   ISBN 0-8047-2179-3 (pbk)
     1. Woolf, Virginia, 1882–1941—Criticism and interpretation.
  2. English fiction—History and criticism.   3. Silence in
  literature.   I. Title.
  PR6045.072Z7728   1991
  823'.912—dc20   90-23636
                                                           CIP

  ⊗ This book is printed on acid-free paper

15 28
    65